Dublin's Bourgeois Homes

In 1859, Dubliners strolling along country roads witnessed something new emerging from the green fields. The Victorian house had arrived: wide red brick structures stood back behind manicured front lawns. Over the next forty years, an estimated 35,000 of these homes were constructed in the fields surrounding the city. The most elaborate were built for Dublin's upper middle classes, distinguished by their granite staircases and decorative entrances. Today, they are some of the Irish capital's most highly valued structures, and are protected under strict conservation laws.

Dublin's Bourgeois Homes is the first in-depth analysis of the city's upper middle-class houses. Focusing on the work of three entrepreneurial developers, Susan Galavan follows in their footsteps as they speculated in house building: signing leases, acquiring plots and sourcing bricks and mortar. She analyses a select range of homes in three different districts: Ballsbridge, Rathgar and Kingstown (now Dun Laoghaire), exploring their architectural characteristics: from external form to plan type, and detailing of materials. Using measured surveys, photographs, and contemporary drawings and maps, she shows how house design evolved over time, as bay windows pushed through façades and new lines of coloured brick were introduced. Taking the reader behind the façades into the interiors, she shows how domestic space reflected the lifestyle and aspirations of the Victorian middle classes. This analysis of the planning, design and execution of Dublin's bourgeois homes is an original contribution to the history of an important city in the British Empire.

Susan Galavan is a qualified architect and holds a first class Masters degree from University College Dublin and a PhD in architectural history from Trinity College Dublin. Her doctorate was a multidisciplinary examination of Dublin's Victorian domestic architecture, funded by a three-year scholarship from the Irish Research Council. She is currently a Postdoctoral Research Fellow at the Department of Architecture, University of Leuven, Belgium.

Dublin's Bourgeois Homes
Building the Victorian Suburbs, 1850–1901

Susan Galavan

First published 2017
by Routledge
2 Park Square, Milton Park, Abingdon, Oxon OX14 4RN

and by Routledge
711 Third Avenue, New York, NY 10017

Routledge is an imprint of the Taylor & Francis Group, an informa business

© 2017 Susan Galavan

The right of Susan Galavan to be identified as author of this work has been asserted by her in accordance with sections 77 and 78 of the Copyright, Designs and Patents Act 1988.

All rights reserved. No part of this book may be reprinted or reproduced or utilised in any form or by any electronic, mechanical, or other means, now known or hereafter invented, including photocopying and recording, or in any information storage or retrieval system, without permission in writing from the publishers.

Trademark notice: Product or corporate names may be trademarks or registered trademarks, and are used only for identification and explanation without intent to infringe.

British Library Cataloguing-in-Publication Data
A catalogue record for this book is available from the British Library

Library of Congress Cataloging-in-Publication Data
A catalog record for this book has been requested

ISBN: 978-1-4724-7172-7 (hbk)
ISBN: 978-1-315-61255-3 (ebk)

Typeset in Sabon
by Keystroke, Neville Lodge, Tettenhall, Wolverhampton

 Printed in the United Kingdom by Henry Ling Limited

For my parents.

Contents

List of figures and colour plates   *ix*
Acknowledgements   *xiii*
List of credits   *xv*
List of abbreviations   *xvii*

Introduction   1

1   The architecture of Dublin's bourgeois homes   13

2   The domestic realm: inside the semi-detached house   57

3   Control: land tenure and infrastructure   77

4   Builders, speculators and labourers   107

5   Process: building materials   133

    Conclusion   151

Index   *161*

Figures and colour plates

Figures

0.1	Ordnance Survey map of Dublin, 1860.	2
0.2	Ordnance Survey map of Dublin, 1860: townships of Rathmines and Rathgar, Pembroke.	6
1.1	Merrion Square North.	15
1.2	Pembroke Road North.	15
1.3	Numbers 39–51 Haddington Road.	16
1.4	Numbers 7–25 Northumberland Road.	18
1.5	Numbers 21–25 Northumberland Road, upper ground-floor and first-floor plans.	19
1.6	Ordnance Survey map of Rathgar, 1882.	21
1.7	Numbers 150–153 Rathgar Road, upper ground-floor and first-floor plans.	22
1.8	Numbers 2–32 Crosthwaite Park East.	23
1.9	Numbers 10 and 12 Crosthwaite Park East.	24
1.10	Numbers 2–6 Crosthwaite Park East, upper ground-floor and first-floor plans.	25
1.11	Crosthwaite Park West.	26
1.12	Numbers 46–52 Northumberland Road, upper ground-floor plans.	28
1.13	Corner of Merrion Square South and Fitzwilliam Street Upper, Dublin city.	30
1.14	Number 2 Crosthwaite Park East.	31
1.15	Numbers 19 and 21 Pembroke Road.	34
1.16	Numbers 16 and 18 Burlington Road.	35
1.17	Numbers 26 and 28 Lansdowne Road.	36
1.18	Numbers 42 and 44 Lansdowne Road.	37
1.19	Numbers 11, 28, 31 and 39 Northumberland Road, drawing comparing upper ground-floor plans.	38
1.20	Numbers 11, 28, 31 and 39 Northumberland Road, drawing comparing first-floor plans.	39
1.21	Numbers 1–19 Ailesbury Road, upper ground-floor plans.	41

1.22	Numbers 1 and 3 Ailesbury Road.	42
1.23	Plans of Number 11 Ailesbury Road.	43
1.24	Numbers 5 and 7 Ailesbury Road.	44
1.25	Plans of Number 8 Rostrevor Terrace.	47
1.26	Numbers 6 and 8 Shrewsbury Road.	50
1.27	Scheme for three terraced houses, detail of cross-section, Rathgar Road, 1851.	51
3.1	Belvedere Terrace, Sandymount.	81
3.2	Longford Terrace.	84
3.3	Belgrave Square.	85
3.4	Ordnance Survey map of Kingstown, 1867: Clarinda Park, Royal Terrace and Crosthwaite Park.	86
3.5	Ordnance Survey map of Rathgar, 1843.	88
4.1	Cartouche of Michael Meade, Meade monument, Glasnevin Cemetery.	111
4.2	Portrait of Mr John Crosthwaite.	112
4.3	Portrait of William Carvill.	113
4.4	Meade's Saw Mills.	115
4.5	St Michael's House, Ailesbury Road.	118
4.6	Joseph M. Meade and family, c.1883.	120
4.7	'The Right Honble. Joseph M. Meade, LL.D., P.C.'	124
4.8	Henrietta Street, Dublin.	125
5.1	John Martin & Son timber merchants, North Wall, Dublin.	145

Colour plates

1. Number 22 Elgin Road.
2. Pembroke Township map of Northumberland Road, c.1865.
3. Scheme for four terraced houses, Rathgar Road, 1851.
4. Numbers 150–153 Rathgar Road.
5. The evolution of the terraced house form.
6. Numbers 34–44 Northumberland Road.
7. Numbers 68–74 Northumberland Road.
8. Numbers 46–52 Northumberland Road.
9. Numbers 10 and 12 Raglan Road.
10. Numbers 22 and 23 Clyde Road.
11. Number 51 Northumberland Road.
12. Number 9 Ailesbury Road, detail of gable end to side return.
13. Numbers 2 and 4 Ailesbury Road.
14. Ordnance Survey map of Rathgar, 1865.
15. Numbers 1 and 2 Rostrevor Terrace.
16. Numbers 1–4 Orwell Park.
17. Numbers 1 and 2 Orwell Park, detail of entrance doorcases.
18. The evolution of the semi-detached house form.

19. Scheme for two semi-detached houses, upper ground-floor plan and front elevation, Rathgar Road, 1851.
20. Scheme for two semi-detached houses, first-floor plan, Rathgar Road, 1851.
21. Scheme for two semi-detached houses, lower ground-floor plan, Rathgar Road, 1851.
22. Numbers 16 and 17 Northbrook Road.
23. Numbers 16 and 17 Northbrook Road, basement and ground-floor plans, 1881.
24. Numbers 16 and 17 Northbrook Road, first- and mezzanine-floor plans, 1881.
25. Proposed semi-detached houses in Shrewsbury Road, ground-floor plan, 1900.
26. Shrewsbury Road, first-floor plan, 1900.
27. Shrewsbury Road, detail of first-floor rear return, 1900.
28. Shrewsbury Road, earlier sketch of first-floor rear return, 1900.
29. Lease map of Ailesbury Road, September 1865, the Earl of Pembroke to Michael Meade.

Acknowledgements

This book was made possible thanks to the support and assistance of the following people and organisations.

This research is based on doctoral work carried out at Trinity College Dublin, which was funded by a postgraduate scholarship from the Irish Research Council for the Humanities and Social Sciences. I owe a great deal of thanks to my supervisor, Christine Casey, for her continuous guidance, enthusiasm and encouragement over the course of this research. Thanks also to David Dickson and Murray Fraser, who provided valuable feedback and advice.

Central to this research is the execution of detailed surveys on a wide range of Victorian house properties in Dublin. I would like to thank the owners, occupiers and conservation professionals who granted me permission to carry out this fieldwork. Thanks, too, to Thomas J. O'Neill for sharing his many years' expertise of working with historic buildings in Dublin. I am grateful to Deirdre McEvoy, who was very generous in granting me access to her genealogical work on the Carvill, Meade and Crosthwaite families, and to John Carvill who entrusted me with the photographs of the families. I am indebted to Eve McAulay, whose doctoral work on the Pembroke estate provided me with a springboard for further research. I would also like to thank the staff of the following libraries and archives who assisted me in my research, and for granting permission to reproduce maps and drawings: the Irish Architectural Archive, the National Library of Ireland, the National Archives of Ireland, Trinity College Library, Public Record Office of Northern Ireland, Glasnevin Cemetery and St Michael's House. Thanks are also due to Routledge publishers for their patience and understanding, and their attention to detail.

Part of this research appeared in the following edited volume by Four Courts Press, who kindly granted permission for the material to be reproduced here:

Galavan, Susan, 'Building Victorian Dublin: Meade and Son and the expansion of the city' in Ciaran O'Neill (ed.), *Irish elites in the nineteenth century* (Dublin, 2013), pp. 51–67.

I have benefited enormously from generous comments and valuable feedback from many people. In particular, I wish to acknowledge the following: Ciarán

Wallace, Yvonne Cullen, Colleen Thomas, Caroline McGee and Conor Lucey, who provided very helpful feedback on final drafts, and Patrick McKay, for his creative insights on the images and the book cover design. Thanks too to Kathleen James-Chakraborty, Ciaran O'Neill, Hugh Campbell and Finola O'Kane for their generous advice and support. I am also grateful to my friends, both inside and outside of Trinity's walls, who encouraged me every step of the way. Finally, I would like to thank my family, to whom my gratitude knows no bounds: my brother Colin and my sisters Gráinne and Barbara. This book is dedicated to my parents: my mum and friend Monica, for her unwavering faith in my abilities, and to my father Dan, a kind and gentle soul who first ignited my passion for history.

Credits

All photographs and drawings are the author's own, unless otherwise stated.

No drawing may be reproduced or utilised in any form or by any means, electronic or mechanical, including photocopying, without permission in writing from the author.

I am grateful to the following organisations for agreeing to reproduce the following maps, drawings and images:

Figures 0.1, 0.2, 1.6, 3.4, 3.5, 5.1: Reproduced courtesy Trinity College Dublin.
Figure 1.27, Plates 3, 19, 20, 21: RIAI Murray Collection, Irish Architectural Archive.
Figure 4.1: Glasnevin Trust.
Figures 4.2, 4.3, 4.6: John Carvill.
Figure 4.4: National Library of Ireland.
Figure 4.7: Dublin City Library and Archive.
Plate 2: Aideen Ireland, Director of the National Archives of Ireland (Pembroke Estate Papers, maps, 'Maps of part of the Estate of the Earl of Pembroke and Montgomery Pembroke Township', sheet 6: Northumberland Road/Beggars Bush, c.1865, Acc. No. 2011/2/6).
Plate 14: Leslie Brown.
Plates 23, 24: McCurdy and Mitchell Collection, Irish Architectural Archive.
Plates 25, 26, 27, 28: Aideen Ireland, Director of the National Archives of Ireland (Pembroke Estate Papers, drawings of proposed semi-detached houses in Shrewsbury Road, 1900, plans, elevations etc., Acc. No. 1011/8/55).
Plate 29: St Michael's College.

Abbreviations

Acc. No.	Accession number
Griffith Valuation, Donnybrook	Griffith Valuation, County of Dublin, County Health District of Dublin, Electoral District of Donnybrook, [i.e. Ward of Pembroke, east and west], valuation lists.
Griffith Valuation, Kingstown	Griffith Valuation, County of Dublin, County Health District of Dun Laoghaire, Electoral Division of Kingstown, valuation lists.
Griffith Valuation, Rathfarnham	Griffith Valuation, County of Dublin, County Health District of Dublin, Electoral Division of Rathfarnham, valuation lists.
IAA	Irish Architectural Archive
KT	Minutes of Kingstown Township
mem.	Memorandum/a
NAI	National Archives of Ireland
NLI	National Library of Ireland
OS	Ordnance Survey of Ireland
PEP	Pembroke Estate Papers
PKS	Patterson Kempster and Shortall Collection
PRONI	Public Record Office of Northern Ireland
RD	Registry of Deeds
Thom's	*Thom's Dublin Street Directory*

Introduction

Dublin in 1865

In 1865, Dublin's International Exhibition opened its doors, in an enormous stone and glass structure facing Earlsfort Terrace. An estimated 725,000 visitors arrived that year, the majority by steamboat from Liverpool and Holyhead.[1] Dublin was ranked as one of the finest in the British Empire, resplendent with a 'long lie of beautiful quays, spanned by many graceful bridges'.[2] Cradled at the centre of a large bay, the River Liffey divided the city in two, weaving its way from west to east (Figure 0.1). Its municipal boundary was marked by a series of circular canals, built towards the end of the last century. Compared to the swarming metropolises of Manchester or Glasgow, the Irish capital was relatively compact, its urban core only two miles wide. Development had clustered around a medieval heart, and spread eastwards from here from the seventeenth century, both north and south of the river. On the west side of the city, large tracts of barren land lay, characterised by green fields and market gardens. Backed by 'a lofty and many-tinted range of mountains'[3] to the west and south, tourist guides drew attention to the city's principal buildings, from its many churches and hospitals, to its banks, barracks and railway stations. The Custom House, Gandon's neoclassical masterpiece, commanded a large site on the north bank of the river, serving the numerous ships docked along the quay. Merrion Square was considered the most fashionable of the many 'spacious squares' in the city, lined with tall brick terraces, facing a private park.[4]

Dublin was known for the 'varied and beautiful scenery' found on its outskirts.[5] Placed in the 'bosom of one of the loveliest bays in the world', the southeastern districts were reported to be 'unrivalled in beauty', nestled in between the mountains and the sea. Visitors wishing to escape the bustling city centre could catch a horse-drawn omnibus a few miles south of here, to the outlying village of Rathgar. The Dublin Mountains formed a fine backdrop for this rapidly expanding suburb, whose main streets were lined with red brick houses.[6] It was a landscape in the process of transformation: in the gaps between the buildings were glimpses of green swathe, which would soon be carved into new streets, crescents and squares. A few miles east of here, steam trains plied the route along the south coast, passing

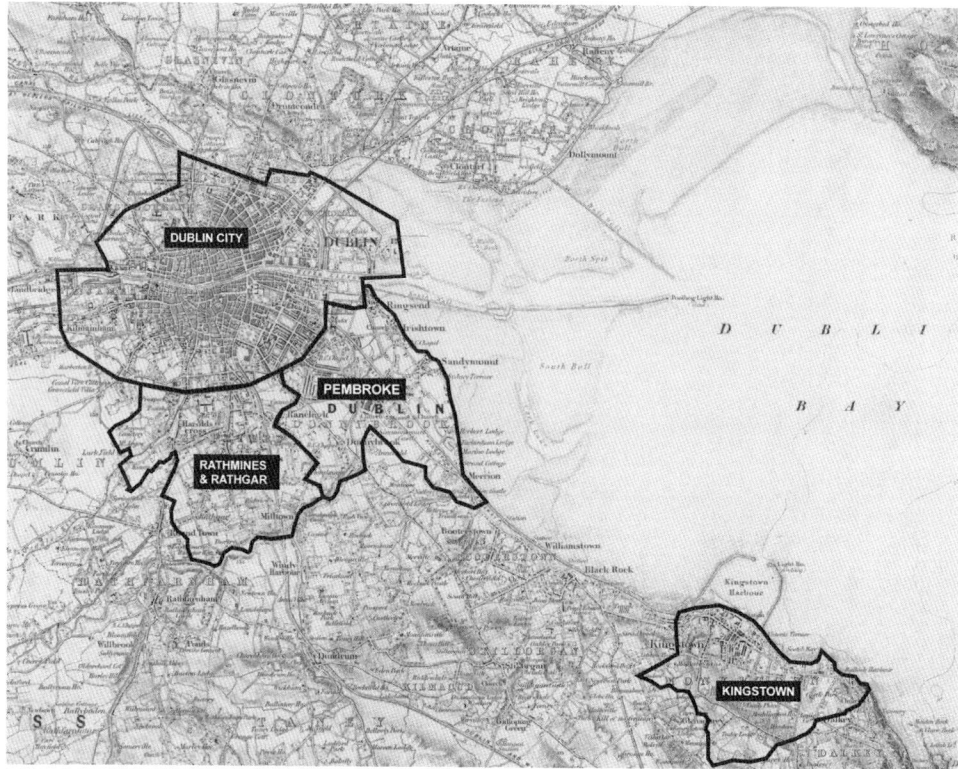

Figure 0.1 Ordnance Survey map of Dublin, 1860 (reproduced courtesy Trinity College Dublin).

by a series of towns and villages, perched along the rocky shore. Bearing the same relationship to Dublin as Ramsgate, Margate, and Brighton did to London, they were backed by 'beautifully wooded hills, sprinkled with villas'.[7] On disembarking in Kingstown, the main port of arrival from Britain, tourists could admire the 'noble harbour, its piers of which are each about a mile in length' and the 'beautiful terraces and numerous public buildings and villas'. In the hills above the town, speculators were laying out new roads, preparing for the building of terraces overlooking the sea. Along the route south from here to the town of Bray, the coastline had been utterly transformed in this way in recent years 'from a state of nature . . . to its present condition of suburban magnificence'.[8]

This book situates itself within this changing landscape outside the city boundary, where over the course of the Victorian age, an estimated 35,000 houses were built.[9] Built for a rising middle class, the suburbs gave birth to new forms of housing, which ranged in scale, materials and quality of workmanship. These streetscapes were built largely on the outskirts of the Victorian city, but are now an integral part of Dublin's identity. In contrast to other cities on these islands, this architecture remains largely intact. Between 1916 and 1923, although the urban core suffered damage due to various conflicts, its Victorian suburbs remained largely unchanged.

Furthermore, Ireland's neutrality during World War II largely ensured the preservation of its historic urban fabric. Today, these houses are some of the capital's most highly valued structures, and are protected under strict conservation laws. Despite their significance, they have received little attention from architectural historians. Furthermore, we know little about those responsible for the creation of the city's Victorian houses, and of the complex processes that brought them into being. This book is the first in-depth analysis to address this lacuna in Irish architectural historiography.

Progress or decay? Dublin in the industrial age

By the end of the eighteenth century, Dublin was second only to London as the most populous city in the United Kingdom.[10] Its status was reflected in the high quality of its public architecture, designed by architects of the first rank, with an impressive network of wide streets and circulatory canals. A number of fine Georgian squares had been laid out, filled with tall brick terraces, distinguished by their grand scale and ornament.[11] With the passing of the Act of Union in 1801, the tide began to turn for the city, as the abolition of the Irish parliament removed political power to Westminster. This led to an exodus of the political classes, and the most wealthy, who were no longer in need of seasonal townhouses. A period of 'partial de-industrialisation' followed: the city's traditional manufacturing base, comprising mainly of textiles, shipbuilding and sugar refining, gradually declined during this period, so that by 1825, most of these products were imported from across the Irish Sea.[12] What is more, there was a progressive shift to commercial enterprise, reflected in the proliferation of banks, insurance buildings and offices. Improvements in communications also saw an expansion of the wholesale trades, with Dublin re-emerging as the epicentre for Ireland. A rise in the status of the professions saw increasing numbers of doctors, lawyers and clerks, part of a burgeoning middle class who also needed to be housed.[13] However, the Great Famine of 1845–1850 struck at the heart of the Irish economy, bringing widespread death, disease and mass emigration. In Dublin, there was a surge in population, as tens of thousands of beggars descended on the city from rural areas.[14] Some were lucky enough to find work; but others found refuge in the workhouses, or emigrated to foreign shores. These factors, along with its declining industrial base, meant that the Irish capital was soon outranked by other cities in the United Kingdom. By 1860, it had slipped to the fifth largest city in the British Isles, while other urban centers were expanding rapidly in size.[15]

How then does Dublin compare with other British cities during the Victorian age? In the context of its reduced industry and marred by the Famine, it has long been viewed as a time of stagnation and decline. Maurice Craig, in his seminal *Dublin 1660–1880*, described the Victorian age as a time of 'slow decay and fitful growth' in the city.[16] Certainly, the decline of its manufacturing economy was in marked contrast to the rapidly industrialising towns of Birmingham, Glasgow or Manchester, which saw huge growth rates during the nineteenth century. In contrast, Dublin's population growth was lacklustre. Compared to Glasgow, which almost quadrupled in size between 1831 and 1911, Dublin's population increased only by half during the same period. However, what differentiates Dublin is that its expansion was largely due to growing commercialisation, rather than rapid industrialisation. In this way, it had more in common with older cities in southern Britain, such as Bristol, a commercial rather than an industrial hub, far away from the coal-fired economies of Northern England and central Scotland.[17]

The Victorian age was also a time of shifting city politics. Although the majority of Dubliners were Roman Catholic, a small Protestant elite had controlled the city government since the late seventeenth century. In 1841, the Municipal Corporation (Ireland) Act brought a gradual transfer of power to a rising Catholic merchant class.[18] In time, Catholic nationalists dominated City Hall, and used the municipal council as a platform for national politics. The Protestant business elite felt increasingly marginalised, and formed new self-governing townships outside the canals, which were subject to lower levels of taxation. This exodus exacerbated the decline of the inner city, parts of which degenerated into diseased and overcrowded slums. A growing middle class further propelled the flight to the periphery, seeking refuge in the 'air and beauty of scenery' advertised in the emerging suburbs.[19] Over the course of the nineteenth century, there was an increased polarisation between the mostly unionist townships outside the city boundary, and the predominantly Nationalist Catholic city council inside.[20] By 1898, ten separate councils surrounded the city, and these bodies raised their own taxes and elected their own commissioners to provide local services.[21] The result was city of contrasts, which was reflected in its homes: an urban core increasingly characterised by crammed tenements, its outskirts featuring elegant suburban villas.

Despite these challenges, Dublin remained the administrative and commercial capital of Ireland.[22] It was the largest Irish city for much of the Victorian age: in 1861, Dublin was still twice the size of Belfast, and was eclipsed by it only in 1891. As in other cities in the United Kingdom, suburbanisation was facilitated by the technological age: the opening of Ireland's first train line in 1834 precipitated the expansion of railway suburbs such as Blackrock, Killiney and Dalkey.[23] New building types appeared: railway stations and factories epitomised the industrial age, and the rise of cultural institutions was reflected in the opening of new museums and library buildings. Meanwhile, released from the restrictions of the penal laws, the Catholic hierarchy set about 'building churches for a whole nation'.[24] The 1850s was a time of increased building activity in the city, as improvements were made in transport and communications, ensuring Dublin's importance as a centre of business and commerce.[25] It was also the era of the public works contracts, as new prisons, hospitals and children's asylums were constructed. In 1869, the city's expansion to the south drew the attention of *The Irish Builder*:

> In our time, and for a city almost devoid of foreign trade, and having to contend with numberless disadvantageous circumstances, its suburban extension

has been truly remarkable, more particularly upon the south and southeaster. sides.[26]

Dublin's domestic architecture

The city is defined more by its houses than its cathedrals, its town halls or its court buildings.[27] All human life is represented in its dwellings – from the row houses to the villas, the artisan cottages to the apartment blocks. For a long time, architectural historians focused on the great palaces and villas of the past, viewed through the lens of a 'great architect', or a wealthy client. After World War II, there was a renewed interest in the historic built environment in Britain. John Summerson was the first to address the eighteenth-century townhouse, in his seminal study *Georgian London*, published in 1945. Since then, the speculative house has featured in many new urban histories of Britain and Ireland.[28] In the 1960s, H. J. Dyos sparked interest in the nineteenth-century house in his publication *Victorian suburb: a study of the growth of Camberwell*.[29] Other enquiries followed suit, providing an economic and social context for the rise of suburbia, right into the twentieth century.[30] Since then, the field of architectural history has continued to expand, attracting scholars from diverse areas such as sociology, engineering, media studies, geography and feminism. This has brought new points of view to the study of domesticity. The pioneering work of Gwendolyn Wright and Dell Upton and others paved the way for a raft of new histories on a wide range of house types in North America, from apartments to speculative houses, vernacular dwellings to mass housing[31] In short, the historiographies of home have unveiled a myriad of factors that shaped a large part of our built environment, while providing a window onto past lives.

In Dublin, the historiography of its architecture tends to focus mainly on the eighteenth-century city, while considerably less attention is paid to its larger nineteenth-century urban fabric.[32] The Georgian townhouses, built in large numbers in Dublin from the 1720s,[33] were influenced mostly by the speculative building system common in Britain, where estate owners teamed up with builders. However, compared to the London model, their exteriors remained relatively plain, and tended to be clad in brick with little decorative treatment in the form of stringcourses, cornices or window surrounds. From the 1860s, the townhouses of Dublin's northeastern quarter, previously the most fashionable district in the Georgian age, fell into tenement use, while the areas to the south remained relatively affluent. Outside the municipal boundary, new streets were carved out in Rathmines and Pembroke, which together contained over half of the total suburban population (Figure 0.2).[34] Compared to the large townhouses of Merrion Square, suburbia reflected the desires of the middle-class dweller: the houses tended to be smaller in scale with more space to the front and side. Pembroke was the most prestigious, containing wide well-planted boulevards, filled with 'the stateliest mansions in Dublin or in any of the other suburbs'.[35] It attracted the wealthiest of

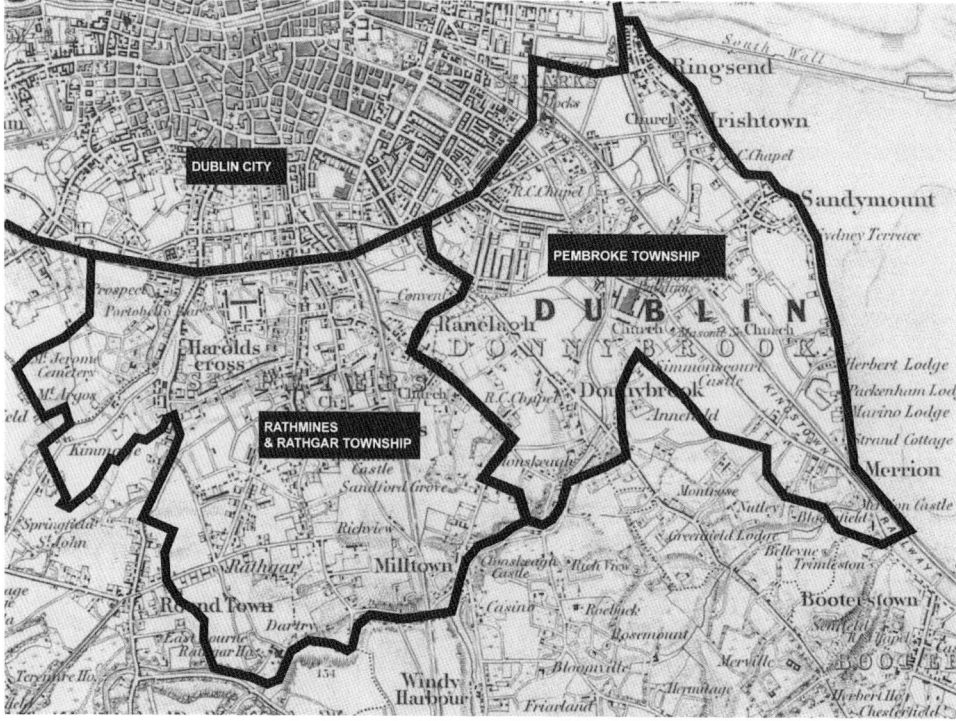

Figure 0.2 Ordnance Survey map of Dublin, 1860: townships of Rathmines and Rathgar, Pembroke (reproduced courtesy Trinity College Dublin).

Dublin's middle-class residents, from its senior civil servants, barristers and business owners, to its merchants, aldermen and bankers. Adjoining it to the west, was the growing suburb of Rathmines, home to the city's banking and commercial clerks. Although there was some middle-class housing built in the northern townships of Drumcondra, Glasnevin and Clontarf, progress there was relatively slow, as noted in 1860:

> Wending our way hence to the suburbs, a new field for our notice – too extended, however, for this sketch – opens before us. Our record has embraced, at least to a considerable extent, particulars of chief items in the neighbourhoods of Rathmines, Rathgar – now virtually a wing of the city – of Kingstown, Dalkey, and Bray – all spreading with wonderful rapidity. Again at the north side, Clontarf, slower by a thousand degrees than the preceding, *yet* improving.[36]

In the post-Famine era, changes in the urban economy produced rising numbers of lower middle-class workers in the city. Many were employed in transport related jobs, with the railways, canals and the steamship companies of increasing importance. It was also a time of investment in public services, with the building of schools, prisons, hospitals and welfare institutions. As Dublin was the administrative capital of Ireland, further employment opportunities were opened up for white-collar workers, in the expanding retail, insurance and banking sectors. New modest red brick terraces were built for this rising lower middle class, primarily to the north and west of the city, both inside the outside the canals. One of the first of these emerged to the south of the inner city, in the Portobello area, from 1845. At Heytesbury Street, a row of modest single-storey over basement houses were constructed, characterised by two-bay red brick façades. Two- and three-storey versions of these were built nearby by the developer Frederick Stokes from 1850. Based on the most common Georgian plan, these narrow terraces were built close to the street, and finished with a minimal degree of classical detailing.

These houses were relatively modest in scale, a reflection of the incomes of the lower middle classes.[37] This prototype continued to remain popular over the following decades, as it continued in streets further west of here, and in the northern sector from the 1860s. In the suburb of Phibsborough, homes were built primarily for skilled workers, clerks, policemen and shop assistants.[38] Some houses were notorious for their 'scamping workmen and bad materials', where road dirt was used for mortar and soft or rotten bricks formed walls and chimneys.[39] By the late 1870s, a new suburb was in the course of formation, built specifically for clerical and skilled workers in Drumcondra, to the north-east of the city. It was the type of home that *The Irish Builder* had been advocating for many years, for a 'man of moderate means'. Although many large houses had been built for the upper middle classes, it reported the dearth of properties for '[t]hose who spend the whole week in gloomy offices . . . [who] would gladly select their habitation in some airy and beautiful locality, apart from the din that assails their ears during business hours'.[40] Meanwhile, to the west of the city were the growing suburbs of Kilmainham and Inchicore, populated mainly by railway workers, prison warders and soldiers.

In contrast to other similarly sized cities in Victorian Britain, comparatively little housing was built for Dublin's working-class population. In Belfast, thousands of houses were built for those working in the linen and shipbuilding industries. However, with Dublin's declining industrial base and a plentiful supply of older housing, the labouring poor had to make do with existing accommodation in the city.[41] A particular blackspot was the southwest inner city, where many of the factories, breweries and distilleries were located. Since the late eighteenth century, this area had had a notorious reputation for abject poverty, where families were crammed into dilapidated houses.[42] Increasingly, larger Georgian terraces, no longer needed by the city's political classes, were subdivided into tenement accommodation. Formerly the comfortable homes of Dublin's aristocratic and upper middle classes, the level of overcrowding was extreme by UK standards, with a high proportion of families living in single-room accommodation. In 1841, a visitor remarked on the sad irony of these 'lofty' and opulent façades, 'deserted by the rich, they were filled by the poor; and as they decayed, they became the resort of the more abject who could find no other shelter'.[43] Within twenty years, a third of the city's housing stock consisted of converted Georgian townhouses, which had become a breeding ground for disease.⁴⁴ By 1890, it was estimated that 30,000 families were packed into 6,000 houses in the city, where they paid excessive rents and lived in 'deplorably unsanitary conditions'.⁴⁵ In 1911, Dublin had the highest rate of single-room dwellings in the United Kingdom, with an average of twenty-two people living in a typical eighteenth-century terraced house.⁴⁶ This had obvious repercussions for public health: in 1906, the city's death rate was twice that of London, and was said to be the worst in Western Europe.⁴⁷

Working-class housing was not confined to the southwest inner city, or the north city streets. Poorer residents could also be found in wealthier districts, particularly near railway lines and gas works.⁴⁸ In 1892, *The Irish Times* reported that a few streets away from the grand boulevards of the Pembroke estate, were 'large numbers of the most wretched hovels that could possibly be imagined, and in which a great portion of the industrious poor are compelled by hard circumstances to reside'.⁴⁹ This was a reference to the low-lying areas of Ringsend and Irishtown to the southeast, where the labouring poor were reliant on small-scale industries, such as fishing, boat building and glassworks. The newspaper reported that life there was worse than in the city tenements, where a number of families shared a couple of small rooms, without sanitary provision, and facing streets or lanes 'made the receptacle for filth and refuse of all kinds'. These housing conditions had a direct bearing on life expectancy: outbreaks of fever and disease were common and by 1911, over one-fifth of working-class children in Ringsend died before the age of five.⁵⁰ Other examples can be found in Dundrum, where families inhabited 'ruinous cabins', while in the salubrious surroundings of Merrion, some of the dwellings were deemed 'not fit for habitation' by the estate landlord.⁵¹ In the seaside resort of Kingstown, six miles south of the city, over a third of the population lived in unsanitary back lanes and courts.⁵² Behind the commercial buildings of the main street, a series of shed roofs ran along the rear garden walls, providing a rudimentary form of shelter for the poor.⁵³ It was a contrast that drew the attention of *The Dublin Builder* in 1863:

> There are lanes and alleys in Dublin into which the rays of the sun never penetrate, dark, gloomy, and vault-like lanes through which a malarious slim oozes, emitting a stench almost unbearable to those accustomed to dwell within its reach . . . The mansions of the rich are being fitted up in a style of the most costly extravagance, while the dwellings of the poor are unnoticed and uncared for.⁵⁴

The scope of this book

This book is the first in-depth analysis of Dublin's upper middle-class houses. Using measured surveys, photographs, and contemporary drawings and maps, it analyses a range of houses in different sectors. It focuses on the two main suburban typologies: the terrace and the semi-detached house. It reveals the many hands that shaped these eclectic façades, from the landlord to the builder, the architect to the leaseholder. Comparisons will be made with similar house types in Britain, showing the unique characteristics of the Dublin house form. Taking the reader behind the façade into its interior spaces, this study also opens a window on to Victorian middle-class life. It shows how domestic space was manipulated to articulate the relationships between master and servant, male and female, adult and child, and explores the role of the architect, who negotiated the boundaries between these different members of the household. In this analysis of the planning, design, execution and occupation of Dublin's bourgeois homes, this book aims to contribute to our understanding of an important city in the British Empire.

Due to the scale of speculative house building, no single volume could analyse all of Dublin's upper middle-class houses. Therefore, a broadly representative sample has been selected here. They were all built in the districts to the south of the city, home to the majority of Dublin's affluent suburbanites. The sample is spread across three different townships, which permits a comparative analysis of local conditions, such as building control, land tenure and the availability of materials. They range in scale and quality from the modest to the prestigious: from the stuccoed terraces of Kingstown to the trophy mansions in the Pembroke estate. Today, the high prices placed on the houses on Ailesbury and Shrewsbury Roads, two of the most expensive streets in the country, are due to the quality of their domestic architecture. Analogous to a section cut through nineteenth-century speculative building activity, these schemes, along with other associated projects and acquisitions, form the basis for investigation.

We know very little about those involved in the creation of these buildings, from the builders to the landowners, the architects to the speculators. Their work now characterises many streetscapes in the city, forming the backdrop for its citizens' lives. This book focuses on the work of Michael Meade, William Carvill and John Crosthwaite: three entrepreneurial developers who built premium homes in different sectors. They were just some of the many city merchants, lord mayors and town commissioners who presided over and shaped the Victorian city. Part of a rising Catholic middle class, the most prominent was Michael Meade, founder of one of Dublin's largest building firms, which was in turn inherited by his son who become an important political and business figure in the city. This monograph follows the lives of these three families, as they speculated in house building, signing leases, acquiring plots, and sourcing bricks and mortar. Challenging the common depiction of Dublin's Catholic commercial class as mere publican-grocers, or petty-bourgeois at best, their achievements are reflected in the high-quality houses that they built around their homes.

Notes

1 D. Dickson, *Dublin, the making of a capital city* (Dublin, 2014), p. 333.
2 J. R. Joly, *Dublin and its environs: with a map of the city and numerous illustrations engraved on wood* (Dublin, 1846), p. 1.
3 W. F. Wakeman, *Tourists guide through Dublin and its interesting suburbs* (Dublin, 1865), p. 2.
4 Joly, *Dublin and its environs*, p. 2.
5 *Ibid.*, p. 161.
6 L. F. Bickerstaffe, R. D. Walshe and F. J. O'Kelley, *Dublin, a historical sketch of Ireland's Metropolis* (London, 1850), p. 191.
7 Wakeman, *Tourists guide through Dublin*, p. 2.
8 *Ibid.*, p. 1.
9 M. E. Daly, 'The growth of Victorian Dublin' in Mary E. Daly, Mona Hearn and Peter Pearson (eds), *Dublin's Victorian houses* (Dublin, 1998), p. 3.
10 A. McLaren, *Dublin, the shaping of a capital* (London, 1993), p. 37.
11 C. Casey, *Dublin, the city within the grand and royal canals and the circular road with the Phoenix Park* (New Haven and London, 2005), p. 1.
12 Dickson, *Dublin*, p. 287.
13 T. Murtagh, 'Henrietta Street in the nineteenth century' (unpublished research paper for Dublin City Council, September 2015), p. 28.
14 Dickson, *Dublin*, p. 317.
15 M. E. Daly, *Dublin, the deposed capital* (Cork, 1984), p. 2.
16 M. Craig, *Dublin, 1660–1880: the shaping of a city* (Dublin, 1952), p. 297.
17 Dickson, *Dublin*, p. 308.
18 S. Jones, 'Dublin reformed: the transformation of a municipal governance of a Victorian city, 1840–1860' (Ph.D. thesis, Trinity College, Dublin, 2001).
19 *General Advertiser*, 20 May 1865.
20 C. Wallace, 'Local politics and government in Dublin city and suburbs 1899–1914' (Ph.D. thesis, Trinity College, Dublin, 2009), p. 73.
21 *Ibid.*, p. 2.
22 A. McLaren, *Dublin: the shaping of a capital*, p. 40.
23 Daly, *Dublin*, p. 176.
24 *The Irish Builder and Engineer Jubilee Number, 1859–1909* (Dublin, 1909), p. 9.
25 Dickson, *Dublin*, p. 366.
26 *The Irish Builder*, 15 December 1869.
27 A. Rossi, *The architecture of the city* (Massachusetts, 1966), p. 70.
28 For example: I. G. Lindsay, *Georgian Edinburgh* (Edinburgh, 1948); A. J. Youngson, *The making of classical Edinburgh* (Edinburgh, 1967); J. Summerson, *Architecture in Britain 1530–1830* (Yale, 1953); D. Cruickshank, *A guide to the Georgian buildings of Britain and Ireland* (London, 1985); Craig, Maurice, *The architecture of Ireland from the earliest times to 1880* (London, 1982); and Craig, Maurice, *Dublin 1660–1860* (Dublin, 1952).
29 H. J. Dyos, *Victorian suburb, a study of the growth of Camberwell* (Leicester, 1961).
30 Examples include: R. G. Rodger, 'Speculative builders and the structure of the Scottish building industry, 1860–1914' in *Business History*, xxi, no. 2 (1979), pp. 226–246; *Housing in Urban Britain 1780–1914* (Cambridge, 1995); D. Fraser (ed.), *Municipal reform and the industrial city* (Leicester, 1982); M. Galinou, *Cottages and villas, the birth of the garden suburb* (Yale, 2011).
31 B. M. Lane, *Housing and dwelling: perspectives on modern domestic architecture* (Oxon, 2007), p. 1.
32 Examples include: Dublin City Council, *The Georgian squares of Dublin* (Dublin, 2006); C. Casey (ed.), *The eighteenth-century Dublin town house* (Dublin, 2010); G. O'Brien

and F. O'Kane (eds); *Georgian Dublin* (Dublin, 2008) and *Portraits of the city: Dublin and the wider world* (Dublin, 2012); M. Craig, *Dublin 1660–1860* (Dublin, 1980); and N. McCullough, *Dublin an urban history, the plan of the city* (Dublin, 2007); C. Casey, *Dublin* (New Haven and London, 2005).
33 Casey, *Dublin*, p. 36.
34 Daly, *Dublin*, p. 152.
35 *The Irish Times*, 4 March 1892.
36 *The Irish Builder*, 1 December 1860.
37 Daly, 'The growth of Victorian Dublin', p. 19.
38 Daly, *Dublin*, p. 120.
39 *The Irish Builder*, 15 April 1878.
40 *The Dublin Builder*, 15 March 1864.
41 *The Irish Times*, 28 January 1890.
42 Dickson, *Dublin*, p. 372.
43 A. Simms and J. Brady, *Dublin through space and time* (Dublin, 2001), p. 160.
44 Dickson, *Dublin*, p. 376.
45 *The Irish Times*, 28 January 1890.
46 M. Fraser, *John Bull's other homes, state housing the British policy in Ireland, 1883–1922* (Liverpool, 1996), pp. 66–67.
47 Dickson, *Dublin*, p. 418.
48 Daly, *Dublin*, p. 280.
49 *The Irish Times*, 4 March 1892.
50 Dickson, *Dublin*, p. 419.
51 I. Kirk, *The artisan dwellings of the Pembroke estate* (Dublin, 2001), p. 24.
52 Dickson, *Dublin*, p. 328.
53 *Report from the select committee on town holdings*, H.C. 1886 (213-Sess. 1), evidence of Mr Stewart, p. 197, para. 5284.
54 *The Dublin Builder*, 15 October 1863.

1 The architecture of Dublin's bourgeois homes

Introduction

By 1859, Dublin's outskirts were in the course of rapid transformation:

> Passing to the south side we find the same steady march in the path of improvement . . . where villas, single and semi-detached, terraces, &c., are springing up with an almost fairy-like rapidity, and the green sward speedily gives way to macadamized roads and populous thoroughfares, justifying the supposition that there is a universal move in that direction.[1]

Dubliners strolling along country roads must have marvelled at this transformation. The Victorian house had arrived: wide red brick structures stood back behind large front lawns. Over the next forty years, an estimated 35,000 homes were built in the fields surrounding the city. Distinguished by their elaborate entrances and imposing granite staircases, Dublin produced its own unique version of the Victorian house form. The most prestigious were the red brick mansions that emerged in the 'boulevards' of the Pembroke estate, located to the southeast of the city (Figure 0.1). Designed for Dublin's upper middle class, they were clad in expensive machine-made brick and cut stone. Various house types emerged here, but the semi-detached house had particular sway, due to specific covenants inserted into the leases. Adjoining the Pembroke estate was the suburb of Rathmines, which, although wealthy, was characterised mainly by smaller-scale development. Although there were some semi-detached schemes, the terrace predominated here. The railway suburb of Kingstown, located six miles further south along the coast, was characterised by a predominance of rendered terraces, jostling for views of the sea.

This chapter will carry out a detailed architectural analysis of a range of houses built in the middle-class suburbs to the south of the city. Built between 1851 and 1865, they are typical of early suburban houses in Dublin, which modified previous house typologies to the fields surrounding the city. The analysis will focus on two main housing types: the terrace and the semi-detached house, focusing on key architectural characteristics such as external form, plan types and decorative detailing. Previous building models will be discussed in detail, particularly those in the Pembroke estate, which was a testing ground for high-quality development.

Showing how house design evolved over time, it then chronicles the development of the suburban house form, as it adapted to a new context. Finally, the buildings will be compared with similar house types in Britain, revealing the unique characteristics of the Dublin house form.

Dublin's suburban terraced houses

The origin of the nineteenth-century terrace in Dublin

The brick terrace emerged in Britain and Ireland in the seventeenth century, and was largely the work of the speculative builder. After the Great Fire of London, a series of building acts introduced a raft of measures that would transform the built environment on these islands. The legislation stipulated that all new buildings in London were to be constructed in brick or stone and established four classes of house.[2] This ushered in new prototypes for urban housing, which influenced development beyond the capital, which, although variable, conformed broadly to a certain type. In the streets of Mayfair in London, flat brick façades were relieved by a restrained form of decoration in brick, stone or timber ornamentation. To European eyes, these exteriors were remarkably plain, compared to the more lavishly decorated fronts popular elsewhere. The German architect Hermann Muthesius, author of *The English house* (1904), attributed this austerity to the Englishman's character whom he surmised 'avoids attracting attention to his house by means of striking design or architectonic extravagance, just as he would be loth to appear personally eccentric by wearing a fantastic suit'.[3] When the brick terrace emerged in Dublin in the early eighteenth century, these relatively modest façades were pared down even further. Noted for their 'consistent lack of ornament', the city's Georgian terraces are characterised by plain brick façades with little decorative treatment in the form of stringcourses, cornices or window surrounds.[4] Instead, builders substituted expensive stone facing with decorative entrance doorcases, whose variety is not matched with any regularity in England or Scotland.[5] Scholars have long debated the reasons for this dichotomy, which is especially intriguing in light of their sumptuously decorated interiors. It is believed that the answer lies in the speculative nature of the urban terrace, where Irish developers economised on expensive stone or brick decoration.[6]

Early suburban terraces in Dublin

When developers began building houses in the green fields outside the city, they turned to a familiar typology in Dublin, the eighteenth-century townhouse.[7] Butted up against each other in rows, these tall brick terraces were an 'infinitely adaptable' template,[8] extending vertically and horizontally to suit both function and purse. In the city squares, they are four storeys high, forming terraces two to three bays wide (Figure 1.1), but in secondary streets, they are of more modest proportions, with narrower frontages only two storeys high. Fulfilling the demands of a dense

Architecture of Dublin's bourgeois homes 15

Figure 1.1 Merrion Square North.

Figure 1.2 Pembroke Road North.

16 *Architecture of Dublin's bourgeois homes*

urban framework, they sit close to the edge of the street, allowing just enough space for a light well, and steps to an embellished entrance doorcase. The standard Georgian townhouse includes a basement floor, which is almost fully submerged below the street.

As Dublin expanded during the nineteenth century, this typology was planted along the existing radial routes from the city. As Eve McAulay has found, the first signs of 'suburbanisation' occurred along Baggot Street Upper, which began to break new ground from 1816.[9] These red brick terraces bear a close resemblance to the townhouses of Merrion Square (Figure 1.1), but are reduced in height and pushed further back from the road (Figure 1.2). In adjacent streets, densities were reduced even further, such as on the south side of Haddington Road, where the houses are only three storeys high (Figure 1.3). What is more, the roof is no longer hidden behind a parapet wall, but now overhangs the front façade. The basement has also risen out of the ground, necessitating a grand flight of steps to the entrance. In short, the tall four-storey over basement terrace, built in an urban

Figure 1.3 Numbers 39–51 Haddington Road.

context, was no longer suitable to the green fields surrounding the city. These early suburban houses, reduced in scale, pushed back from the street and rising out of the ground, were already adapting to a new suburban context, over twenty years before Queen Victoria's reign.

Dublin's Georgian streetscapes are characterised largely by minimalist façades, consisting of tall brick fronts punctured with a series of window openings. This began to change in the nineteenth century, as a move away from classical prototypes saw experiments in architectural style. Publications by John Ruskin in the late 1840s and early 1850s, inspired by Italian medieval architecture, brought polychrome decoration to house façades in bands of coloured brick or stone.[10] Furthermore, the advancing technological tide brought a profusion of coloured brick and stone to the market, and this, combined with the rise in mechanisation, encouraged increased decoration in house façades. In time, bay windows (also approved of by Ruskin) began to push through façades. At Elgin Road, diaper brickwork patterns and stone stringcoursing enlivened façades in 1863 (Plate 1),[11] their entrances framed with round-headed archways of brick and stone, and flanked by colonettes topped with foliated capitals. These polychromatic façades had quite an impact on new suburban streetscapes, and contrasted sharply with the relatively plain brick fronts of their neighbours. This classical sobriety was becoming increasingly unfashionable, as Charles Cameron, chief medical officer for Dublin, alluded to in 1870, describing Merrion Square as 'simply two long dirty brick walls, provided with oblong holes for the admission of light'.[12]

Case studies of terraced houses in Pembroke, Rathgar and Kingstown

The previous section provided a broad overview of the origin and early development of Dublin's Victorian terraces. The following section will build on these findings by analysing a number of terraced schemes in detail. Built between 1834 and 1865, these early suburban houses were in the process of adapting to a new and evolving suburban landscape.

1. Pembroke: Numbers 7–25 Northumberland Road (1834–1862)

Northumberland Road was laid out just outside the Grand Canal, to the southwest of the city in c.1830. It was planned by the Pembroke estate to make a 'great leading passage' from Dublin to the port of Kingstown.[13] Formally, it was designed as a logical extension of Mount Street, to form another major radial route from the city, laid out with plots twenty-four feet wide and 200 feet deep. Despite these early plans, Northumberland Road was slow to develop and took approximately fifty-four years to finally reach completion. In so doing, the street's architecture tells the story of the Victorian house, from its early fruition in the 1830s, to its full emergence by the late 1880s.[14] The first three houses were built by 1837 (Figure 1.4: on the right): Number 7 was leased to barrister Llewellyn Nash, while the adjoining Numbers 9 and 11 were leased by the architect/builder John Gibson. As

18 *Architecture of Dublin's bourgeois homes*

Figure 1.4 Numbers 7–25 Northumberland Road.

McAulay has shown, this typology is typical of contemporary building schemes outside the canals: the suburban development of the Georgian terrace, consisting of two-bay brick façades over a rendered basement, with flat parapets.[15] Compared to the houses in Merrion Square, they are one storey lower and are risen out of the ground, requiring nine or ten steps to the entrance. Reduced in scale and grandeur, this building type was already in force in nearby streets such as Percy Place, Haddington Terrace and Pembroke Road. This terrace of ten houses was finally complete in 1862, after twenty-five years of speculation in the Pembroke estate, and they are all based on the same template (Plate 2).

Internally, these houses are laid out using the most common two-room plan found in the eighteenth-century Dublin townhouse,[16] consisting of one space to the front and another to the rear, alongside a continuous hall and stair compartment (Figure 1.5: e.g. Number 23). The ground floor consists of two reception rooms of equal width: a parlour to the front and a dining room to the rear. A spine wall divides these two reception rooms, rising up through the building to provide support for floor and ceiling joists, terminating at roof level where it forms a bearing for the double-pitched roof structure and valley gutter. All of the houses on the terrace were built with two-storey rear returns accessed off the half-landing level, a common feature of the late Georgian/early Victorian townhouse, which was often separated from the main house by a vestibule or anteroom. Externally, the houses are faced with plain brown brick in a Flemish bond pattern, with stone quoins

Architecture of Dublin's bourgeois homes 19

defining the sides of the earlier houses. The windows on the upper floors are determined by the largest and most important space in the house, namely the first-floor reception room, which runs the full width of the plot (Figure 1.5: Number 21). These openings are located centrally in the room, and are the tallest, reflecting the spatial hierarchy of the 'piano nobile', where the richest decoration is found. On the floor below, the window to the front reception room shifts to the left, thereby sacrificing an alignment with those above in order to locate the opening central to the room. In other words, form follows function, as the plan takes precedence over the façade. An exception to this is the layout of Number 25, located at the end of the terrace, at the junction with Haddington Road. This plot exploits the corner site, by inserting the hall in an extension to the side, allowing the front ground-floor room to run the full width of the plot. The windows then align on all floors, resulting in the satisfactory termination of the terrace.

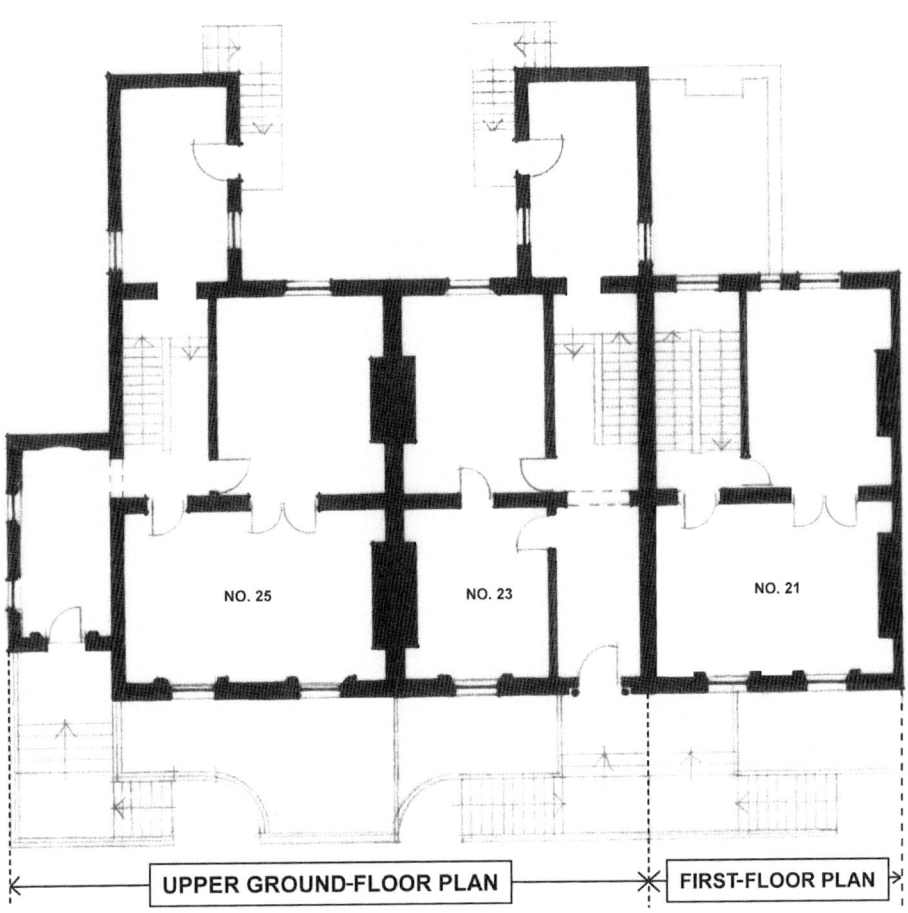

Figure 1.5 Numbers 21–25 Northumberland Road, upper ground-floor and first-floor plans.

2. Rathmines and Rathgar: Numbers 132–135 Rathgar Road (1851)

In 1862, *The Dublin Builder* reported on development in the growing suburb of Rathmines and Rathgar, where 'villas detached and semi-detached, cottage residences, and terraces in various designs and styles here stud the soil, and the several roads and approaches seem to have been laid out with much judgement' (Figure 0.2).[17] The terrace was the dominant form of domestic suburban building,[18] although it was not always seen in a favourable light. In 1904, the German architect Hermann Muthesius described Bedford Park in London, which had been laid out in the 1870s in a mix of house types. Muthesius conceded 'even the terraced houses made a pleasant impression' and that they were inserted 'where extreme cheapness was required'.[19] They were certainly a more profitable form of building than paired houses, as speculators could accommodate twice the number of units on the same width of plot. An example is the scheme designed in 1851, by architects Murray and Denny for a site on Rathgar Road. The road connected the suburban villages of Rathmines and Rathgar, which by this time was characterised by terraced houses with uniform setbacks from the street (Figure 1.6). Arthur Murray, a younger brother of one of the architects and a builder by trade, was presented with three options for the site.[20] The first scheme maximised the density on the site by providing four terraced houses with narrow plot widths (Plate 3). The second option formed three wider terraces, while the third was generously laid out in a pair of semi-detached houses. The higher-density scheme was finally chosen, and the four terraced houses that stand there today match those originally conceived by the architects. As with the earlier houses on Northumberland Road, the scheme has inherited the common two-room plan.

3. Rathmines and Rathgar: Numbers 150–153 Rathgar Road (1857–1859)

The next building to be examined is Numbers 150–153 Rathgar Road, just north of the Murray and Denny scheme (Figures 1.6 and 1.7). The plot was acquired by the builder Michael Meade, founder of one of the largest building empires in the city. His site on Rathgar Road stood at an important intersection with Frankfort Avenue, opposite the site for a new Catholic church. By 1859, Meade had completed a scheme of four terraced houses, while he was in the process of constructing a new saw mill in the city, at New Brunswick Street.[21] Work began on the Church of the Three Patrons the following year, designed by the architect Patrick Byrne (builder unknown) to cater for the numerous domestic servants who worked in the area. Father Meagher commissioned the project to provide for what he called 'these poor creatures', whose employers allowed them only 'a miserable driblet of time' to attend mass in Rathmines.[22] However, the building of a large Catholic institution in a primarily Protestant middle-class area was controversial to say the least. On the laying of the foundation stone in 1860, *The Irish Times* reported: 'Under the windows of the Protestant gentry all the paraphernalia of Popery was ostentatiously displayed'.[23] The best view of the proceedings was from the windows of Meade's houses at 150–153 Rathgar Road.

Architecture of Dublin's bourgeois homes   21

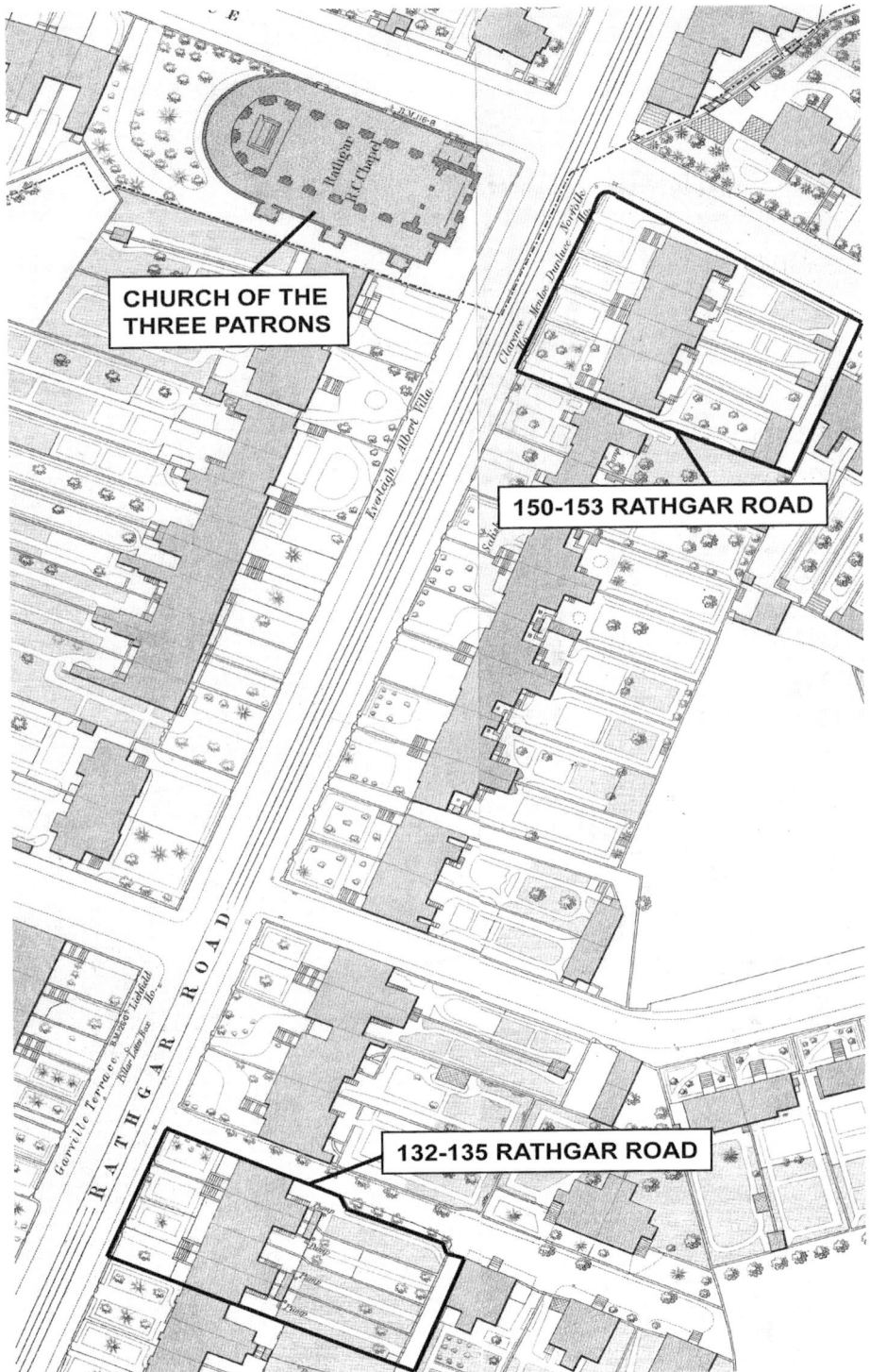

Figure 1.6 Ordnance Survey map of Rathgar, 1882 (reproduced courtesy Trinity College Dublin).

22 *Architecture of Dublin's bourgeois homes*

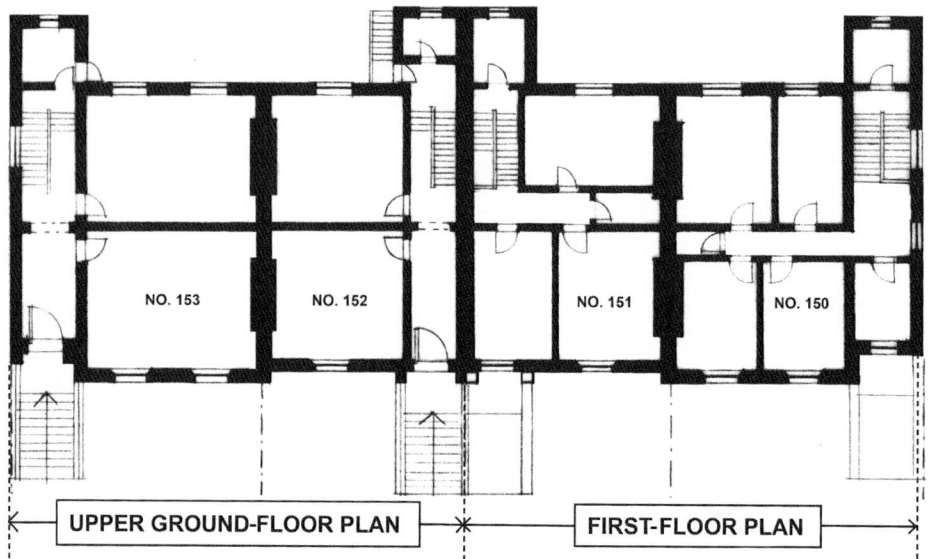

Figure 1.7 Numbers 150–153 Rathgar Road, upper ground-floor and first-floor plans.

Compared to the earlier scheme described above at 132–135 Rathgar Road, Meade's site was wider by thirty-two feet. He could have accommodated five of the houses designed by Murray and Denny, but instead he opted for a lower-density scheme. The site was divided in four, with the two end plots seven feet wider than the two central plots. At ground-floor level, the plans are similar to Murray and Denny's, with two similarly sized reception rooms at entrance level, a continuous hall and stairwell to the side and full-height rear returns. At first-floor level, three bedrooms are provided in the central plots, but the wider end bays allow for a five-bedroom layout.

Externally, Murray and Denny's scheme is a simple expression of the plan. There is no attempt to embellish the façade, by providing decorative brick, stone or stringcoursing. The building has been designed from the inside out: the windows have been centred on the rooms behind, but they do not line up on the front façade (Plate 3). Formally, it reads as a horizontal plane of yellow brick, relieved only by flat-headed windows and round-headed doorcases. Meade's street elevation is more successful, as it has been manipulated to provide vertical breaks in the front façade. This has been done by manipulating the plan: the end houses project out beyond the line of those adjacent, and then recess back in to form the entrance at the side (Plate 4). These projections are then framed in bands of render; on the entrance floor they are lined out to resemble quoins, while a smooth finish is used on the upper level. The whole composition is tied together by wide bands of stringcoursing, with a generously proportioned cornice at parapet level. Care has been taken to align the windows on all floors, just one of many indications of a desire to form a harmonious street façade, suggesting the hand of an architect.

4. Kingstown: Crosthwaite Park (1860–1878)

Both of the previous two schemes addressed Rathgar Road, which was a main arterial route through one of the city's adjoining suburbs. Crosthwaite Park emerged in quite a different context, on an elevated site in Kingstown, a railway suburb located six miles from the centre of Dublin (Figure 0.1). Kingstown was known for its 'scenic beauty'[24] and so its housing was concerned with providing views over the surrounding landscape. They were mostly terraced in form and constructed with local rubble stone, finished in a lime render. Crosthwaite Park consists of three terraces, beginning with the east and west sides, which were designed to face each other across a park. They are all rendered and of two bays, rising two to three storeys over a raised basement (Figure 1.8). The scheme was planned to exploit its elevated location, by attempting to frame views of the surrounding landscape. This was an important marketing tool for owners: when Number 12 was advertised in 1861, the notice claimed that the house was 'most cheerfully situated, commanding extensive and varied views'.[25] It was also of interest to valuers: soon after the completion of Numbers 2, 4 and 6, it was noted that there was a 'good view from the rear of these houses'.[26]

We have discussed the manner in which façades could be manipulated by providing vertical breaks, or by introducing a variety of materials and features such as stringcoursing. The east and west sides of Crosthwaite Park each comprise

Figure 1.8 Numbers 2–32 Crosthwaite Park East.

24 *Architecture of Dublin's bourgeois homes*

Figure 1.9 Numbers 10 and 12 Crosthwaite Park East.

sixteen houses, resulting in low horizontal façades. The east side is three-and-a-half times the length of Meade's façade in Rathgar Road, presenting a much greater challenge to the designer. At Crosthwaite Park East, different formal devices are introduced to create a compositional rhythm across the façade. Each house features at least one bay window, which provide a regular vertical accent across the terrace. These were an important feature of Victorian house design, as they flooded the rooms with light and provided angled views down the street. It appears that they were also an attraction to prospective residents, as 'bay windows all through' were advertised at Number 4 in 1885.[27] Like the sea views, they also increased the value of Victorian house property, as they were factored into the calculations in Griffith's Valuation.[28] Other compositional features are the paired entrances, which are framed by carved console brackets supporting a projecting frieze.

The east side of Crosthwaite Park was built by a number of local builders, who took at least three plots each. On signing the lease, they were required to build within a plot width of twenty-five feet. However, not all speculators were

Architecture of Dublin's bourgeois homes 25

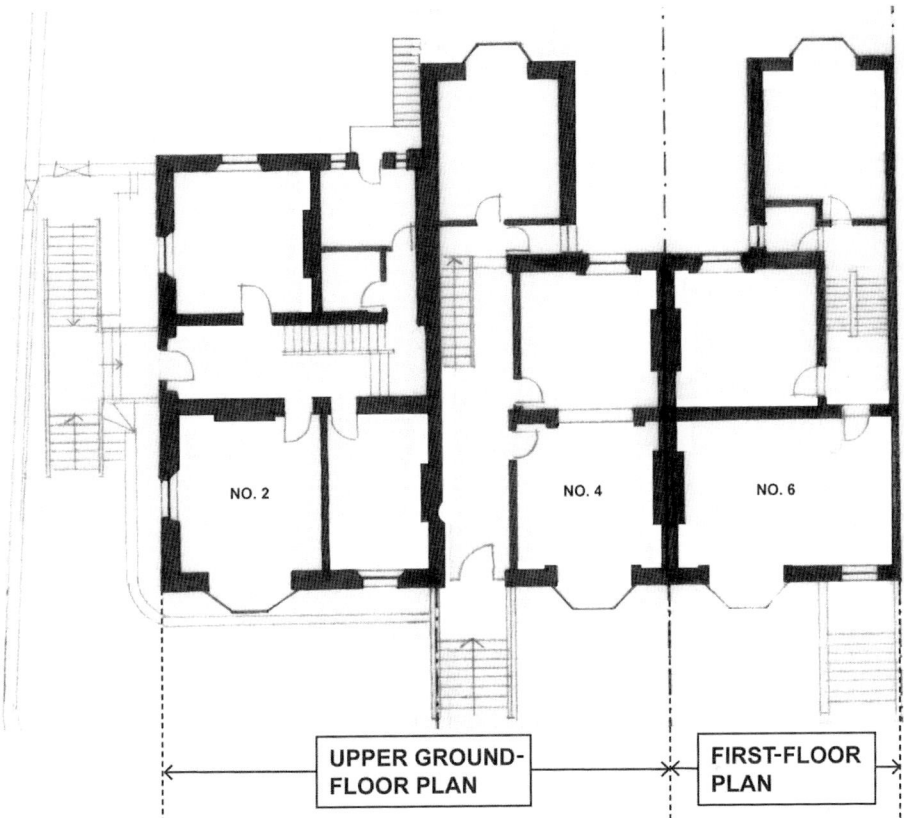

Figure 1.10 Numbers 2–6 Crosthwaite Park East, upper ground-floor and first-floor plans.

compliant. The architect and engineer Peter Joseph Moran acquired three adjoining sites on the east side of Crosthwaite Park in the early 1860s. However, it seems that a mistake was made in setting out the buildings, as Number 8 is wider by over one foot. In order to comply with the overall plot width specified in the lease, the two adjoining houses were narrowed accordingly.[29] This indicates how housing schemes built to broad guidelines could be compromised by the decisions of individual developers. Other anomalies can be found on the front elevation, which on first glance appears to be a homogeneous façade, characterised by a succession of paired entrances and oriel windows. Most of the houses feature two-storey oriel windows, but on three of the properties they appear only on the first floor. Thus, these speculators focused their efforts on the provision of a feature window to the most important room in the house: the first-floor drawing room. However for the elevation, it creates a 'top-heavy' house front, which breaks the regularity of the façade. Added to this is the peculiar 'huge bow-shaped pediment'[30] over the entrances to Numbers 10 and 12, Moran's attempt to put his stamp on the terrace (Figure 1.9). It's possible that he designed Crosthwaite Park: he leased three adjoining plots on the east side, and appears in the records at the time as an auctioneer, a surveyor, an architect and engineer, with an office nearby in Clarinda Park. In 1861, just as Crosthwaite Park was rising out of the ground, Moran advertised his services as an architect to speculators in the area. He could supervise 'Works of every description' for a fee of 2½% but he could include plans at a cost of 5%. When a newly built house was put up for sale at Clarinda Park South in 1862, it was reported to be built 'in a superior manner under architectural supervision'.[31]

The houses at Crosthwaite Park are planned in a similar manner to the schemes described thus far, with two reception rooms, one front and one back, alongside a hall and stair compartment (Figure 1.10: Number 4). In both Rathgar Road schemes, the highest ceilings were recorded on this floor, where the main reception rooms were located. However, at Crosthwaite Park, the higher ceilings are reserved for the floor above, where a large drawing room runs the full width of the plot (Figure 1.10: Number 6). It is a feature of nearby Clarinda Park and Royal Terrace and is inherited from the eighteenth-century townhouse: the first floor or 'the drawing room storey' was where typically guests were entertained. Thus, three reception rooms are provided in these houses: two on the ground floor and a primary space at first-floor level. To the rear, full-height rear returns are large enough to accommodate bedrooms, capturing views of the Dublin sea and mountains.[32]

An extra storey was added to Crosthwaite Park West, most likely to capture views over the roofs of the east side (Figure 1.11). To this day, this floor enjoys panoramas to the sea and the mountains, which must have been even more

Figure 1.11 Crosthwaite Park West.

dramatic in the 1860s, when there was little to obscure the view. However, in formal terms, this attic storey appears as an afterthought, rather than an intended part of the design. It is punctured by a succession of round-headed windows, which are not in keeping with the remainder of the fenestration, and accentuate the horizontality of the façade. On the floors below, the elevational treatment is a copy of the east side, with a rhythm of paired entrances and two-storey oriel windows. We have seen how successful this was on the opposite terrace, where a long façade was balanced by the introduction of a series of vertical devices. It would have been more successful to continue the oriel windows to the top storey of the west side, to help to integrate this level with the floors below.

Other differences in the west side relate to the rear returns, which are smaller on Numbers 15, 17, 19 and 21, providing only a small extension to the stair landing. These houses were built by the local builder John Galvin of Kingstown between 1863 and 1865.[33] Elsewhere on the terrace other variations can be found: Number 29 for instance is over four feet wider than one of the Galvin houses.[34] This has obvious benefits for the interior layouts of these houses, where the two-room plan is stretched to suit the wider plot. These distinct differences show the influence of the individual leaseholder.

The terraced house: a summary of findings

These early suburban terraces bear close resemblance to their predecessors: the eighteenth-century townhouse (Plate 5). Although they each emerged in different districts, they share common characteristics. They are all of the two-room plan, clad in plain brick and finished with parapet roofs. Number 11 Northumberland Road (1837) is a simple adaptation of the Georgian terrace, but reduced in scale and risen halfway out of the ground. The two schemes on Rathgar Road reveal further changes: the houses have risen almost entirely out of the ground, are reduced by one storey, and are pushed further back from the street. The earlier scheme at Numbers 132–135 Rathgar Road (1851) is characterised by a relatively plain façade, with minimal decoration focused on the entrance doorcases. Numbers 150–153 Rathgar Road (1857–1859) are further along in the process of transformation, as they are in marked contrast to the plain brick façade of their neighbours. The plot widths were varied to form a pair of two-bay houses in the centre, flanked by a three-bay house, one either side. The end houses were used to create vertical breaks in the façade, by forming a series of projections and recesses on the front elevation. Other devices provide variety at Crosthwaite Park (1860–1865), such as the oriel windows and paired entrances, which provide a vertical rhythm across this much longer façade. Thus, by introducing a range of materials and/or formal devices, the Victorian terrace has broken away from the 'unadorned stock brick'[35] of its Georgian past.

In time, Victorian terraces were increasingly imbued with a greater range of decorative and formal devices. At Numbers 34–44 Northumberland Road (1872),

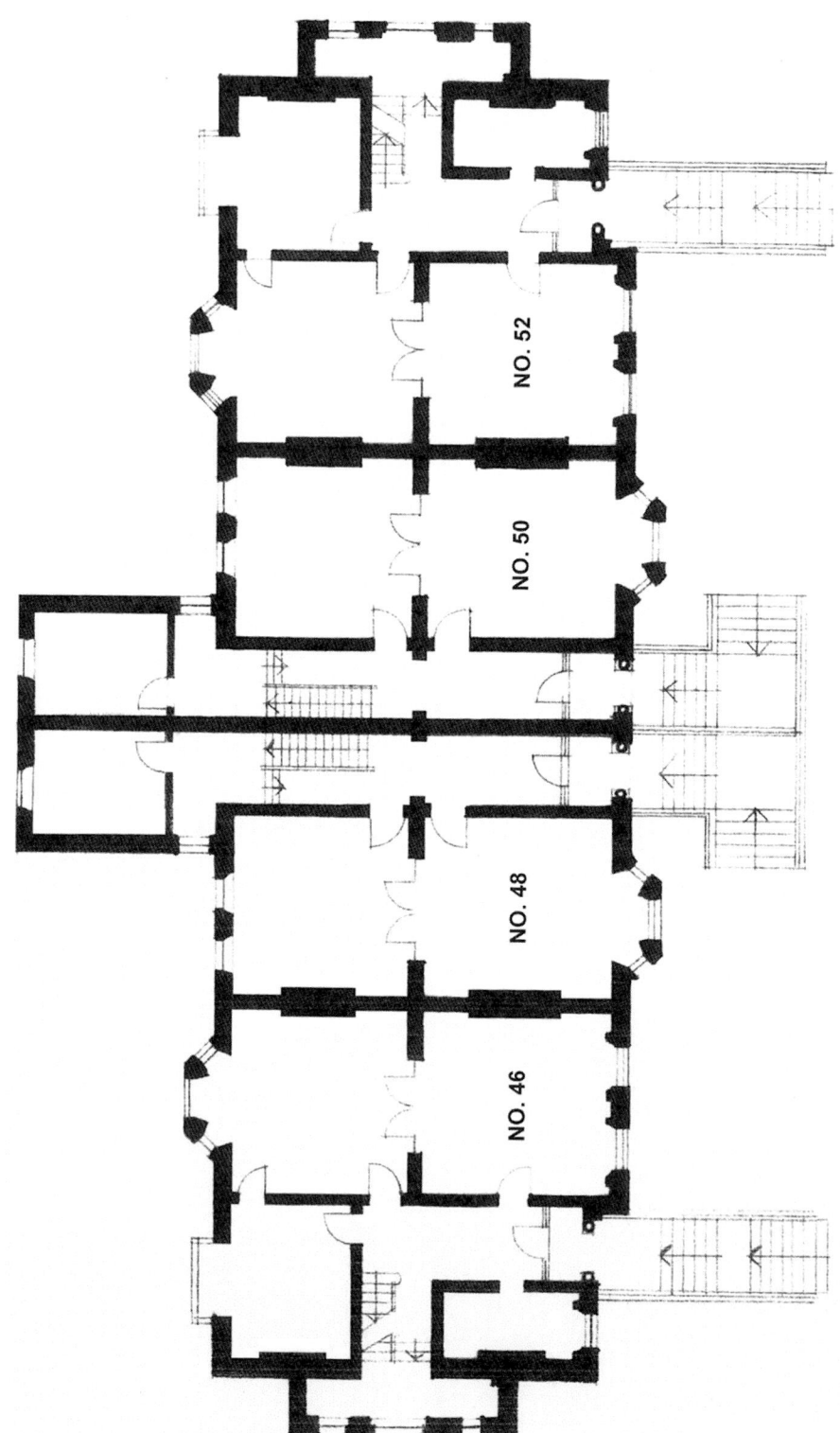

Figure 1.12 Numbers 46–52 Northumberland Road, upper ground-floor plans.

the parapet was substituted by overhanging eaves and a hipped roof profile (Plate 6). This provides the opportunity to display a more exposed roof form, and so polychromatic brick is introduced under the eaves, and wrapped around the chimney stacks. Announcing the arrival of the red brick front, increasingly fashionable from the 1860s, this façade contrasts with the brown/yellow brick finish of the previous terraces on the road (Figure 1.4). Nevertheless, the decoration is restrained, limited to some embellishment of the entrance doorcases. They are also fully emerged out of the ground, requiring a full flight of steps to the main entrance. A similar architectural language can be found at Numbers 68–74, built five years later, with the addition of an oriel window that dominates the entrance floor (Plate 7). When Numbers 46–52 Northumberland Road emerged in the 1880s,[36] it marked the pinnacle of development of the suburban terrace in Dublin (Plate 8 and Figure 1.12). The scheme is in the High Victorian Gothic style and displays a high degree of architectural sophistication.[37] The careful modelling of the façade, including the recessed ends and raised gable break fronts, is successfully integrated with stone stringcoursing, eaves bracketing and polychromatic brick. Completed in 1885, the Meades were instrumental in creating the most successful architectural composition on the road. It also marked the metamorphosis of the terrace into a new Victorian house typology, fully adapted to its suburban context.

Turning the corner

Dublin's Victorian homes were inspired by the eighteenth-century townhouse, characterised as a two-dimensional building form, 'a space between two cross walls'.[38] Externally, it is expressed as a continuous brick façade, running from party wall to party wall (Figure 1.1). For the mid-terrace, the house was simply organised, consisting of 'boxes of rooms harmoniously arranged around lobbies and halls'.[39] They were constructed mainly by speculative builders, who focused their attention on two parallel façades: one to the street and another to the rear. However, the formation of the corner was a more complex problem that required the resolution of two façades running in different directions. In many of the principal streets or squares, the main terraced front dominated the corner, producing blank gables and garden walls to the side streets. These gabled ends were sometimes alleviated by bows, bay windows or blind windows, with varying degrees of success (Figure 1.13).[40] In some cases, an effort was made to continue the façade around the corner, but this was often offset by sacrifices to the layout inside, and/or the loss of a garden space to the rear. This awkward relationship between the house and the urban plot began to change in the nineteenth century.

The Georgian house emerged from a tight urban framework, which demanded a dense form of development, forming long cliff-like façades close to the street. When this house type was adapted to the green fields surrounding the city, speculators were no longer constrained by the rigidity of the urban plot. Reduced in scale and pushed back from the street, these new suburban prototypes stood in individual

Figure 1.13 Corner of Merrion Square South and Fitzwilliam Street Upper, Dublin city.

blocks, with space in between (Figure 1.6). Early Victorian houses remained in the Georgian tradition, sparsely decorated except for the entrance doorcases, their ends finishing abruptly in blank gables (Plate 3).[41] In other cases, the end plots widened to take advantage of a less space conscious suburb, forming a single-storey addition to the side. At Number 25 Northumberland Road, this was used as an entrance hall, allowing the front reception room to run from party wall to party wall (Figure 1.5). Alternatively, it could extend the full height of the building to house both the hall and stairs, providing for additional bedrooms on the first floor (Figure 1.7). These early experiments were a simple 'tack-on' of a block to the side, lit by a window or two in the side wall, but gradually the side extension was fully absorbed into the plan. If we compare the plan of Numbers 46–52 Northumberland Road, built by the Meade builders twenty-five years after their scheme on Rathgar Road, a clear metamorphosis is evident (Plate 8 and Figure 1.12). While the central plots are of the standard two-room plan, forming two-bay façades, with extensions to the rear, the end houses have been widened by fourteen feet. This results on wider four-bay façades on the ends, with large side extensions stepped back from the main façade. The stairs has been turned to run parallel to the front façade, providing space for additional rooms to the front and rear, with smaller ancillary spaces lit from the side. In contrast to the largely blank gables of the past, the Victorian house type had now begun to turn the corner, exploiting the exposed ends of the suburban plot. It also represents a successful fusion of the terraced and semi-detached house.

At Crosthwaite Park, this device was taken one step further, by forming grand set pieces on the ends facing Tivoli Road (Figure 1.10). To do this, the layout was manipulated to serve this grand entrance front, by moving the entrance to the side, accessed by a T-plan stairs. The depth of the building was also increased, forming a double-loaded entrance hall. Notably, the chimneys were placed on the internal walls, allowing the rooms to face all three sides. These changes affected the façade to Crosthwaite Park: the last two houses on the block step up in height, with increased ornamentation to the parapet (Figure 1.14). The façade then wrapped itself around the end, marking this transition by a number of pilasters on the upper level. The entrance front is reminiscent of many of the detached Victorian houses in the area: a three-bay, two-storey over raised basement structure with a central entrance doorcase and decorative window surrounds. A similar template is produced at Crosthwaite Park West, where a straight stairs and projecting entrance

Figure 1.14 Number 2 Crosthwaite Park East.

was inserted on the end wall (Figure 1.11). It is not a feature at the other ends of these blocks, and has as much to do with capturing views of the sea at first-floor level, as creating an imposing elevation to Tivoli Road.

Dublin's suburban semi-detached houses

Early forms of semi-detachment

Today, the semi-detached house is a familiar form of housing on these islands. However, it is largely a nineteenth-century phenomenon, when large numbers of paired houses were built around towns and cities in Britain and Ireland. Compared to the detached villa, paired housing made sound structural and economic sense, as a shared party wall and chimney stack reduced the amount of heat loss from a building.[42] 'Double' cottages or farmhouses had been built in rural locations in Britain since the seventeenth century, the earliest recorded being in the village of Norfolk in c.1600. The first street of semi-detached houses was built at The Grove, Highgate, London in 1688, where three paired dwellings were developed by the merchant William Blake.[43] During the eighteenth century that followed, paired villas were sometimes built in and around both London and Dublin, but not in enough numbers to signify the emergence of a new form of domestic architecture.[44] The first large-scale planned scheme for semi-detached houses dates from 1794, when the Eyre estate was laid out in north London. Consisting of two-storey houses all laid out in pairs, this development marked a new departure for the English house form. Summerson considered this 'a revolution of striking significance and far-reaching effect', indicating a willingness to forgo the terrace for the semi-detached villa.[45]

Despite these early aspirations towards the end of the eighteenth century, it took at least another twenty-five years for the plan for the Eyre estate to come to fruition. Construction began in the 1820s and the final scheme, named St John's Wood, contained a mixture of both detached and semi-detached houses. Number 20 Hamilton Terrace, dating from 1832, was the first of these 'double' houses to be built, characterised by a three-storey brick façade, reminiscent of the eighteenth-century terrace. Later examples were reduced in height to two storeys and clad in stucco, such as the houses at Clifton Hill, which were finished in Regency style fronts (1854–1858). This stucco finish had a unifying effect on the paired form, by making two houses appear as one. Architect John Nash had been the pioneer of this 'two for the price of one' idea in the early nineteenth century, by adding centralised pediments and gables to paired houses.[46] An Irish example can be found at Harcourt Terrace in Dublin, comprising five pairs of Regency style houses built in 1830. The central bays are articulated with an assortment of pediments, niches and columns, emphasising the singularity of each pair.[47] The garden designer J. C. Loudon continued the trend in 1833, with the publication of a number of seminal guides to suburban house design. He claimed that the paired house could give 'dignity and consequence to each dwelling by making it appear to have the magnitude of two houses'.⁴⁸ Creating an illusion of grandeur, he advised designers to locate the two entrances so they could not be seen at once. By forming a recessed porch on either side, or combining two entrances into one, visitors could perceive a house as twice its size. Loudon practised what he preached, as he lived in such a home in London, with side porches and a conservatory to the front, which concealed the duality of the house.⁴⁹

Compared to terraces that sit on comparatively narrow plots, semi-detached houses require sites that are often double the width. They are not the most economical form of speculation, as compared to terraces, half the number of houses were possible in the same width of plot. It was a more expensive form of building, which tended to attract a higher class of tenant. In the Dublin suburbs, they were more common in prestigious areas such as the Pembroke estate, which attracted prosperous professionals. The terrace remained the dominant house type in the Kingstown estate, but large-scale semi-detached houses were built on Monkstown hill, capturing dramatic views of the sea. They were also a feature of certain parts of Rathmines, such as in Belgrave Square and Palmerston Park. We have seen how the Victorian terrace was derived from the eighteenth-century townhouse, and retained the two-room plan and parapet roof detail. The semi-detached house used the same template but went through greater changes, as it widened to three bays and formed its own distinctive plan. What then was the driving force for this new house type, and how did it evolve during the nineteenth century in Dublin? The next section will trace its gradual development in the Pembroke estate, which was a testing ground for the semi-detached house form.

The development of the semi-detached house in the Pembroke estate

By the early nineteenth century, Dublin had already begun to break beyond the traditional city limits of the canals, so that by 1816 its hinterlands were characterised by what has been described as 'a steady scattering' of development lining the major radial routes out of the city. We have seen how these houses closely resembled the eighteenth-century terrace, but were reduced in scale and pushed back from the street (Figure 1.2). In 1830, the Pembroke estate followed trends elsewhere by commissioning its first scheme for semi-detached houses, located on the south side of Pembroke Road.⁵⁰ In an ambitious plan to create a 'very handsome approach' to the city, it indicated large plots over four times the width of the terraces opposite, with generous setbacks, forming deep front gardens. The estate explored two options: the first were paired versions of the terraces opposite, comprising two-bay, three-storey structures, with parapet roofs and half basements. The second option marked a shift in form: these houses were reduced by another storey and the parapet was replaced by an overhanging roof. In the years to come, this building form would characterise many of the surrounding streets and is an indication of the estate's vision for its suburban ground.⁵¹ It seems that it came too early for Pembroke Road, as the road developed thereafter using the first taller option (Figure 1.15).

34 *Architecture of Dublin's bourgeois homes*

Figure 1.15 Numbers 19 and 21 Pembroke Road.

It took another thirty years for the semi-detached house to emerge fully formed in the Pembroke estate. Over the following decades, a number of streets were laid out, mainly in terraces. In 1853, John Vernon was appointed agent of the Pembroke estate, and brought in a stricter level of building control, particularly

Figure 1.16 Numbers 16 and 18 Burlington Road.

in the more valuable western sector. During the 1860s, the majority of housing built there was semi-detached, which he ensured through a condition in the lease. The earliest of these to survive are Numbers 16 and 18 Burlington Road, built between 1856 and 1859 (Figure 1.16).[52] Formally, they are a paired version of the Victorian terrace described above at 132–135 Rathgar Road (Plate 3), characterised by plain brick façades, simple round-headed doorcases and parapet roofs. However, the sites are double the width, forming wider houses with a porch extension to the side. While the paired house is in the process of adapting to a more spacious plot, the roof is still hidden behind a parapet wall, harking back to its terraced predecessor. It remains two-dimensional in character: only the dominant street façade is articulated, with the roofs hidden behind blank lateral walls.

As with the terrace, it took some time for the semi-detached house to surrender the parapet detail, which until then had characterised so much of the city's domestic architecture. John Vernon was determined to eradicate it from paired housing in the estate, as he was insisting on a 'Cantilever roof' to Numbers 26 and 28 Lansdowne Road by 1859 (Figure 1.17).[53] Formally, this presented a fundamental change in the architectural character of the semi-detached house, expressing the roof form on the front façade. In this example, the side returns

36 *Architecture of Dublin's bourgeois homes*

Figure 1.17 Numbers 26 and 28 Lansdowne Road.

were two storeys high, making an efficient use of the additional space to the side. However, it is interesting to see how speculators grappled with the roof over this adjunct to the main building volume. The earlier houses form either a gable or parapet over the side return, both of which sit awkwardly with the hipped roof profile of the main volume. It was only by 1867 when Numbers 42 and 44 were built that a solution was found, where the hipped roof was continued around the side extension, integrating it with the main building (Figure 1.18).

These changes in the external form had implications for the plan, as illustrated in Northumberland Road, where the first paired houses emerged by 1865. These plots were double the width of the earlier terraces with large setbacks forming generous front gardens (Plate 2). These early semi-detached houses adapted in various ways to suit the wider plots. Numbers 31 and 33 (leased by Patrick O'Toole) retained the common Georgian plan, but added extensions on either side, slightly recessed from the front façade (Figure 1.19: C). Numbers 26 to 32, (leased by James Farrell) emerged at the same time on the opposite side of the road. Here, the plan was stretched out fit the wider plot, forming two elongated receptions rooms, one front and one back (Figure 1.19: B). These were early experiments, making awkward compromises between old and new typologies.[54] It was particularly evident at first-floor level, where the provision of bedrooms demanded further subdivision of the floor plate. Compared to the narrower terrace where the rooms were accessed

Architecture of Dublin's bourgeois homes 37

directly off the stairwell, a corridor was required to access the centre of the wider semi-detached plan (Figure 1.20: B). This was a transitionary phase where the simple two-room plan, designed for a narrower plot, was no longer suitable to the paired house site. At Number 12 Raglan Road, a solution had been found in 1862, by disassociating the stairs from the entrance hall, and moving it to the rear centre of the plan, as found at Number 39 Northumberland Road in 1877 (Figure 1.19: D).[55] This marks the emergence of a distinctive plan for the semi-detached house, reconfigured to its new suburban context.

One resounding feature of the early semi-detached form is the sparse ornamentation of the façade. These early templates suffer the monotony of large expanses of brick wall, punctured only by simple window openings and entrance doorcases. Although lively polychromatic brick was used in terraced houses by 1863 (Plate 1), it was not until the end of the decade that it reached semi-detached façades in the Pembroke estate. This was first recorded in 1869 in Clyde Road, where lines of stone stringcoursing, Venetian Gothic doorcases and eaves brackets appeared on façades (Plate 10).[56] However, it was not until the 1870s that the semi-detached house began to embrace the eclecticism of the Victorian era. Projecting bay windows began to push through the front walls of houses in Lansdowne Road in 1873, helping to balance out the horizontality of the paired house form. Over the following

Figure 1.18 Numbers 42 and 44 Lansdowne Road.

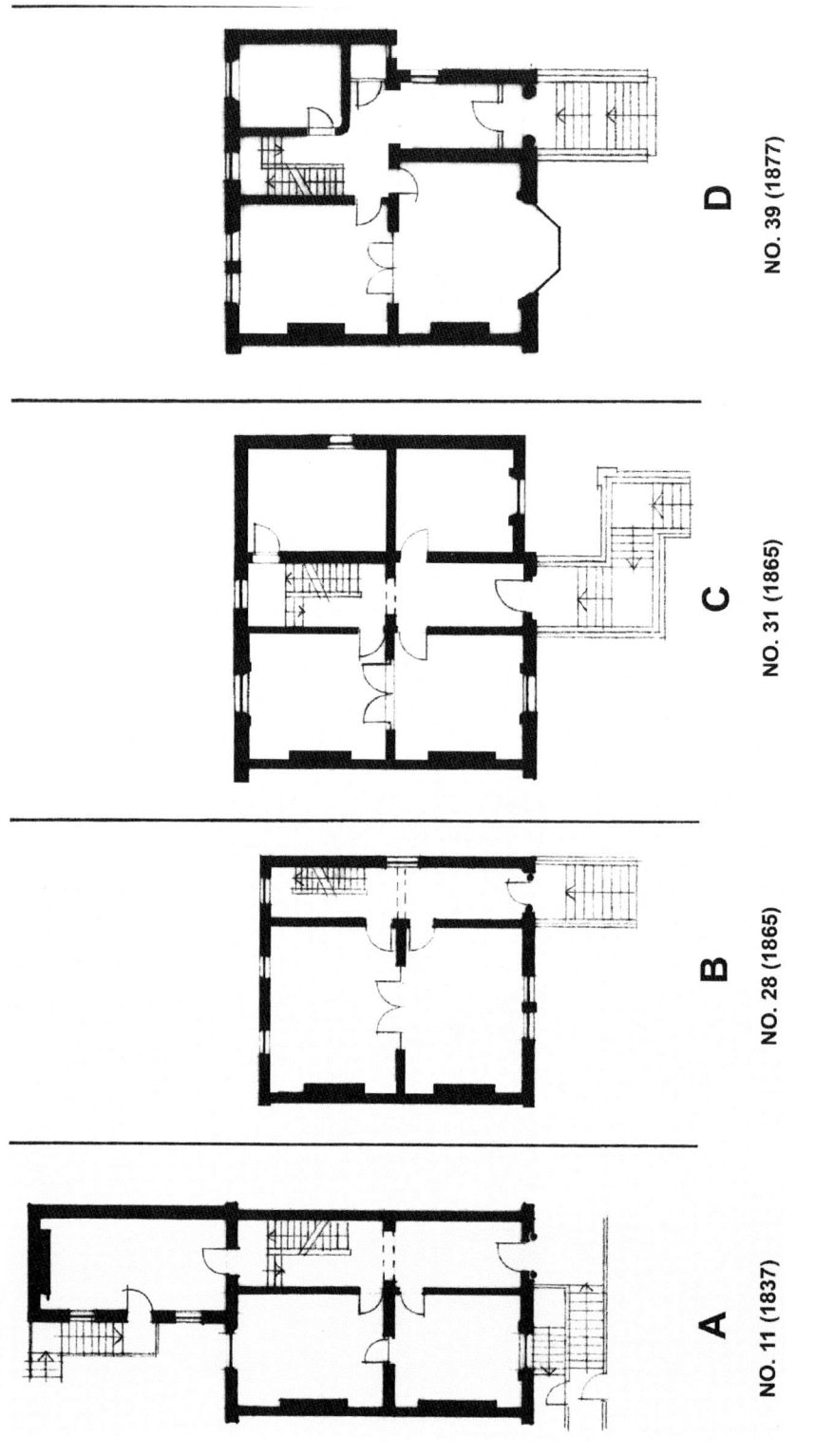

Figure 1.19 Numbers 11, 28, 31 and 39 Northumberland Road, drawing comparing upper ground-floor plans.

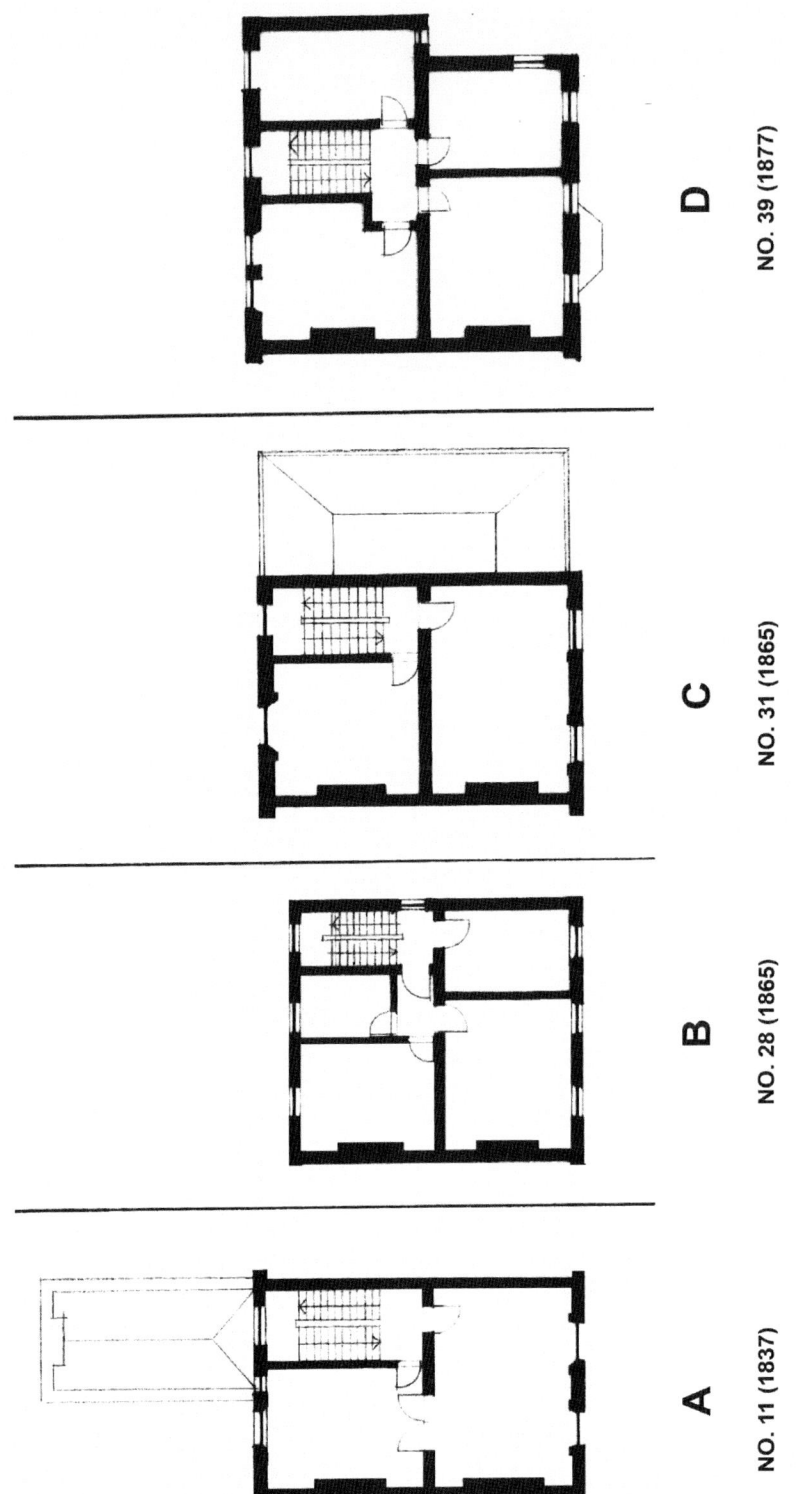

Figure 1.20 Numbers 11, 28, 31 and 39 Northumberland Road, drawing comparing first-floor plans.

years, houses were infused with a greater variety of materials, such as black brick, limestone and glazed white brick, stitched across façades in lively stone string-coursing, with coloured brick laid to form chevron or diaper patterns across the façade (Plate 11). By the 1870s, the semi-detached house now had its own distinctive decorative style on Northumberland Road, a major arterial route through the Pembroke estate.

Case studies of semi-detached houses in Pembroke, Rathgar and Kingstown

As producers of high-quality housing schemes, the work of Michael Meade and William Carvill provides a focus for this analysis. In 1865, these men began building semi-detached houses in the fields around their homes, during a decade of record growth in suburban building in Dublin. While the average speculator acquired two or four plots, Carvill and Meade were building twelve to sixteen houses each. Built at the same time but in different sectors, they illustrate how location had an influence on the final building form. A total of twenty-eight buildings will be analysed: twelve built by Meade on the Pembroke estate and eighteen by Carvill in Rathgar. Meade's houses were constructed over a fourteen-year period, illustrating how house design changed over time.

1. Pembroke: 1–19 Ailesbury Road (1865–1879)

By the 1860s, the semi-detached house was the dominant form of domestic architecture in the western side of the Pembroke estate. When Ailesbury Road was laid out in this sector in 1863, it cut through green fields and market gardens, three miles south of the city. Extending for over a mile in length, Meade was the first to build on the street, acquiring a prime corner site of over two acres on the junction with Merrion Road. Michael Meade acquired his first plots there in 1865, where he built twelve semi-detached houses: ten on the south side of the road (Figure 1.21: Numbers 1–19, built 1865–1870), and two on the north side (Numbers 1 and 2, built 1877–1879). In terms of their overall massing and scale, the first ten houses bear a resemblance to those built a few years earlier at Raglan Road, located closer to the city (Plate 9). A product of the building lease, they are all three-bay, two-storey over raised basement structures with overhanging eaves. However there are differences in the form of the houses at Ailesbury Road: the roofs are gabled rather than hipped, and the side returns do not rise the full height of the building (Figure 1.22). These variations reflect the choice of the speculator: the lease required him to project the roof over the external walls, but he could choose to finish the ends in either a gable or a hip. There are also few attempts to form openings in the side walls, and so they are characterised primarily by blank gable ends. All efforts are focused instead on the front façade, which is clad in red brick with large window openings framed in decorative stone surrounds.

While the external form clings to earlier traditions, the internal layout has evolved with its own distinctive plan. A modest side return accommodates the

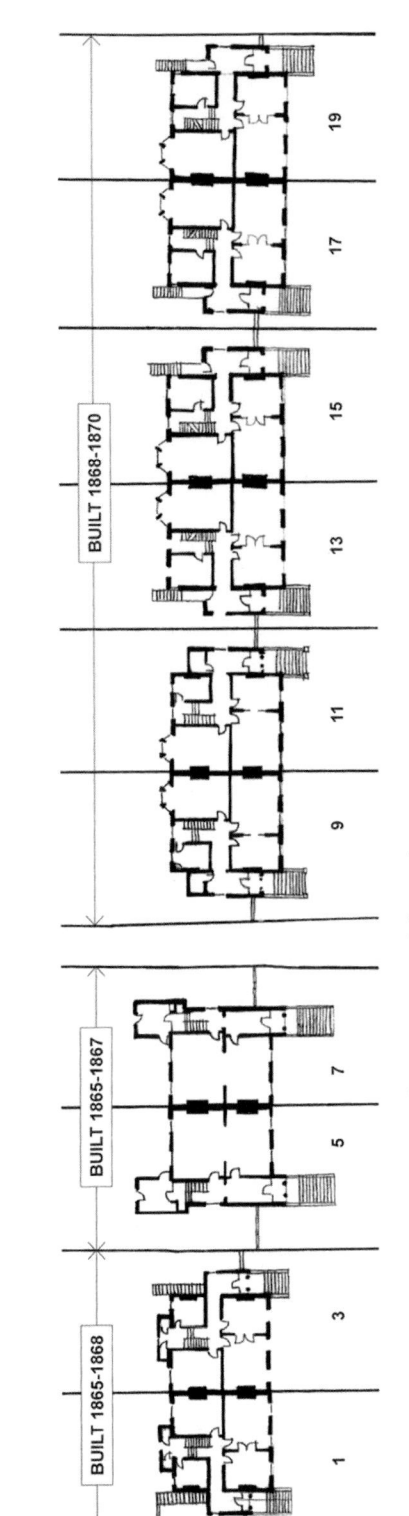

Figure 1.21 Numbers 1–19 Ailesbury Road, upper ground-floor plans.

42   *Architecture of Dublin's bourgeois homes*

Figure 1.22 Numbers 1 and 3 Ailesbury Road.

entrance hall, allowing the front of the plan to be devoted to living space (Figure 1.22). Three reception rooms are provided: two interconnecting spaces to the front, and a separate room to the rear. The later houses (Numbers 9–19: built 1868–1870) benefit from two-storey canted bay windows to the rear, which provided views over south facing fields. The stairs is located in the rear centre of the plan, similar to that recorded at Raglan Road in 1862 (Figure 1.23). This had implications for other parts of the design, forming a new space where the stairs used to be, accessed off the half landing. In some houses, this space extends into a full-height side return, but in Ailesbury Road it is a comparatively small space, contained within the existing volume. The upper level benefits from the central location of the stairs, where three bedrooms are accessed directly off a modest first-floor landing. Sanitary accommodation is inserted in the left over spaces: at the centre of the gable at first-floor level (Numbers 9–19), or by projecting a space to the rear of the stairwell (Numbers 1 and 3).

While these first ten houses are volumetrically similar, Numbers 5 and 7 are quite different in plan. They were all most likely built by the Meade building firm, but these are the only two houses leased to Michael Meade's son Joseph. Instead of a separately defined side return, a projecting entrance portico is inserted to the third bay, similar to houses in Raglan Road (Figure 1.24). In contrast to the houses

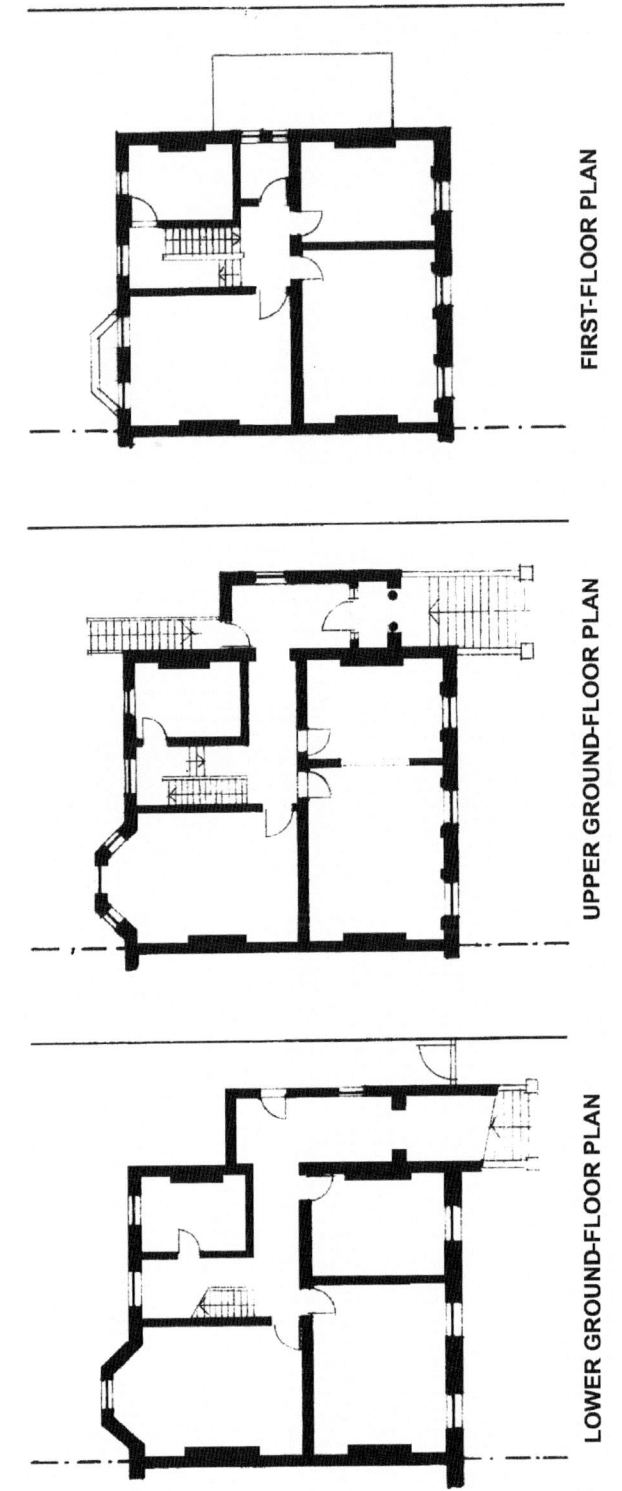

Figure 1.23 Plans of Number 11 Ailesbury Road.

leased by his father, Joseph Meade's plan harks back to the Georgian terrace. The location of the stairs means that a corridor is required to access the centre of the plan at first-floor level. This is offset by a full-height extension to the rear, an unusual feature for a semi-detached house at the time, providing additional rooms off the half-landing level. This house shows that despite the confines of the building lease, variations could be inserted by the leaseholder. These two houses formed part of Joseph Meade's marriage settlement in 1870, although he does not appear to have lived there.[57]

These are beautifully crafted buildings, which present their best side to the street, while economising on the less prominent faces. In accordance with the building lease, the front façade is clad in 'the best red bricks', while the basement storey is finished in granite ashlar.[58] A cheaper stock brick is to the side, forming the transition to the red brick front in either of two ways (Plate 12). Granite quoins define the corner of the main volume, but a cheaper route is taken for the less exposed porch extensions, where the red brick front is 'toothed' into the grey brick side. The eaves are characterised by decorative timber brackets, where care has been taken to space them at regular intervals, while relating to the window openings. An unusually extravagant feature is the sandstone window surrounds, which echo those on Meade's villa adjacent. Their varying designs tell the story of the phased

Figure 1.24 Numbers 5 and 7 Ailesbury Road.

construction of the scheme. Those to the later houses are more ornate, reflecting a general trend for house designs to become increasingly decorative. There is similar variation in the entrances: Numbers 1 and 3 (built by 1867) are simple in design with a semi-circular archway and foliated capitals. Numbers 5 and 7, as we have seen, are in contrast to the other eight houses, where the entrance is inserted in a projecting sandstone portico, framed by a recessed archway and limestone columns. The remaining six houses (built by 1870) are more ornate, where segmental arches and decorative keystones sit above polished stone columns with stylised capitals. Despite the use of the window surrounds, timber brackets and entrance doorcases, the external ornamentation is generally restrained. By the time the second set of houses were complete in 1870, polychromatic brick and stone string coursing had been in use in other areas of the estate for at least two years.[59] Clearly, they were not uniformly dispersed throughout the suburbs: it wasn't until 1877 that they were introduced in Northumberland Road.

After completing the first ten houses, Meade waited another seven years to lease a plot on the north side of Ailesbury Road. By 1879, he had completed another pair of semi-detached houses, which he could see from the windows of his villa across the street. Numbers 2 and 4 were very different to his earlier experiments on Ailesbury Road, with wider plots and more generous volumes (Plate 13). The two houses are imbued with the increased eclecticism of the 1870s, with Bath stone stringcoursing, imposts and keystones. The canted bay windows found to the rear of the houses opposite are inserted here on the front elevation, robustly expressed in brick and stone. Michael Meade abandoned the blank gables of the 1860s, instead adding hipped roofs, full-height side extensions and windows in the side walls. Number 2 takes advantage of its corner site by increasing in width and inserting the entrance in the gable, in a two-storey projection to the side. An unusual feature here is the continuation of the expensive red brick and granite finish to the side *and* rear elevations, which was above the requirements of the lease. The scheme has all of the hallmarks of a client-led design and Number 2 is the only one of Meade's houses that appears to have been sold, rather than let to tenants, to a former British army captain in 1879.

The design for Numbers 2 and 4 Ailesbury Road is not successful in terms of its overall composition, and seems to have been compromised by a larger site. It is approximately ten feet wider than the earlier houses, requiring vertical breaks to balance this elongated façade. Admittedly, there is an attempt to provide relief by the addition of bay windows and ornamentation, but the stone stringcourse only serves to accentuate the horizontality. There is a curious projection in the façade of Number 4, which is not mirrored in the adjoining property. Experimentation continues with the side return, but the eaves level does not match that of the main volume, forming awkward junctions between the two elements. The design of this block therefore suggests amateur meddling, rather than the hand of a competent architect. Following the pattern found at Crosthwaite Park, speculative building was open to idiosyncratic departures from the broad design brief provided in lease agreements.

2. Rathmines and Rathgar: Rostrevor Terrace (1865–1870)

Rostrevor Terrace and Orwell Park were developed by the timber merchant William Carvill on his forty-six-acre estate in Rathgar. Carvill and Meade, who were related to each other by marriage, both began building semi-detached houses in the mid-1860s, in different suburbs three miles south of the city. While Meade's development emerged in the prestigious Pembroke estate, Carvill's ground was in the growing suburb of Rathgar, which was dominated by the terraced house (Figure 0.2 and Plate 14). Previously, we discussed the two terraced developments, at 132–135 and 150–153 Rathgar Road. In 1862, Carvill's land was absorbed into the township of Rathmines and Rathgar, which no doubt provided him with the incentive to begin speculating. From 1865 he built eighteen semi-detached houses on his estate: fourteen at Rostrevor Terrace and four at Orwell Park. By the time the houses were completed in 1871, his daughter had married Michael Meade's son at a ceremony nearby. Each family brought two properties to the marriage: Joseph Meade entrusted Numbers 5 and 7 Ailesbury Road and Catherine Carvill conveyed two of the houses built by her father at Rostrevor Terrace.

Rostrevor Terrace is similar in form to the houses described earlier in Lansdowne Road, which emerged in the Pembroke estate from 1860 (Figures 1.17 and 1.18). They are two-bay, two-storey over raised basement structures with the entrance inserted in a full-height side return (Plate 15). In the context of suburban development in general, they were reported to be 'well-built superior houses'. Compared to Ailesbury Road, however, the plots are reduced in scale and pushed eighteen feet closer to the street. He repeated the same template across the seven pairs of houses at Rostrevor Terrace, forming a regular rhythm of uniform façades. Characteristics of the terrace continued to appear, as parapets and gable ends are both in evidence here. It does however provide another solution to the problems discussed at Lansdowne Road, where the parapet is continued across all three bays, successfully integrating it with the remainder of the house. The step in the façade is purely cosmetic, bearing no relation to the plan, forming curious projections in the front rooms (Figure 1.25). It has clearly been inserted to provide vertical breaks in a wide expanse of brick, but also gives uniformity to each pair, perhaps a nod to the 'two for the price of one' idea advised by Loudon in 1838.

A comparison of the plans of Rostrevor Terrace and Ailesbury Road shows that they are almost identical in overall size (Figures 1.23 and 1.25). At Rostrevor Terrace, the entrance is inserted into the third bay, instead of in a separate side extension. This results in two (instead of three) reception rooms, which are turned at right angles to each other: the larger space to the front and a smaller room lit by a bay window to the rear. Otherwise, the plans are virtually identical: the position of the stairs, and third room in the rear corner and the first-floor layouts are all in common here. Externally, however, the houses are very different. At Rostrevor Terrace, the basement is finished with a lime render lined out to resemble ashlar

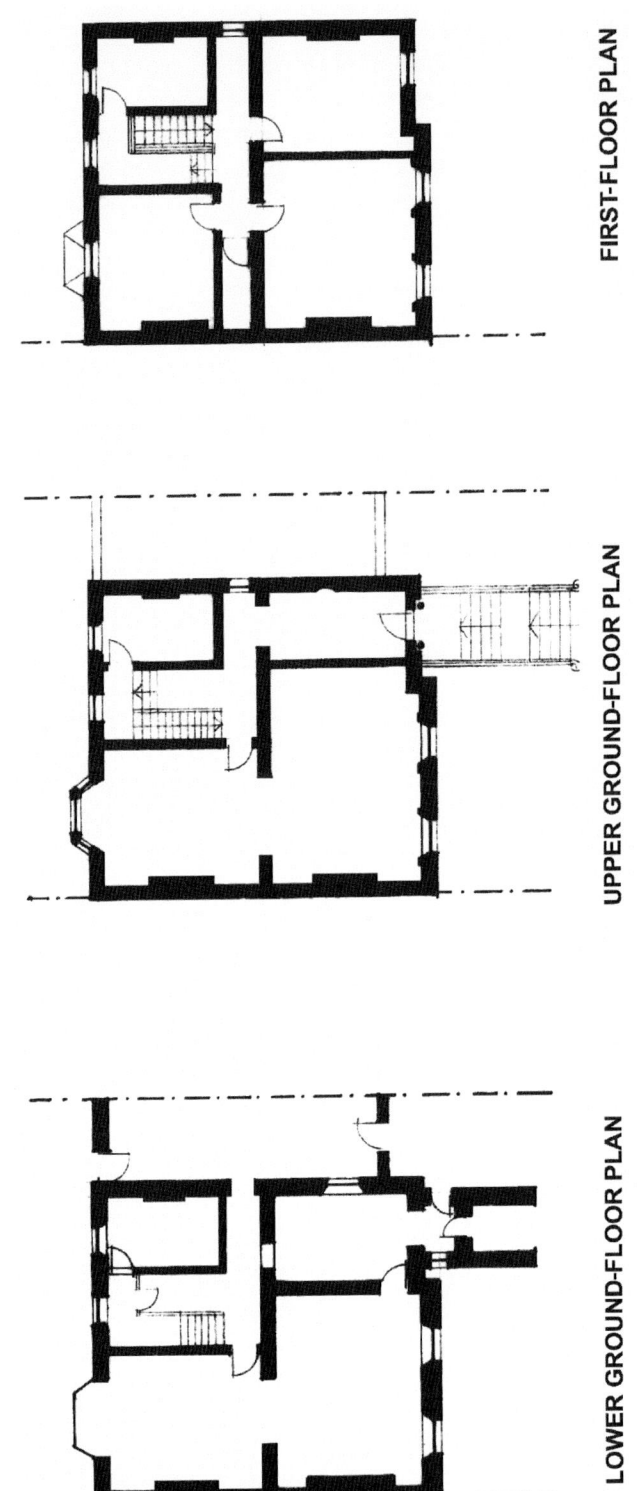

Figure 1.25 Plans of Number 8 Rostrevor Terrace.

stonework, while the transition between the red brick front and the rendered sides are articulated with vermiculated quoins made of 'patent pre-cast stone'.[60] The window lintels are of brick rather than stone, and the parapets are characterised by cornices of brick dentils and dog-toothed corbels. This is repeated on the chimneys and is indicative of the beginnings of a very Victorian phenomenon: the integration of decorative brickwork in façades.

3. Rathmines and Rathgar: Orwell Park

While Rostrevor Terrace was in the course of formation, William Carvill was erecting houses in another holding nearby (Plate 14). Compared to the schemes thus described, these plots are significantly reduced in scale, about 40% narrower than Rostrevor Terrace, relating to their secondary location on a tributary road. They are a simple pairing of two terraced houses, each two bays wide, rising two storeys over a raised basement, with parapet roofs (Plate 16). Unusually, the oriel windows are inserted on the uppermost floor, instead of the more common location on the floor below. This was most likely done to capture sunny views, from this south-facing façade on an elevated site, as evidenced by advertisements for neighbouring houses that boasted 'a splendid view of the Dublin mountains'.[61] Despite the gains for their interiors, these windows take away from the integrity of the exterior, appearing somewhat top-heavy and incongruous on this floor.

The front elevations are clad in red brick, with granite quoins marking the transition to the gable ends. The treatment of the service floor follows that at Rostrevor Terrace, delineated as a rendered base, with the same brick cornicing repeated at the parapet level and on the oriel windows. Other ornamentation is focused on the entrances: curved and straight edged bricks alternate with decorative stone and timber to frame the openings (Plate 17). While in Ailesbury Road and Rostrevor Park the plan has adapted to the wider plot, the Orwell Park houses are still firmly entrenched in the terraced form. It is a scaled-down version of the standard Dublin Georgian terrace: two reception rooms are formed alongside the hall/stair compartment, with a large return to the rear.

The semi-detached house: a summary of findings

In summary, the houses built by Michael Meade and William Carvill stand on the cusp between Georgian and Victorian building practices. They are reflective of the changing shape of the Dublin suburb, which was in the process of adapting familiar building models – the terrace – to a wider suburban plot. Some clung tighter to the terrace (Orwell Park), whereas others were further on in the process of transformation (Plate 18). Meade's earlier experiments on Ailesbury Road (1865–1871) had widened to three bays, but gabled roofs and sparse ornamentation indicate a building form in the early stages of transition. Carvill's houses at Rostrevor Terrace were similarly influenced by earlier models, but managed to create cheaper stripped down versions of houses in the fashionable Pembroke estate. Builders had not yet begun to exploit the new open-ended form offered by the suburban plot, and so the houses remain somewhat two-dimensional in form. All of this changed in 1879 when Meade laid out plots on the north side of Ailesbury Road. Here, gable ends and parapets gave way to hipped roofs, characteristics of the fully developed semi-detached house. Openings were inserted in the end walls, while full-height returns fully exploited the space at the side. In accordance with the fashion of the time, bay windows pushed through the front façade, while new lines of polychromy were introduced. In Northumberland Road, polychromy and bay windows were combined, bringing the semi-detached façade to a new level of sophistication (Plate 11 and front cover). The façade was no longer a flat expanse of brick, but instead was broken by projecting oriel windows and recessed entrances. Two lines of smooth limestone were wrapped across the façade, lifting the overall hue of the brick front, while joining the whole composition together.

A comparative analysis of the suburban house form in Dublin and England

How do these houses compare with similar classes of homes built in other Irish and British cities? Certainly, the formal evolution of the house is similar, such as the lower density of development and the use of hipped roofs, projecting bay windows and decorative detailing. While some of these details appear generic, it is the mixture of materials used on the front elevations and the treatment of the service floor that make Dublin's suburban houses unique. In the brick-rich cities of London and Belfast, many Victorian terraces were clad either in stucco or in brick, or a combination of the two. Where there was a plentiful supply of local stone, this material often became the dominant front for houses in other cities, such as the yellow sandstone homes of Glasgow and the limestone houses of Bath. However, in the wealthier suburbs adjoining Dublin city to the south, both brick and stone was often used to clad the front of houses, a combination not commonly found in England.[62] The origin of these materials will be explored further in Chapter 5.

The most striking difference between Dublin's Victorian houses and their British counterparts is the location of the service floor. In the eighteenth-century townhouse, the basement was an integral part of the 'space-conscious, urban Georgian terrace', containing all of the functional accommodation.[63] It was the 'engine room' of the home, where the kitchens, sculleries and pantries were hidden away from view. This was done by submerging the service floor almost entirely below ground, lit by a small light well to the front, with just a few steps up to the entrance door. Between 1840 and 1850, this functionary floor began to rise out of the ground, elevating the entrance about half a level up from the street. This occurred mainly in suburban semi-detached houses and villas in England, but there were also terraced examples of this 'half basement'.[64] In time, the basement was eradicated altogether: by the 1870s, basements were being omitted from houses in London's city and suburbs, displacing service accommodation to enlarged rear extensions.[65] Thus, the lowest floor of the house now contained the living spaces, which were entered

Figure 1.26 Numbers 6 and 8 Shrewsbury Road.

directly off the street. This prototype became a feature of the Dublin suburbs from the 1880s,[66] as exemplified by Meade's houses in Shrewsbury Road, designed in 1900 (Figure 1.26 and Plate 18).

Since the seventeenth century, basements had been providing protection from the adversities of a wet climate, acting as a buffer zone between the damp earth and the living spaces above. Architect Isaac Ware (1704–1766), advised raising the principal apartments above ground, considering it 'more wholesome also as they are more out of the reach of damps'.[67] The idea was also rooted in the grammar of classical architecture, where the basement was expressed as a rusticated plinth, over which was raised the main reception floor, or 'piano nobile'.[68] In the Georgian city, the basement was hidden below the street, but there were serious implications in sinking a floor entirely below ground level. Apart from dangers of excavating below the water table, a subterranean floor incurred the risk of flooding from burst river banks, or excessive rainfall. Builders circumnavigated the problem in Georgian London, by artificially raising the road above the natural ground line.[69] To do this, they excavated ground for the houses, and used this soil to build up the road, thereby creating space for an almost fully hidden basement. This practice continued on into the nineteenth century, evidenced by one observer in 1857:

The level of the land is too low to allow of the required drainage, and has to be raised perhaps ten or a dozen feet . . . the roads were built up to the level of the ceilings of the basement-rooms – such being the practice the general rule. The floor of the so-called underground kitchen of a London house was never really underground, but was laid originally a trifle above the level of the soil, and even in many cases at a considerable elevation above the level. As fast as the roads are formed, the houses, built according to a certain plan, . . . rise rapidly on either side of them.[70]

Similar construction methods were used to build Dublin's nineteenth-century suburbs, as evidenced by designs by architect William Murray in 1838. In a scheme for twenty houses in Kingstown, Murray explained: 'It is proposed to build those houses two stories high one storey partly underground. The ground on which the houses are to stand to be cut down to the level of the road and the earth used for levelling the remainder.'[71] Thirteen years later, Murray had similar plans for houses on Rathgar Road (Figure 1.27), where he proposed raising the front garden by three feet above the 'natural surface'. Compared to the eighteenth-century townhouse, where the basement was almost fully submerged, this suburban service floor was now located mostly above ground.

In the English Victorian suburbs, the basement emerged only a half level out of the ground, but in Dublin it continued to rise up. The first known evidence of this in Dublin was at Haddington Terrace, located just outside the canal to the south of the city. Fourteen house plots were leased in the first year of the nineteenth century and were complete by 1816. They are all three storeys high, with the service

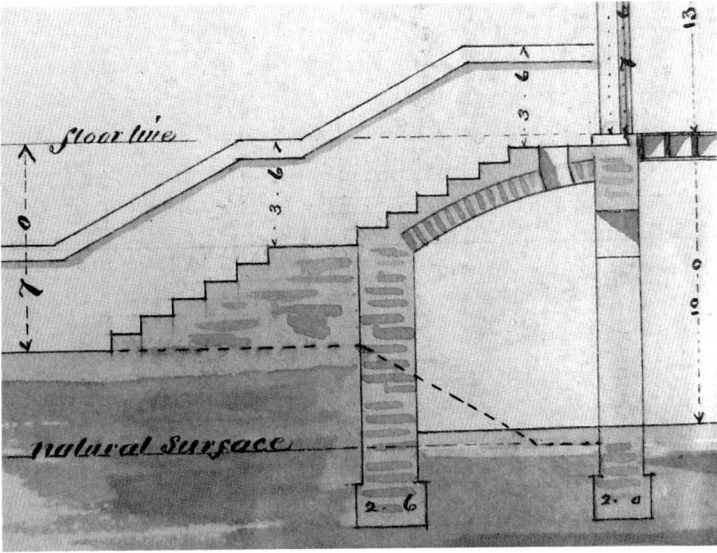

Figure 1.27 Scheme for three terraced houses, detail of cross-section, Rathgar Road, 1851 (RIAI Murray Collection, Irish Architectural Archive).

floor entirely above ground, and long flights of straight steps leading to an elevated entrance floor. (Figure 1.3). Where the basement was omitted in other streets, the main entrance tended to remain in the floor closest to the street, as was the general practice in other British and Irish cities. A distinctly Dublin feature, this is most commonly found in the wealthier houses, particularly in the prestigious western side of the Pembroke estate.

Why did the service floor emerge out of the ground in the Victorian suburb? A number of suggestions have been put forward: such as the desire to emit more light, to create space for a bay window, or longer stairs.[72] However, it seems unlikely that these minor modifications were the driving force for such a radical change in building practice. Subterranean rooms were problematic living spaces, due to adverse conditions created by rising damp, condensation, poor ventilation and lack of adequate light. These problems were extenuated during the nineteenth century, when rising populations led to increased pressures on housing. By 1842, one-third of Liverpool's labouring poor were living in small, damp cellars submerged below the street, often with low ceilings and little light or ventilation.[73] The Public Health Act of 1848 included measures to deal with these problems, by stipulating minimum standards for underground rooms that were separately occupied as dwellings. The act applied to England and Wales and required that cellars be adequately provided with windows, drains, a fireplace and surrounded by an open area at least two feet six inches wide.[74] It specified minimum room heights of seven feet, with the ceiling located at least three feet above the street, i.e. half a level out of the ground. Thus, this is the most likely reason for the emergence of the basement floor in the English Victorian suburbs in the 1840s. Although the regulations were not applicable to Ireland, they were absorbed into the 1866 Sanitary Act.[75]

Clearly, legislation was an influence in forcing the service floor out of the ground. However, it does not explain why it rose entirely out of the ground in Dublin, as this occurred many years before legislation was introduced. Furthermore, the full eradication of the basement is not a requirement of either the 1848 or the 1866 Sanitary Acts.[76] The most probable explanation relates to the practical considerations of building in undrained areas outside the municipal boundary. Between 1860 and 1879, the period of greatest suburban growth, development was carried out without a proper main drainage system in Rathmines and Pembroke, the most affluent of the Dublin suburbs. This was in marked contrast to London, where the metropolitan area was fully drained by 1868.[77] In the meantime, speculators in Dublin were digging for foundations in undrained green fields. Low-lying marshy land was not appropriate for house building, as the architect Thomas Morris advised in 1860:

> Out of the area involved in our boundary must be deducted, not only the busy nucleus, but several tracts which are low, marshy or otherwise unsuitable for residential purposes. For such objects the slopes and elevated tables are chiefly in request, commanding as they necessarily do, the advantages of dryness, prospect and ventilation ... In undrained districts it is generally inexpedient to adopt a sunk or basement storey ...[78]

In the Pembroke estate, the western side was higher and better drained, but much of the eastern side was reclaimed land and prone to flooding from the Dodder canal. Within the context of Dublin's low-lying coastal location, subterranean floors presented a number of difficulties: they were susceptible to flooding, but they also made it difficult to provide a sufficient fall for drains to the sea. In light of these challenges, the estate agent John Vernon regulated development in his characteristically strict manner, prohibiting any underground accommodation, as he explained: 'I never allow the basement of any house to be lower than the road, and this is for drainage purposes.'[79] Before his agency, leases for plots on higher ground in Wellington Road in 1847 stated that the houses were not to be less than 'two stories high above the cellars',[80] but by the 1860s, Vernon had substituted the word 'cellars' with 'elevated basement storey'. This was the case for the leases in Ailesbury Road, which dictated that the service floor was almost entirely above ground, clad in a granite finish (Figure 1.22).[81] These divergences result in a distinct Dublin version of the same template, producing a unique Victorian streetscape.

Notes

1 *The Dublin Builder*, 1 January 1859.
2 E. McKellar, *The birth of modern London, the development and design of the city, 1660–1720* (Manchester, 1999), p. 155.
3 H. Muthesius, *The English house* (repr. 1979, eds D. Sharp, J. Posener and J. Seligman, London) (Berlin, 1904), p. 10.
4 C. Casey, 'The Dublin domestic formula', in Christine Casey (ed.), *The eighteenth-century Dublin townhouse* (Dublin, 2010), p. 58.
5 A. Rowan, 'The irishness of Irish architecture', in *Architectural History*, xl (1997), p. 16.
6 Casey, 'The Dublin domestic formula', p. 58.
7 J. D. Murphy, *The semi-detached house: its place in suburban housing* (Dublin, 1977), p. 21 and E. McAulay, 'The origins and early development of the Pembroke estate beyond the Grand Canal 1816–1880' (Ph.D. thesis, Trinity College, Dublin, 2003), p. 59.
8 N. McCullough, *Dublin, an urban history, the plan of the city* (Dublin, 2007), p. 191.
9 McAulay, 'Pembroke estate', p. 59.
10 H. Long, *Victorian houses and their details* (Oxford, 2002), p. 42.
11 McAulay, 'Pembroke estate', p. 198.
12 *The Irish Builder*, 1 June 1870.
13 NAI, PEP, Letter Books, vol. 3, Sullivan to the Hon. J. Pomeroy, Grand Canal Company, 24 December 1831 (Acc. No. 97/46/3/3).
14 S. Galavan, 'Northumberland Road, the story of a Dublin street 1833–1888' (M.A. thesis, University College, Dublin, 2008), p. 64.
15 McAulay, 'Pembroke estate'.
16 McCullough, *Dublin, an urban history*, p. 172.
17 *The Dublin Builder*, 1 January 1862.
18 McAulay, 'Pembroke estate', p. 200.
19 H. Muthesius, *The English house*, p. 135.
20 IAA, Arthur Murray Collection, Rathgar Road, plans, elevations, sections and details depicting three schemes for houses for Arthur Murray Esq. by William G. Murray and Abraham Denny, 1851 (Acc. No. 92/46.753–8).

21 *Thom's*, 1857 and Griffith Valuation, 1855–1864, vol. 2, p. 94.
22 B. Grimes, *Majestic shrines and graceful sanctuaries, the church architecture of Patrick Byrne 1783–1864* (Dublin, 2009), p. 127.
23 *Ibid.*, p. 128.
24 *The Dublin Builder*, 1 January 1862.
25 *General Advertiser*, 15 June 1861 and *The Irish Times*, 31 May 1864.
26 Griffith Valuation, Kingstown 1855–1859, vol. 3, p. 332i.
27 *The Irish Times*, 16 May 1885.
28 '2 Oriel windows' are noted to Numbers 1, 3, 7, 15 and 17, adding ten shillings to the rateable valuation of each house. Griffith Valuation, Kingstown, 1855–1859, vol. 3, p. 332h.
29 RD, 1861, vol. 22, mem. 146 and 1862, vol. 26, mem. 173.
30 P. Pearson, *Dun Laoghaire, Kingstown* (Dublin, 1981), p. 100.
31 *The Irish Times*, 10 May 1862.
32 Soon after the completion of Numbers 2, 4 and 6, valuers noted that there was a 'good view from the rear of these houses'. Griffith Valuation, Kingstown 1855–1859, vol. 3, p. 332i.
33 RD, 1863, vol. 16, mem. 76 and 77, and *Ibid.*,1864, vol. 23, mem. 107.
34 This is based on building widths taken from Numbers 15 and 21, both built by Galvin.
35 C. Casey, *Dublin, the city within the grand and royal canals and the circular road with the Phoenix Park* (New Haven, NJ and London, 2005), p. 37.
36 RD, 1882, vol. 6, mem. 76, and *Thom's*, 1885, Northumberland Road.
37 McAulay, 'Pembroke estate', p. 210.
38 McCullough, *Dublin, an urban history*, p. 191.
39 *Ibid.*, p. 172.
40 E. McParland, 'The geometry of the stable lane', in Christine Casey (ed.), *The eighteenth-century Dublin townhouse* (Dublin, 2010), p. 135.
41 McAulay, 'Pembroke estate', p. 155.
42 Murphy, *The semi-detached house*, p. 19.
43 G. Gater and W. H. Godfrey (eds), *Survey of London, The Village of Highgate*, Vol. XVII (London, 1936), p. 77.
44 F. Jenson, *The semi-detached house* (Cambridgeshire, 2007), p. 31.
45 J. Summerson, *Georgian London* (London, 1988), p. 50.
46 J. Summerson, *Architecture in Britain, 1530 to 1830* (London, 1953).
47 Murphy, *The semi-detached house*, p. 14.
48 J. C. Loudon, *The suburban gardener and villa companion* (London, 1838), p. 314.
49 R. Dixon and S. Muthesius, *Victorian architecture* (London, 1978), p. 60.
50 I am grateful to Eve McAulay for information on the development of housing on the Pembroke estate. McAulay, 'Pembroke estate', p. 46.
51 *Ibid.*, p. 47.
52 *Ibid.*, p. 200.
53 *Ibid.*, p. 202.
54 Galavan, 'Northumberland Road', p. 99.
55 *Ibid.*, p. 124.
56 McAulay, 'Pembroke estate', p. 206.
57 *Thom's*, 1865–1885.
58 St Michael's House archive, original lease from March 1868, piece of ground on the south side of Ailesbury Road, the Earl of Clanwilliam and Marquis of Ailesbury and Earl of Pembroke and Montgomery and Michael Meade and RD, 1869, vol. 24, mem. 136.
59 McAulay, 'Pembroke estate'.
60 M. Craig, 'Rostrevor Terrace, Rathgar', unpublished report, Dublin, 15 February 1977, p. 1.

61 *General Advertiser*, 3 September 1864.
62 In the coastal suburbs of Monkstown and Kingstown, stucco was the main facing material. These areas were emulating the great Victorian resort towns such as Brighton, where grand monumental stucco terraces were built overlooking the sea.
63 S. Muthesius, *The English terraced house* (New Haven, NJ and London, 1983), p. 88.
64 *Ibid.*, p. 179 and H. J. Dyos, *Victorian suburb: a study of the growth of Camberwell* (Leicester, 1977), p. 183.
65 S. Muthesius, *The English terraced house*, p. 88.
66 M. E. Daly, 'The growth of Victorian Dublin', in M. E. Daly, M. Hearn and P. Pearson (eds), *Dublin's Victorian houses* (Dublin, 1998), p. 53.
67 I. Ware, *A complete body of architecture* (London, 1756), p. 322.
68 M. Craig, *Classic Irish houses of the middle size* (London and New York, 1976), p. 20.
69 Summerson, *Georgian London*, p. 50
70 C. M. Smith, *Curiosities of London life* (London, 1857), p. 346.
71 IAA, Arthur Murray Collection, Victoria Square, Surveys, plans and elevations for houses on proposed Victoria Square for T. M. Gresham by William Murray, 1838. (Acc. No. 92/46/838).
72 S. Muthesius, *The English terraced house*, p. 89.
73 E. D. Mapother, 'The sanitary state of Dublin', *Journal of the Statistical and Social Inquiry Society of Ireland*, Vol. IV Part XXVII, 1864, p. 73. [www.tara.tcd.ie/handle/2262/6639, accessed 3 August 2016].
74 W. C. Glen, *The law relating to the public health and local government in relation to sanitary and other matters* (London, 1858), p. 110.
75 P. C. Cowan, 'Notes on byelaws as to new streets and buildings', in *The Irish Builder and Engineer Jubilee Number, 1859–1909*, p. 60 and C. Noonan, 'Residential development and the making of streets in late nineteenth-century Dublin city' (M.U.B.C. thesis, University College Dublin, 2007). In Dublin city, cellar dwellings were regulated by Dublin Corporation who took a more active role in sanitary health after leglislation enacted in 1847. A bye-law was passed banning any cellar, two-thirds of which lay below ground, leading to the closure of over 3,000 cellars by 1864.
76 J. O. Byrne, *Compendium of Irish sanitary law: containing the Sanitary Act, 1866* (Dublin, 1870); and T. W. Grimshaw, J. E. Reynolds and R. O'B. Furlong and J. W. Moore, *Manual of public health for Ireland* (Dublin, 1875) [https://archive.org/details/b28062516, accessed 3 August 2016].
77 S. Ó Maithú, *Dublin's suburgan towns* (Dublin, 2003), p. 100.
78 T. Morris, *A house for the suburbs, socially and architecturally sketched* (London, 1860), p. 25.
79 *Municipal Boundaries Commission (Ireland), Part I, Evidence, with appendices. Dublin, Rathmines, Pembroke, Kilmainham, Drumcondra, Clontarf, and also Kingstown, Blackrock and Dalkey*, [C.2725], H.C. 1880, evidence of Mr Arthur H. Robinson, p. 279, para. 34.
80 McAulay, 'Pembroke estate', p. 120.
81 St Michael's House archive, original lease from March 1868, piece of ground on the south side of Ailesbury Road, the Earl of Clanwilliam and Marquis of Ailesbury and Earl of Pembroke and Montgomery and Michael Meade.

2 The domestic realm

Inside the semi-detached house

Introduction

This chapter moves the discussion beyond the city's Victorian façades, to the interior spaces within. It was here that the lives of Dublin's upper middle class played out: they entertained guests in their drawing rooms, their children were born in the upstairs bedrooms and their servants toiled in their kitchens and sculleries below. But how people lived and worked in such houses, how social relationships were managed within the domestic interior, remains largely unexplored territory.[1] The analysis focuses on three sets of contemporary drawings, which throw new light on the functional requirements of the semi-detached house. The first is an unrealised design for two houses in Rathgar dating from 1851, the second is for houses in Northbrook Road (Rathmines) built thirty years later, and the third is for homes in Shrewsbury Road (Pembroke) in 1900. These rare drawings provide insights into Victorian house design at three snapshots in time, from the mid-Victorian period to the emergence of a new Edwardian era. In particular, it considers the way in which domestic space was manipulated to articulate the relationships between the different members of the household: between master and servant, male and female, adult and child. How did the use of decoration, fittings and furniture relate to these boundaries, while giving meaning to domestic space? Showing how architects negotiated the boundaries between different members of the household, this chapter aims to open a window on to daily Victorian middle-class life in Dublin.

The interior world of Dublin's Victorian semi-detached houses

Thus far, the analysis has focused on houses built between 1851 and 1879, whose origins were the eighteenth-century townhouse. Dublin's Georgian townhouses were an expression of 'social hierarchy': the service areas were located at basement level, the family rooms on the ground floor, the formal reception rooms on the piano nobile, and the bedroom accommodation on the second floor (Figure 1.1).[2] This was in turn reflected in the spatial character of the interior: the basement contained low ceilings and sparse decoration, while the first floor was characterised by lofty and ornate spaces. When this typology was applied to Dublin's nineteenth-century suburbs, it inherited this spatial hierarchy, expressed through a division of functions by floor. However, we have seen how it tended to reduce in height, its basement emerging out of the ground, elevating the entrance a full storey up from the street. A common three-storey template was the result: starting with a service floor at ground level, with reception rooms above, and a second floor of bedrooms. The reception floor remained of primary importance: often accessed by a grand flight of steps, it contained the highest ceilings and most elaborate ornamentation. At first-floor level, there was a distinct change in character, where lower ceilings and simpler cornices signalled a less formal purpose. The service level was simplest in decoration, with little or no cornices, and ceiling heights reduced to the minimum.

Chapter 1 discussed the development of the semi-detached house on Northumberland Road where, by 1865, paired dwellings stood back from the street and widened to three bays, with extensions to the side (Plate 2). Early house plans were reminiscent of the Georgian townhouse, but eventually the stairs moved to the centre rear of the plan, forming a new space, accessed off the half-landing level. This plan was found in a number of streets in the Pembroke estate, but it also emerged in other suburbs, such as in Rostrevor Terrace in Rathgar. How was space organised on each floor? Advertisements for houses in Northumberland Road indicate that the entrance floor typically contained three reception rooms: a drawing room, a dining room and a study.[3] At first-floor level, four bedrooms were generally provided, but sometimes a dressing room, a bathroom and/or a W.C. were mentioned.[4] The service floor contained a number of rooms, including a kitchen, a 'servant's room' and ancillary spaces labeled as 'china' and 'pantry'. Outdoor amenities were equally important, as estate agents were keen to promote large gardens, or tennis lawns to the rear.

Analysis of original design drawings for Rathgar Road (1851)

Chapter 1 introduced the drawings by architects William Murray and Abraham Denny, who experimented with three options for a site in Rathgar in 1851: one for semi-detached houses and two for terraces.[5] Although the semi-detached version was never realised, the drawings provide a rare insight into the internal organisation of this house type (Plate 19). Compared to the narrower terraced plots, this design was intended for a more exclusive class of occupant, with a large floor area and a generous coach house to the rear. In plan, they are an example of the semi-detached template described to date, with the stairs in the centre rear of the plan. The form is articulated to the front in two bays, with the third bay set back to the side, similar to the houses at Rostrevor Terrace and Lansdowne Road (Figures 1.17 and 1.18; and Plate 15). A series of steps provides access to the main entrance, while a separate service entrance is provided to the side, leading to stables, a coach house and a yard to the rear.

The upper levels

J. C. Loudon would have approved of the semi-detached scheme at Rathgar Road. The central bays have been unified and crowned by a raised parapet, and the entrances have been recessed to the side. The scheme bears the closest resemblance to one of Loudon's designs for what he called 'double detached houses',[6] with back-to-back fireplaces serving the main reception rooms: a drawing room to the front and a dining room to the rear. The drawing room was the most important space in the house, and should be 'lofty' and well ventilated, declared Loudon, to accommodate large parties. It should upstage all other living rooms, he believed, with elegant furniture of a 'lighter, and yet superior, description'.[7] Decorative detailing was at its best here, with ceiling and cornice enrichments 'light and pleasing' and of a 'gayer and more fanciful description' than in the dining room. He suggested making a white marble chimneypiece the focal point in the room, with carvings of 'fanciful and graceful groups of flowers, foliage, or fruits, or graceful mythological figures'. The best paintings adorned the walls, while a French clock, vase or ornament could be placed on the chimney-shelf. The drawing room was also the realm of the woman of the house, where she could exercise her 'taste and good sense' by her choice of card tables, sofas in plain rose wood, the occasional sofa table, chairs and other cushioned seats and footstools. No drawing room was complete without a pianoforte, which Loudon claimed was a feature of almost every dwelling, 'from that of the humble tradesman, to that of the palace'.[8] Walking in the London suburbs in 1857, Charles Manby Smith noted the impact this had on the Victorian streetscape. When twilight fell, the suburban dwellings came to life, where 'candles are lighted in the drawing-rooms, and from a dozen houses at once pianofortes commence their harmony'.[9] Music was also a feature of the Dublin suburbs: the drawing room of Number 19 Ailesbury Road contained a 'grand square pianoforte, in rosewood case, by Cadby, London'.[10]

Returning to the 'principal plan' at Rathgar Road, two entrances are provided to the drawing room: one from the hall and another from the stairwell. Guests were brought in here directly from the hall, where they assembled before dinner. Loudon confirmed that in larger mansions, the dining room served only one purpose, but in suburban villas it could also function as a second family room, or a library, advising that the space be comfortable, 'as much of the family enjoyment depends on it'.[11] He advised a rectangular shaped space, entered by a door inserted into the longer wall, opening diagonally opposite the fireplace, either side of which were 'handsome bookshelves'. The dining table, located in the centre of the room, was to be solid but plain, made of uncarved mahogany, and 'beautifully French-polished'. The dining room at Rathgar Road would have complied with Loudon's plan, as it is of similar proportions, with the door in the desired location, opening directly opposite the fireplace. The wall adjoining the drawing room was the probable location of another essential piece of furniture: the sideboard. This was a series of cabinets used for storing and serving food, and displaying serving dishes during dinner, familiar to diners since the eighteenth century. According to Loudon, 'closets' were not permitted here, so the sideboard was to be fitted with 'every possible convenience', such as a receptacle underneath for cooling wine. At night, diners were lit by lamps suspended from the ceiling, or a chandelier 'with candles and metallic wicks'. In some houses, servants communicated with the kitchen via a 'speaking tube', located in a recess in the hall and fitted with a hinged door.[12]

While the bulk of this floor is reserved for entertaining, the extension to the side contains a number of functions. Located half a level below the 'principal floor', this area is strategically out of sight and sound of the main reception rooms. To the front is the main entrance and 'vestibule', but to the rear is a small toilet and pantry. The latter is a probable close relation of the 'Lady's Store-room', located close to the dining room for stocking serving dishes and preserves.[13] Larger pantries were fitted with a dresser (complete with drawers underneath, some lockable) and closets to store 'all the china, glass, and dessert service, and also the pickles and preserves'. A line of storage is shown running along three of the walls in Rathgar Road, a likely indication of the deep shelving advocated by Loudon, its edges fitted with hooks for hanging up cups and jugs. After dinner, serving dishes were brought down to the basement to be washed, and then returned here to be securely stored. Family and guests used the W.C. off the half landing, but the toilet in the stable yard was reserved for the servants. At first-floor level, this side return is divided into two small bedrooms, which are without fireplaces (Plate 20).[14] The remainder of this level is simply laid out, where two principal bedrooms follow the layout of the reception rooms below.

The lower level

The service quarters are located on the lowest floor, supporting the efficient organisation of the other levels (Plate 21). This was the domain of the servant, signalled by sparse ornamentation and low ceilings. At Rathgar Road, the largest rooms are arranged around the fireplaces: comprising a kitchen to the front and a bedroom to the rear. In between these rooms is a cellar, in its ideal location at the centre of the plan, subject to the least fluctuations in temperature.[15] According to Loudon, the kitchen should be a 'lofty' space, and provided with good light for working, its door opening towards the chimney to prevent it smoking.[16] The architects have widened the fireplace to accommodate the kitchen range, which, if deep enough, would fit a 'proper boiler' at the rear, producing hot water all day long. The cook would prepare food on a large table in the centre of the room, with access to additional storage in a dresser close by. This would be fitted with lockable drawers and cabinets, their ends fixed with mills for coffee, pepper and other finer spices. Around the walls, rails could be fixed with hooks to hang 'dish covers', while the back of the doors might feature 'round or jack-towel rollers' (paper towel holders).

Food was prepared and cooked in the kitchen, but washing up was reserved for a separate area. This was the purpose of the scullery at Rathgar Road, which was usually fitted with a stone sink under the window, complete with a plate rack and drip-board. Adjacent to the scullery is the coal store, inserted under the entrance steps and fitted with a cast iron grate and chute. In Dublin's Victorian suburbs, the delivery men had to haul their sacks from horse-drawn carts, across the front garden and up quite a number of steps to the entrance (Figure 1.27). Compared to the city townhouses, located close to the path and only a few steps up from the street, Dublin's Victorian domestic architecture created an increased workload for these workers. Inside the house, frequent trips were required between the coal store and the kitchen range, and Loudon recommended that the store be large enough to hold nine months' supplies. Resilient floors were required here: Loudon advised a rubbed Yorkshire stone to the kitchen, with a stone or brick floor to the scullery and coal store. Adjoining the coal store is the servants' pantry, with a line of storage running around the three walls. General provisions were stored here, but Loudon recommended hanging 'strong iron-bearers' across the ceiling, fitted with hooks to hang meat. Adjacent to here is the 'servants' room', which probably functioned as a second staff bedroom.

At the rear of the stairhall, servants could exit the house and proceed to the stable yard through an opening in the side wall. It was here that the paths between master and servant crossed: while the family ascended the stairs from the garden, servants could pass unseen below (Plate 19). A generous stable building was provided to the side, with space for one coach and two horses, and a hay loft above. According to Loudon, stable windows were permissible but should be high 'to prevent careless or bad grooms from knowing when their master is coming to look after them'.[17] In the yard is a water trough for horses and an external toilet placed against the garden wall.

Analysis of original design drawings for Northbrook Road (1881)

Thirty years after the designs for Rathgar Road were complete, a set of drawings were prepared for houses in Northbrook Road, just a few miles away. Located close to the city boundary, the street was largely built upon by the time the plans were prepared. The houses were designed by William Mansfield Mitchell, who was in partnership with John McCurdy, architect to Trinity College Dublin.[18] The committee of the Adelaide Road Presbyterian Church commissioned the project, located nearby on a site inside the municipal boundary. The builders were J. and W. Beckett, one of the leading contracting firms in the city, who in a few years' time would build one of the city's most important projects: the National Museum and Library.[19] When Mitchell's houses were complete in 1882, they commanded a prominent corner site facing Cambridge Terrace (Plate 22). In the previous scheme, a coach house and stable was provided to the rear of each site, to accommodate residents travelling by horse-drawn vehicles. However, stables were omitted from the houses in Northbrook Road, which were built a mile and a half closer to the city centre, where residents could travel by horse-drawn trams. The continued growth of the suburbs had led to an expansion of transport services, with omnibuses running along the nearby Ranelagh Road. These changes are reflected in the designs for Northbrook Road, as only a pedestrian entrance is indicated at the side, leading to an outdoor WC and ash pit at the rear (Plate 23). A separate servants' or tradesmen's entrance was an important feature in any suburban house, and was used as a marketing tool in advertisements.[20]

Externally, these houses bear some resemblance to the houses previously described in Ailesbury Road, as the third bay is now absorbed into the main volume (Figure 1.22 and Plate 22). Internally, they are a variation of the semi-detached plan described previously, where the stairs is located towards the centre of the plan (Plate 23). However, instead of placing it on the rear wall, it is turned lengthways and located directly behind the entrance hall, which appeared in Number 43 Northumberland Road in 1877. The third space at entrance level is inserted behind (rather than next to) the stairwell, whose proportions are enlarged by projections to the side and rear. The remainder of the entrance level is identical to Rathgar Road, forming a drawing room to the front, and a dining room to the rear. Spatial hierarchy is reflected in the scale of decorative fittings and finishes. Eleven-inch 'double face moulded skirtings' were specified for the three principal rooms, hall and stairs, but were to reduce down to nine-inch single faced on the bedroom floor above.[21] The simplest joinery was reserved for the basement level, where seven-inch beaded skirtings were stipulated.

The upper levels

The English Gentleman's Country House was the seminal guide to English mid-Victorian house planning. It was first published in 1864 by Robert Kerr, a Scottish architect who analysed the functionalities of 'a convenient and comfortable English Residence of the better sort, on whatever the scale'.[22] He excluded what he considered inferior dwellings such as cottages, farmhouses and business premises and the house types being discussed here were deemed small under Kerr's classification. However, regardless of the scale, there was one overriding principle governing the design of all English homes: their division into two departments, one for the family and one for the servants. Kerr began his analysis in the dining room, which was almost always used for luncheon and dinner, but could sometimes function as a breakfast room. According to Kerr, it should be somewhat secluded for privacy, but not overlooked by the main entrance. He advised that the room should be placed out of direct sunshine and without a door leading to the lawn. Its size was determined by the number of diners, with a minimum width of sixteen feet, by a length of between eighteen and twenty feet. This was to allow enough room for a fully occupied table, with space for servants to pass behind, as well as extra chairs, a hearth-rug, a screen and a sideboard.[23] Similar to Loudon, Kerr advised against locating the door on the same wall as the fireplace, as this would create a draught, considering this 'an arrangement generally fatal to a Sitting-room'.[24] In Rathgar and Northbrook Roads, the door was inserted in Kerr's preferred position, opening opposite the fireplace.

By 1865, the dining table and sideboard were still the main pieces of furniture in the dining room, which according to Kerr were to be ideally 'massive and simple'.[25]

The sideboard was usually located behind the master's chair, with the entrance door nearby 'for ease of service' and opening towards the sideboard, rather than to the diners. The sideboard should never be placed too close to a window, he advised, as this might highlight the servants' movements, or cast expensive dinnerware in shadow.[26] Other key items include 'dinner-waggons or chiffoniers' (the latter is smaller than a sideboard and enclosed by doors on the front), located in the corners of the room. According to the architect, the dining room should be masculine in appearance, both in the choice of furniture and style of decoration. Taking account of both Loudon and Kerr's advice, the dining room in Northbrook Road was likely laid out as follows: the dining table in the centre of the room, the sideboard against the spine wall, with bookshelves on either side of the fireplace and other pieces of movable storage on either side of the window.

While the dining room was ostensibly male in character, the drawing room was the domain of the female, being 'the status indicator, the mark of gentility, the room from where the woman governed her domain. The wife, the family and the house were the outward indicators of a man's success in the world.'[27] The drawing room was used as a family sitting room in the evening, but it was also a space for visitors to gather before and after dinner, 'the modern form of the Lady's Withdrawing-room', according to Kerr.[28] In 1882, Mary Heyden entertained her friends in the drawing room of her house in the Dublin suburb of Rathmines: 'After tea there was a good deal of music and singing; then some round games, then more music and more games. At 12 o'clock the people left, except Bernard who remained smoking with John till nearly 1 o'clock; when he left I went to bed.'[29] During the day, ladies could receive visitors there, so Kerr advised that the drawing room face the morning sun, but be shaded during the hottest part of the afternoon. Only one wall of windows was required in an ordinary drawing room, but their heights were to be maximised to create a 'cheerful character', looking out on 'the very best view that the house commands'.[30] Adequate wall space was required for furniture, which was to be 'comparatively delicate', reflecting the 'ladylike' character of the room:

> a centre table, perhaps with a chandelier over, the usual chairs and couch, occasional table, sofa-table, or writing-table, occasional chairs, a chiffonier generally, or one or more fancy cabinets, perhaps one or more pier-tables, a what-not or the like, one or more mirrors, and a cabinet pianoforte. If there be sufficient space there may be an ottoman settee; perhaps a pair of wall settees also.[31]

To Kerr, the relationship between the spaces was as important as the detailed layout of each individual room. He advised against a direct link between the two reception rooms, to maximise privacy and minimise the transmission of sounds and smells.[32] However, he conceded that in suburban villas, a connecting door might be unavoidable for the occasional large gathering, although he considered this 'a grievous informality, but one which nevertheless will yield to contrivance'. Furthermore, the approach from the hall to the drawing room should be direct and 'sufficiently stately', but the onward route to the dining room was even more important. First impressions were made here: the route was to be short and spacious, with no turnings, the reception rooms easily discernible to visitors.[33] The Northbrook Road houses have been planned in this way, with wider doors to the 'best rooms' (drawing and dining), with a narrower door to the library/study.[34] Moulded cornices 'of 27" girth with two well relieved enrichments' are specified for the reception rooms and hall, but are reduced down to twenty-one inches in the library/study. On ascending the stairs, one bedroom is provided on the half landing, while another three rooms complete the layout on the first floor (Plate 24). The 'three principal bedrooms' are to be fitted with twenty-one-inch cornices, with fifteen-inch cornices for the smallest room, located to the front corner of the building. At the top of the rear return, the staircase continues to a bathroom and toilet. Since the Rathgar Road scheme thirty years earlier, residents in Northbrook Road benefited from a separate bathroom. Notably, all of the habitable rooms are provided with fireplaces, including the small bedroom to the front and the second-floor bathroom.

Returning to the ground floor, there is a third room inserted behind the stairs, labelled the 'Library or Study'. In larger homes, this was used by the gentleman of the house, who spent his mornings in practical affairs, but in a smaller home it was used for reading and writing. As for the room's internal layout, the relationship of the desk, fireplace and window was of primary importance to Kerr. For good natural light, the window was to be placed in front of the desk and to the left of the sitter. Another wall was to house bookshelves for serious reading, but lighter material for the family could be stored in the main reception rooms. The study was to be somewhat secluded so that 'casual visitors need not be tempted to look in upon the student in passing – "just to say how-d'ye-do"'.[35] It should be located near the dining room, as it also served as an occasional waiting room for gentleman visitors. Accessibility from both primary and secondary entrances was also important, so that a range of people could be admitted discreetly. Kerr suggested that it be located at the division point between the main house and the service quarters, with direct access from both, and a 'judiciously-contrived route of entrance through each'.[36] The plan at Northbrook Road would appear to satisfy this complex design brief, as set out by Kerr. The library/study is accessed from the main stairhall, but it is somewhat removed being three steps lower, its door inserted under the soffit of the main stairs. Located directly above the service entrance, it is conceivable that tradesmen could approach the house from the servants' entrance, and proceed directly up the basement stairs to the hall. This would avoid what Kerr referred to as 'that most unrefined arrangement whereby at one sole entrance door the visitors rub shoulders with the tradespeople'.[37]

The lower level

In the suburbs of Victorian London, a street of thirty 'genteel' suburban terraces were described by Charles Manby Smith in 1857. There was, he observed, a 'daily succession of nomadic industrials' calling to the houses, from the baker and butcher delivering goods, to the greengrocer and watercress man.[38] Travelling tradesmen offered their skills mending chairs, glass, bells or umbrellas, while others called to gravel paths or polish silverware. The service entrance played an important role in the successful operation of the Victorian house, as it was here that deliveries were made, and tradesmen pegged their wares. This is reflected in the novel *Diary of a nobody*, set in the home of Charles Pooter, a city clerk who lived in a two-bay terrace in the London suburb of Holloway in 1888. Pooter remarked on the numerous tradesmen who called to the servants' entrance, whether it was the butcher, the ironmonger or the butterman. One day, he expressed his annoyance at the grocer's boy, who had the 'impertinence' to bring his basket to his hall door, marking the newly cleaned doorstep with his dirty boots.[39] In Dublin, a new consumer culture emerged to serve a 'dynamic urban middle class', expressed in the arrival of the department store, otherwise known as the 'monster' store.[40] The 1850s was a decade of particularly rapid growth in commerce, as department stores increased in size to cater for a rising upper middle class. The firm of Pim Brothers & Co., located in a premises in the city at South Great Georges Street, appealed to Dublin's bourgeoisie, and were delivering to addresses in the southern suburbs by 1869. Smaller shops could also be found delivering to the prosperous upper middle classes: in 1878, Mrs Atkinston, who lived in Number 11 Clyde Road – one of the premier streets in the Pembroke estate – was a customer of a chandler shop in Grafton Street, which supplied candles and colza, a lamp oil used in domestic lighting. Their carts delivered goods on a daily basis, both in the city and in the wealthier suburban districts of Rathmines, Rathgar, Sandymount and Clontarf.

At Northbrook Road, the service floor is labelled the 'Basement Plan', but in reality it is only a slight drop down from the street. Kerr noted the challenges in planning this floor, admitting that the relative position of each room required careful consideration.[41] Comparisons may be drawn with Rathgar Road: the location of the kitchen in the front near the coal cellar, the provision of a scullery and pantry are all in common here (Plates 21 and 23). In Rathgar, the room to the rear was a bedroom, but here it functions as a 'breakfast parlour', a room dedicated to the early part of the day, or for an early luncheon or dinner for a small family.[42] Furthermore, the china is stored on this floor, rather than on the half-landing level above. By this time, *The Irish Builder* reported on the growing patronage in art in Ireland, as it was 'no longer confined to the nobility or wealthy merchants, but now extended to the middle class, whose members in addition to expensive pictures could by this time be found in possession of respectable "china closets", and to have some knowledge of Wedgwood ware'.[43] The architect specified presses and shelving in the china closet, with a glazed screen to transmit secondary light to the adjacent kitchen lobby. Behind these two rooms is the cook's pantry, where three rows of shelving were specified, and tall cupboards for the recesses in the kitchen, breakfast room and servants' bedroom.

For eighteen years, Number 16 was the home of Reverend Robert McCheyne, minister of the Adelaide Road Presbyterian Church for thirty-seven years.[44] By

1901, the house was occupied by a Mr Louis Shaw, a 'Class I Clerk' for the Local Government Board, who lived there with his wife and one-year-old daughter. The couple employed at least four servants: a nurse, a cook, a parlour maid and a housemaid. Adjoining the Shaws was Miss Catherine Jones and her sister who employed a cook, a parlour maid and a dressmaker.[45] By 1911, only two servants were resident in these two houses.[46] Number 16 was the home of William McNeill, a Presbyterian minister with four children, who kept a general domestic servant and a nurse. His neighbour was the solicitor Edward C. Jameson, who lived there with his wife, a cook and housemaid. All except one of these eleven servants were Roman Catholic, while all of their employers were of the Protestant faith.

Analysis of original design drawings for Shrewsbury Road (1900)

Chapter 1 discussed the houses built by Michael Meade, who was the first to develop on Ailesbury Road. After Michael's death in 1886, his son Joseph moved his family into 'St Michael's', a villa on the junction with Merrion Road. Within three years, a new street had been laid out nearby, running in a southwesterly direction from Merrion Road. While Michael Meade had been the pioneer of development in Ailesbury Road, his son carried on his legacy on this newly emergent street. By the close of 1894, architect Charles Ashworth had completed drawings for him on Shrewsbury Road, just north of his family home. Ashworth was architect to the Dublin Artisan's Dwelling Company and although there is no record of previous collaborations, he and Meade were certainly acquainted, as he paid a number of visits to him during his first year as Lord Mayor.[47] By 1900, Shrewsbury House was complete, a fine detached six-bedroom residence on the junction with Merrion Road. Electric trams now served the area, with steam trains running to nearby Sandymount and Sydney Parade stations. Four adjacent semi-detached houses followed, also designed by Ashworth, all complete by 1906 (Figure 1.26).[48]

In contrast to the previous examples, which were located in the suburb of Rathmines and Rathgar, the Shrewsbury Road houses were built in the prestigious Pembroke estate. This is reflected in the status of their residents, who were members of the higher professions, the merchant class, or in the upper levels of public service. The first of these semi-detached homes (named 'Rossbegh') was completed in 1901, and occupied by Joseph Keogh from Wicklow, a member of Dublin's Stock Exchange.[49] By the time of the 1911 census, he lived there with a wife and seven children, who ranged from one to thirteen years of age.[50] Also resident on the night of 2 April 1911 were five staff: a governess, a nurse, a housemaid, a cook and a chauffeur. The adjoining house was occupied by his neighbour Arthur Hignett, an English civil engineer, who lived there with his wife and five staff: a cook, a parlour maid, a housemaid, a nurse and a nursery maid to look after their two young children. Jane E. Ferguson, a fifty-eight-year-old English widow, lived in the next house 'Fernhurst', with her son and two servants: a cook and a parlour maid. Next door was Hugh Perry, an English colonel, who lived there with his wife, his eighteen-year-old daughter and three servants. Perry worked in the army ordnance department and went on to become Major General Sir Hugh Whitchurch Perry. Of the four houses, Keogh was the only Roman Catholic in 1911, with the remaining residents of the Anglican faith.

Ground-floor level: the family quarters

These homes, built twenty-four years after Numbers 16 and 17 Northbrook Road, represent a dramatic shift in house design (Figure 1.26). In the previous examples, the entire ground floor was dedicated to service, over which were two levels for the family: one for living and one for sleeping. This raised the main entrance a full storey up from the street, accessed by a flight of granite steps. However, at Shrewsbury Road, the entrance floor is only just a few steps up from the street, as the service areas have been displaced to enlarged rear extensions. Furthermore, bay windows are a feature of the front and back, and a robust break-front gable has been added to the street elevation, bringing a strong vertical emphasis to this façade. However, the house is planned in a similar manner to the halls of the previous houses, providing two reception rooms, with the stairs to the rear centre, and a study to the side (Plate 25). There is an awkward step in the plan between the entrance hall and stair hall behind, and this is dealt with by splaying the wall to the study, providing a back-to-back fireplace. Although fireplaces were not provided in the halls of the previous houses, it was advised by Kerr 'for few things have a less hospitable effect in winter than the chill on an Entrance (sic) that has never known warming'.[51] He also suggested a small table for the hall, where visitors could leave their cards, as shown on the drawings for Northbrook Road (Plate 23).[52] Although no inventories have been found for these houses, a silver card tray was stolen from the hall of Shrewsbury House in 1908 (also designed by Ashworth).

In 1860, *The Dublin Builder* welcomed a new publication by the English architect Thomas Morris named *A House for the Suburbs*. Morris was keen to capitalise on the unprecedented expansion of London's outskirts due to what he deemed as 'the modern Genius of Speed and the Science of the Rail'.[53] To cater for this growing market, he presented a number of designs for suburban homes, including one for semi-detached houses, where instead of an entrance to the front, Morris inserted a projecting hall and stairs to the side. To the rear of the stairhall, he placed a store and 'wash-hand place for gentlemen', and a study or 'master's room' to the front corner of the house. The remainder of the plan was similar to Shrewsbury Road, with a drawing room to the front, a dining room to the rear, and bay windows to both of these reception rooms. According to Morris, the drawing room was 'for lady visitors, morning calls, and evening use'. He located the dining room close to the stairs, to enable 'easy service of dinner without crossing the guests'.[54] This was crucial to the practical functioning of the suburban house, providing servants with a direct route from the kitchen below. It is also a feature of Shrewsbury Road: the dining room is located to the rear of the plan, close to the service quarters.

London suburbanites were known for their love of entertaining. In one district, eight neighbouring families threw a party once a fortnight, from the beginning of winter to the end of spring. Morris exuded: 'Delightful alike to Spinster and Matron, Youth and Sage, are the suburban soirees'.[55] Guests arrived at seven, and entertained each other through music, song, dance and drama; the hosts displayed objects of art and science and offered refreshments of sandwiches and cake. The drawing room was where all embellishment was 'most liberally devoted', making it the obvious setting for such festive occasions. At Shrewsbury Road, guests entered the drawing room from the front hall, and then proceeded to the rear hall to access the dining room. Bay windows were provided in the two reception rooms, which Loudon advised should extend down to within six inches of the floor 'so that a view of the adjoining flower-garden, or of the distant prospect, if in the country, might be commanded from it'.[56] On the other side of the hall is the study, which has its own bay window to the side passageway. A previous sketch shows that this room was originally planned as a breakfast room, showing the flexibility of this space. Just beyond the study door, there is a drop in level, providing the first break between the family and servant quarters. Beyond this point, more functional spaces appear: first is a cloakroom, complete with toilet and wash hand basin, and a hanging space for hats and coats. Kerr maintained that 'a roomy Closet' was the minimum for any moderately sized house, located near the entrance for the use of 'gentlemen visitors'.[57] A large return then extends significantly to the rear, containing the service quarters of the house.

Ground-floor level: the service wing

Kerr maintained that the most important consideration in designing a gentleman's home, whatever the size, was the separation of the family and the servants. He explained: 'The family constitute one community; the servants another. Whatever may be their mutual regard and confidence as dwellers under the same roof, each class is entitled to shut its door upon the other, and be alone.'[58] This was the purpose of the service wing, which had an entirely different function to the other parts of the house, being space mainly dedicated to work. In the previous two designs, the division was articulated in section, by elevating the family rooms a full storey above the service floor. In Shrewsbury Road, the two classes inhabit the same plan, but the boundaries are articulated by changes in level. Thus, the main volume to the front of the house is reserved for the family, and the rear return is the domain of the servant (Plate 25). A lobby is formed at the rear of the stairs, providing access to the main 'engine room' of the house. A number of doors off this space provide access to the kitchen, a 'Lady's store' a 'Butler's Pantry and China', and the garden. This space was most likely a buffer zone between the family rooms and the potentially noisy and odorous spaces behind:

> how objectionable it is we need scarcely say when a thin partition transmits the sounds of the Scullery or Coal-cellar to the Dining-room or Study; or

when a Kitchen window in summer weather forms a trap to catch the conversation at the casement of the Drawing-room; or when a Kitchen doorway in the Vestibule or Staircase exposes to the view of every one the dresser or the cooking range, or fills the house with unwelcome odours.[59]

In Rathgar Road, the cellar and pantry were housed in separate spaces, but here they are combined into a Butler's pantry, used for the storage of wine, linen and plates. It is conveniently located close to the dining room, fitted with a sink under the window, and storage along the flank wall. Plates were stacked on open shelving, table linen was stored in drawers, while locked cupboards secured valuable china and stoneware.[60] Householders in Shrewsbury Road were the owners of fine dinnerware: the occupants of Number 16 possessed 'morning and evening china', a dessert service, Dresden and an afternoon tea service,[61] while the master of Shrewsbury House owned 'Ornamental China', a service of 120 pieces of cut glass and a 'Long China Dinner Service'.[62] Similarly, when the contents of Number 19 Ailesbury Road (built by Michael Meade) were sold in 1873, 'dinnerware, dessert ware; china, glass, and delph' formed part of the sale.[63] Near the Butler's Pantry is the 'Lady's Store', fitted with shelving running along three of the walls. In Loudon's time, this was a repository for serving dishes and preserves, but here it was most likely used as a secure storeroom. Managed by the mistress of the house, it housed foodstuffs and cleaning provisions, distributed to the cook either on a daily or a weekly basis.[64] This would enable her to monitor the leftover food from the day before, in order to strictly control her food stock. In Shrewsbury Road, the line of storage continues through to the lobby, possibly for holding soiled boots when entering from outside. Natural light is admitted to this lobby through a glazed door and sidelight.

The fourth door from the lobby leads to the heart of the servant quarters: the kitchen where 'the administration of the culinary art' took place (Plate 25).[65] Located as close as possible to the dining room, this room also overlooks the side entrance, where deliveries were received. To the back of this space is a recess for the range, inserted into the fireplace to form an exit for the flue. Natural light was particularly important for this room, with preference for one large window to the side of the range, as is the case in Shrewsbury Road. The kitchen table was placed in the centre of the room, while shelves, pin-rails and small cupboards stored a variety of kitchenware. A kitchen dresser, used to store utensils, 'ordinary dinner stoneware', jugs and copper pots probably rested against the wall to the lady's store. A 'cook's pantry' is shown off the kitchen, while a narrow stairs rises in the corner of the kitchen, providing access to the servant bedrooms above.

Kerr advised that the door to the scullery be located next to the kitchen range, because of the 'constant passage to and fro while cooking'. In a small house, he recommended the provision of one stone sink here, with a plate rack above, and a grooved 'drip-board' to the side. A smaller cooking-range was probably provided in the alcove at the back of the range, in order to supplement the kitchen appliance. If there was adequate space, the scullery might also accommodate a small table in the centre of the room, which could be used for baking, or preparing vegetables. A door from this room to the outside was necessary for, as Kerr put it 'various incidental matters of out-door cleansing' – a reference to the weekly laundry wash.[66] To the right of the sink, a door leads out to an external yard, which is enclosed on all sides by full-height brick walls, segregating this very functional part of the house from the leisurely enjoyment of the garden. A coal shed, cycle store and lavatory are provided, in some rudimentary outbuildings against the back wall. The location of the coal shed facilitates delivery, but servants were also frequent visitors here, refilling buckets throughout the day to serve both the range and the nine fireplaces in the house. The lavatory ensured that the servants were separately catered for, instead of using the facilities in the main house. Only one opening is shown from the yard to the outside, leading to the side passageway. The kitchen, scullery and larder address either the side passageway or the yard, showing the architect's clear intention to screen the service quarters from the garden.

Kerr preferred a separate exit to the garden to what he deemed 'that inconvenient substitute': a door leading directly from the rear reception room.[67] This is provided at Shrewsbury Road, where the family entered the garden through the rear lobby (Plate 25), an indication of the increased importance of the rear garden, now that the family rooms were on the same level. This is in contrast to Northbrook Road, where no direct access was provided at the rear. Outdoor recreational space was a 'social priority' for Dublin's suburban dwellers;[68] advertisements for Shrewsbury Road promoted the availability of a 'large garden back and front', with the one to the rear of particular importance, providing a private space for adults and children. In the London suburbs, many of the 'lords' of the terraces described by Charles Manby Smith could be found 'strolling leisurely in the gardens in the rear of the dwellings, and amusing themselves with their children, whose prattling voices and innocent laughter mingle with the twittering of those suburban songsters, the sparrows, and with the rustling of the foliage, stirred by the evening breeze'.[69]

The plans at Shrewsbury Road show that servants were commuting to work by bicycle. Furthermore, at least two of the residents employed chauffeurs, heralding the arrival of another technological breakthrough: the motor car. Horses had been the main means of transport for centuries: they pulled coaches and carriages and transported goods across the length and breadth of the country.[70] Introduced into Ireland in 1895, the motor would in the future transform cities throughout the world, but for now it was the preserve of the wealthy.[71] The well-known jeweller Walter Sexton, who lived in one of these houses, operated from a premises in Grafton Street, the main shopping street in the city.[72] He had been the owner of a motor car since 1898, and drove the three-and-a-half-mile trip to town twice a day from his home in Shrewsbury Road.[73] There was certainly sufficient space in front of these houses to facilitate the parking of motor cars on the front driveway. One spring evening in 1905, he was returning from an excursion at Howth, when his car collided with a bicycle. Sexton had been travelling in the front with his chauffeur James Shannon, while his wife sat in the back seat. The victim was Thomas Fenelon, a malt-worker in the city who subsequently took Sexton to court, claiming substantial personal injuries. The case rumbled on until the spring of 1906, but Fenelon lost the case, as he was travelling without bicycle lamps.[74]

The upper levels: the family quarters

These houses cater for larger families, compared to the four-bedroom properties described previously. Six bedrooms are provided: two on the first floor, and four on the second floor. Priority has been given to the master bedroom to the front of the house, complete with a large bay window and a separate dressing room (Plate 26). This was in accordance with Kerr's 'universal standard plan': one principal bedroom for a married couple, with a dressing room attached for the man. The bedroom should be designed mainly for sleeping, but it should also be suitable for its occasional use during illness. To avoid draughts, the entrance door should open at the furthest possible distance from the bed and fireplace. The bed should be turned with its side facing the window, but its end opposite the fireplace 'to give character of fireside comfort to the light half of the room'.[75] The space in front of the window was the woman's sphere, with her dressing table and washstand placed close to the natural light. The wardrobe should be located directly opposite the window, since it was 'the best position for the effect of a handsome piece of furniture'.[76] Other bedroom furniture might include a small table near the fire, a 'pier-glass with its back to the light', a couch, chairs, chest of drawers, cabinet, side-table and chiffonier. Every morning, the lady of the house washed and dressed in this room. Meanwhile, her husband retired to the dressing room, which had two purposes: it took the man's sanitary needs 'out of the lady's way', but it was also a legacy inherited from larger houses, allowing the lady's maid to attend to her employer. Nevertheless, as Kerr conceded, dressing rooms were not always used for their original purpose. When the newly built 'Ellesmere' was advertised in 1906, it was to be let as a seven-bedroom house, so it is likely that the first-floor dressing room was converted to a bedroom.[77] In later years, these spaces were converted to en-suite bathrooms.

The main guest bedroom was next in importance to the master's bedchambers, although it was 'seldom expected to have all the completeness'. At Shrewsbury Road, this bedroom is of a similar size to the master suite, but it does not benefit from a large bay window, or dressing room. On the level above, a steep roof profile allows for the insertion of four smaller bedrooms. A 'Cistern Room' houses the cold water storage tank, and a room for 'Boxes' is provided off the landing level. According to Kerr, sleeping accommodation was divided into three classes: those for the family, for guests and for the children:

> The chief Guests' Chambers will in a manner take precedence of all others; the rooms of the heads of the family will follow; those of the more familiar guests and the rest of the family may come next; and so on to the accommodation of

72   *Inside the semi-detached house*

the dependents in their order; the apartments of the young children being taken separately as the Nurseries.[78]

The upper levels: the service wing

Kerr advised that servants' sleeping quarters were to be grouped together and 'of small size, suitable for not more than two persons'.[79] At Shrewsbury Road, two bedrooms are provided above the kitchen, each at least half the size of the family bedrooms to the front (Plate 26). Servants climbed a narrow stairs in the corner of the kitchen, arriving at a small lobby on the first floor, with just enough space to negotiate the doors to the two bedrooms (Plate 27). On the night of 2 April 1911, between two and five domestic servants were living under these roofs. Some residents made do with a cook and a parlour maid, but Arthur Hignett also employed a housemaid, a nurse and a nursery maid. With two to three domestic servants occupying each of the servant bedrooms, this would have made for very cramped living. They were simply furnished rooms, with an iron bed and a wardrobe, and if space allowed, a chest of drawers and wash-hand basin.[80] The architect has insured that there is no overlooking of the garden, by inserting the windows in the side walls, rather than in the gable. Each bedroom is fitted with a small fireplace, which Kerr concedes to in a servant bedroom 'for use in case of illness if no more'.[81]

A linen room is located on the other side of the servant stairs. This room housed the hot water cylinder, which fed the taps in the adjacent sanitary facilities.[82] At Number 8 Shrewsbury Road, the remnants of a dumb waiter were found in this location, used to pass laundry to the Butler's Pantry on the ground floor. This space was usually fitted with drawers and presses, and Kerr suggested placing a dresser under the window to fold clothes. Outside this room, a glazed screen borrows natural light from the stairwell. The corridor then rises up five steps, signalling the boundary between the main house and the rear extension, between the servant and the served. The main bathroom, and a separate toilet and sink are located here, grouped together for convenience. The location of the bathroom complies with Kerr's recommendations: 'in a retired position amongst the Bedrooms, and not too far off the Principal Staircase', complete with a 'reclining-bath', a fireplace and a generous area for dressing. Kerr confirmed that gentlemen visitors tended to use the ground-floor toilet, while the ladies used the facilities on the first floor.[83] Staff would have been prohibited from using either, as even in the smallest house they were separately accommodated. In Shrewsbury Road, the architect provides for one toilet (but no sink) in outbuildings off the rear yard.

The most striking aspect of the first-floor plan is the amount of area given over to circulation. With two staircases and two sets of corridors, it shows the importance of segregation, even in a house of limited size (Plate 26). Thus, while the family and guests negotiated the main stairwell, their servants passed unseen along hidden corridors and separate staircases. Nevertheless, an earlier sketch shows that the negotiation of this boundary was not always easy to maintain. Previously, the architect considered cutting off the servant bedrooms from the family rooms at the front of the house, as a solid wall is shown between the two sectors of the household (Plate 28: outlined in white). But this would have had other consequences, as housemaids would have had to use the main stairwell to service the family bedrooms. It appears that this was a step too far either for the architect or the client, and in the final layout the connection was maintained.

Conclusion

The spatial organisation of Dublin's semi-detached houses derived from that of the eighteenth-century townhouse, which was adapted to a new suburban context in the nineteenth century. The semi-detached form was wider than its terraced precedent, but gradually it evolved into its own distinctive plan. While the two adjoining reception rooms found their way into the Victorian paired form, in many cases the stairs had moved to the rear centre. Two out of three of the bays were devoted to the reception rooms, while the entrance was often inserted in a third bay to the side. Behind the hall was a new space, where the stairs used to be: in some houses it was a pantry (Rathgar Road), in others a study or library (Northbrook Road), while in Shrewsbury Road it was originally planned as a breakfast room. Spatial hierarchy was expressed in section: in Rathgar Road (1851) and Northbrook Road (1881), the lower level was reserved for service, over which were two floors for family. These upper levels were further divided into private and public realms: the entrance level contained the public rooms of the house (drawing room to the front, dining room to the rear), with the upper level reserved for sleeping. The main entrance door was accessed by a grand flight of granite steps, rising up above the service floor. By the time the Shrewsbury Road houses were designed in 1900, the suburban house form had made some remarkable changes. The reception floor was now entered directly off the street, displacing the service functions to enlarged rear extensions.

These suburban houses negotiated the boundaries between different constituents of the household, between master and servant, adult and child, man and woman. The gendering of space began at the entrance level: the dining room was the primary realm of the master of the house, while the drawing room was the domain of his wife. It seems that sleeping accommodation could also be gendered, as evidenced in the master suite in Shrewsbury Road, which provides for a separate dressing room for the man of the house. The emergence of a separate bathroom in Northbrook Road is indicative of developments in indoor sanitation, as well the means of disposal through a system of main drainage. Emerging from this analysis is also a clear negotiation of the boundaries between the Victorian family and their domestic staff. In Rathgar Road, they occupy different levels, but the insertion of a breakfast room in the service floor at Northbrook Road suggests that these boundaries were not always so clearly defined. In Shrewsbury Road, both family and servants occupy the same floor, requiring a careful manipulation of the plan. The servant quarters operate independently from the remainder of the house, with their own separate stairs and bedrooms, yet close to the family rooms that they serve. In all three case studies, the domestic staff enter the house by means of a separate servants' entrance to the side. Despite these carefully manipulated boundaries, the paths of master and servant must inevitably cross, and it is here the architecture is carefully manipulated, so that discreteness is ensured. At Rathgar Road, the family climb the external stairs from the garden, while the servants enter through a separate rear entrance below. A mostly solid wall screens the garden from the operations of the coach house and yard, while in Shrewsbury Road, the 'engine room' of the house is similarly shielded from view. Within the relatively limited confines of suburbia, domestic space was sacrificed to maintain these ever important boundaries, as Kerr explained in 1864:

> It becomes the foremost of all maxims, therefore, however small the establishment, that the Servants' Department shall be separated from the Main House, so that what passes on either side of the boundary shall be both invisible and inaudible on the other.[84]

Notes

1. P. Borsay, 'Why are houses interesting?' in *Urban History*, xxxiv, no. 2 (2007), pp. 345–346.
2. N. McCullough, *Dublin, an urban history, the plan of the city* (Dublin, 2007), p. 168.
3. *The Irish Times*, 15 August 1874 and 1 May 1875.
4. *Ibid.* 20 August 1878.
5. IAA, Arthur Murray Collection, Rathgar Road, plans, elevations, sections and details depicting three schemes for a terrace of houses for Arthur Murray Esq. by William G. Murray and Abraham Denny, 1851 (Acc. No. 92/46.753–8).
6. J. C. Loudon, *The suburban gardener and villa companion* (London, 1838), p. 320.
7. *Ibid.*, p. 103.
8. *Ibid.*, p. 102.
9. C. M. Smith, *Curiosities of London life* (London, 1857), p. 346.
10. *The Irish Times*, 13 October 1873.
11. Loudon, *suburban gardener*, p. 86.
12. *Ibid.*, pp. 91–92.
13. *Ibid.*, p. 85.
14. Fireplaces were not always found in bedrooms during this time. J. Flanders, *The Victorian house: domestic life from childbirth to deathbed* (London, 2004), p. 72.
15. Loudon, *Suburban gardener*, p. 76.
16. *Ibid.*, p. 67.
17. Loudon, *Suburban gardener*, p. 81.
18. IAA, McCurdy and Mitchell Collection, Northbrook Road, pair of semi-detached houses, plans, elevations, sections, specification for the committee of Adelaide Road Presbyterian Church by W. M. Mitchell, 1881 (Acc. No. 82/49.83).
19. William Beckett was the grandfather of the writer Samuel Beckett. IAA, Dictionary of Irish Architects 1720–1940, James Beckett.
20. *The Irish Times*, 16 May 1885.
21. IAA, McCurdy and Mitchell Collection, Northbrook Road, pair of semi-detached houses, specification for the committee of Adelaide Road Presbyterian Church by W. M. Mitchell, 1881 (Acc. No. 82/49.83).
22. R. Kerr, *The gentleman's house* (London, 1864). Reprint, Cambridge, 2012, p. iii.

23 *Ibid.*, p. 103.
24 *Ibid.*, p. 106
25 At Number 19 Ailesbury Road (built by 1870), the dining room contained a 'Set of massive mahogany dinner tables', in 2 parts on 'pillar and claw', an enclosed sideboard and bookcase in mahogany, a range of chairs, a couch, an oak plate chest and 'lots of books' and ornaments. *The Irish Times*, 13 October 1873.
26 Kerr, *The gentleman's house*, p. 104.
27 Flanders, *The Victorian house*, p. 131.
28 Kerr, *The gentleman's house*, p. 119.
29 M. Hayden, *The diaries of Mary Hayden 1878–1903*, vol. 1 (1878–1883), ed. C. Kennedy (Killala, 2005), p. 304.
30 Kerr, *The gentleman's house*, p. 122.
31 *Ibid.*, p. 123. The best furniture appears to have been reserved for this room. At Number 19 Ailesbury Road, the following drawing room furniture and effects were put up for sale in 1873: 'suit (*sic*) of walnut framed furniture, comprising 6 chairs, lady's, and arm chair; and couch, in striped tabouret, two ladies' chairs and arm chairs in green repp (*sic*), two walnut davenports; walnut chess, wine, spider, and work tables; mahogany yacht table; rosewood sofa table; 2 ottomans, rich velvet pile and tapestry carpets; hearth rugs; suits (*sic*) of brocatelle window curtains; 2, 3 and 5 light gaseliers, engravings, ornaments, fenders, fire irons, &c.' *Irish Times*, 13 October 1873.
32 Kerr, *The gentleman's house*, p. 124.
33 *Ibid.*, p. 109.
34 IAA, McCurdy and Mitchell Collection, Northbrook Road, pair of semi-detached houses, specification for the committee of Adelaide Road Presbyterian Church by W. M. Mitchell, 1881 (Acc. No. 82/49.83).
35 Kerr, *The gentleman's house*, p. 136.
36 *Ibid.*
37 *Ibid.*, p. 75.
38 Smith, *Curiosities of London life*, p. 339.
39 G. and W. Grossmith, *The diary of a nobody* (London, 1892), p. 37.
40 S. Rains, *Commodity culture and social class in Dublin 1850–1916* (Dublin, 2010), pp. 12 and 29.
41 Kerr, *The gentleman's house*, p. 222.
42 *Ibid.*, p. 118.
43 G. Crookes, 'The genesis of an archive, forty years of *The Irish Builder*, 1859–1899' (unpublished Ph.D. thesis, University College Dublin, 1994), p. 164.
44 *Thom's*, 1882–1900 and Mount Jerome Cemetery, Headstone No. 9733 (www.igp-web.com/IGPArchives/ire/dublin/photos/tombstones/1headstones/mt-jerome66.txt; ae).
45 NAI, Census of Ireland, 1901, Numbers 16 and 17 Northbrook Road.
46 *Ibid*, 1911, Numbers 16 and 17 Northbrook Road.
47 NLI, Visitors' book of Alderman Joseph Meade, Lord Mayor of Dublin, 27 January 1891 to 2 August 1892 (Acc. No. Ms. 19,707, Acc. 3383).
48 *Thom's*, 1906.
49 *The Irish Times*, 14 January and 19 October 1901.
50 NAI, Census of Ireland, 1911, 3 Shrewsbury Road.
51 Kerr, *The gentleman's house*, p. 181.
52 *The Irish Times*, 3 August 1908.
53 T. Morris, *A house for the suburbs, socially and architecturally sketched* (London, 1860), p. 1.
54 *Ibid.*, p. 112.
55 *Ibid.*, p. 72.
56 Loudon, *Suburban gardener*, p. 88.

57 Kerr, *The gentleman's house*, pp. 166–167.
58 *Ibid.*, p. 76.
59 Kerr, *The gentleman's house*, p. 75.
60 *Ibid.*, p. 264.
61 *The Irish Times*, 2 December 1905.
62 *Ibid.*, 24 May 1919.
63 *Ibid.*, 13 October 1873.
64 Flanders, *The Victorian house*, p. 82.
65 Kerr, *The gentleman's house*, p. 227.
66 *Ibid.*, p. 236. The residents of Number 19 Ailesbury Road were the owners of a 'patent mangling, wringing and washing machine'. *The Irish Times*, 13 October 1873.
67 Kerr, *The gentleman's house*, p. 182.
68 P. Bowe, 'Dublin suburban gardens: Loudon's influence', in *Irish Architectural and Decorative Studies*, ix (2006), p. 151.
69 Smith, *Curiosities of London life*, p. 4
70 P. McCarthy, 'Stables and horses in Ireland c.1630–1840', in Trinity College Dublin, *The Provost's House Stables, building and environs* (Dublin, 2008), p. 52.
71 M. E. Daly, 'The growth of Victorian Dublin', in M. E. Daly, M. Hearn and P. Pearson (eds), *Dublin's Victorian houses* (Dublin, 1998), p. 127.
72 *The Irish Times*, 15 April 1905.
73 *Ibid.*, 16 November 1905.
74 *The Irish Times*, 26 April 1906.
75 Kerr, *The gentleman's house*, pp. 145–146.
76 *Ibid.*, p. 147.
77 *The Irish Times*, 31 May 1906.
78 Kerr, *The gentleman's house*, p. 152.
79 *Ibid.*, p. 277.
80 M. Hearn, *Below stairs, domestic service remembered in Dublin and beyond, 1880–1922*, (Dublin, 1993), p. 54.
81 Kerr, *The gentleman's house*, p. 278.
82 An advertisement for one of these houses promotes the availability of hot and cold water in the bathroom. *The Irish Times*, 31 May 1906.
83 Kerr, *The gentleman's house*, pp. 168 and 170.
84 *Ibid.*, pp 74–75.

1. Number 22 Elgin Road.

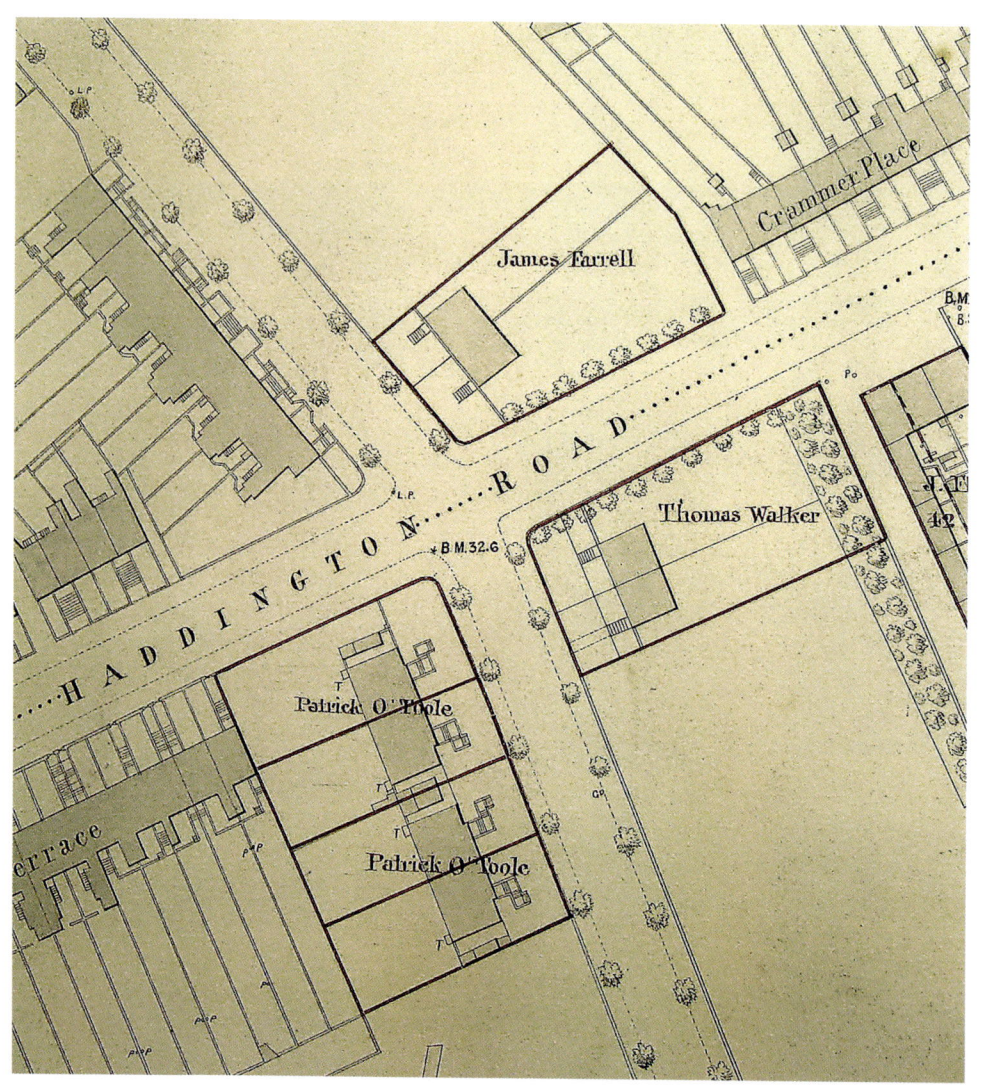

2. Pembroke Township map of Northumberland Road, c.1865 (National Archives of Ireland).

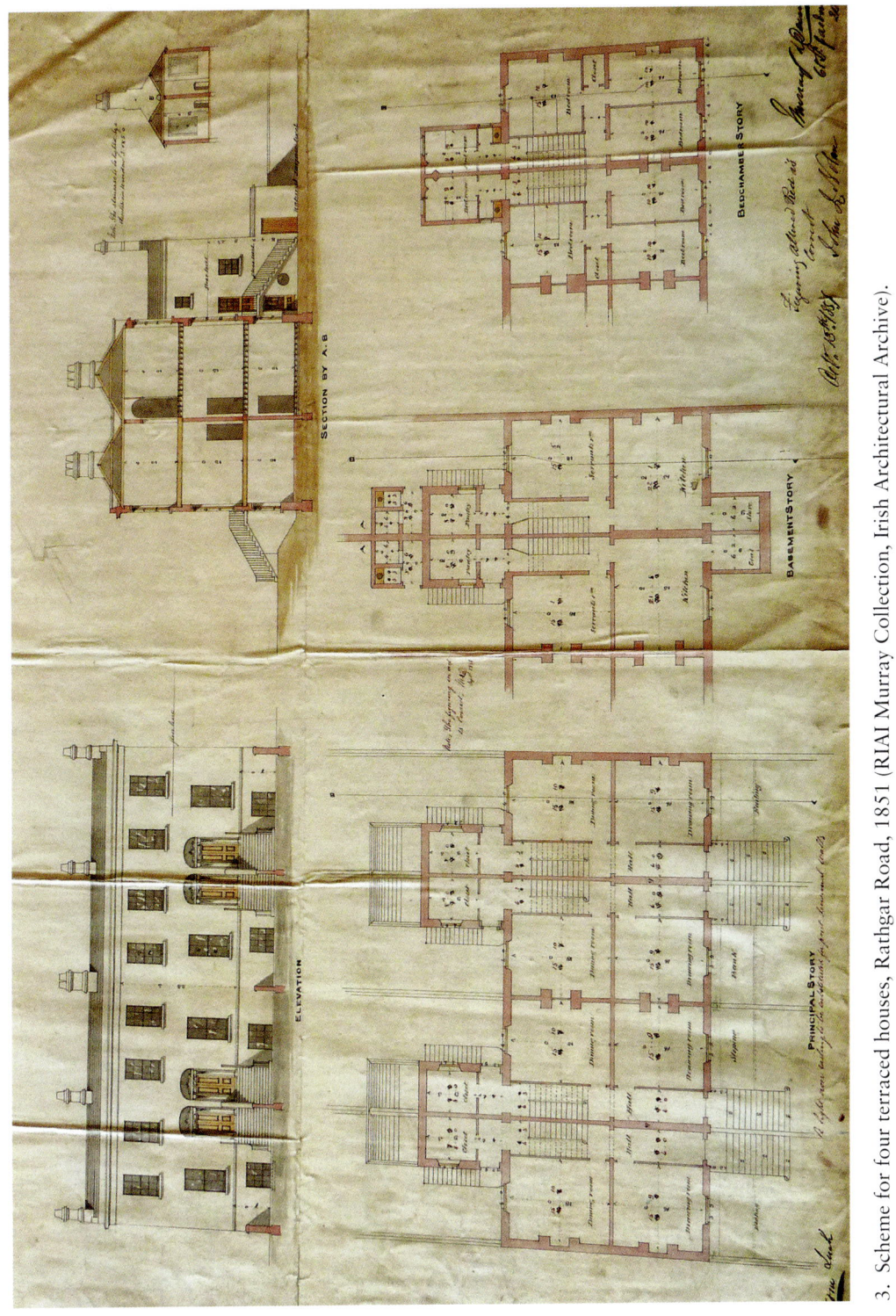

3. Scheme for four terraced houses, Rathgar Road, 1851 (RIAI Murray Collection, Irish Architectural Archive).

4. Numbers 150–153 Rathgar Road.

5. The evolution of the terraced house form.

6. Numbers 34–44 Northumberland Road.

7. Numbers 68–74 Northumberland Road.

8. Numbers 46–52 Northumberland Road.

9. Numbers 10 and 12 Raglan Road.

10. Numbers 22 and 23 Clyde Road.

11. Number 51 Northumberland Road.

12. Number 9 Ailesbury Road, detail of gable end to side return.

13. Numbers 2 and 4 Ailesbury Road.

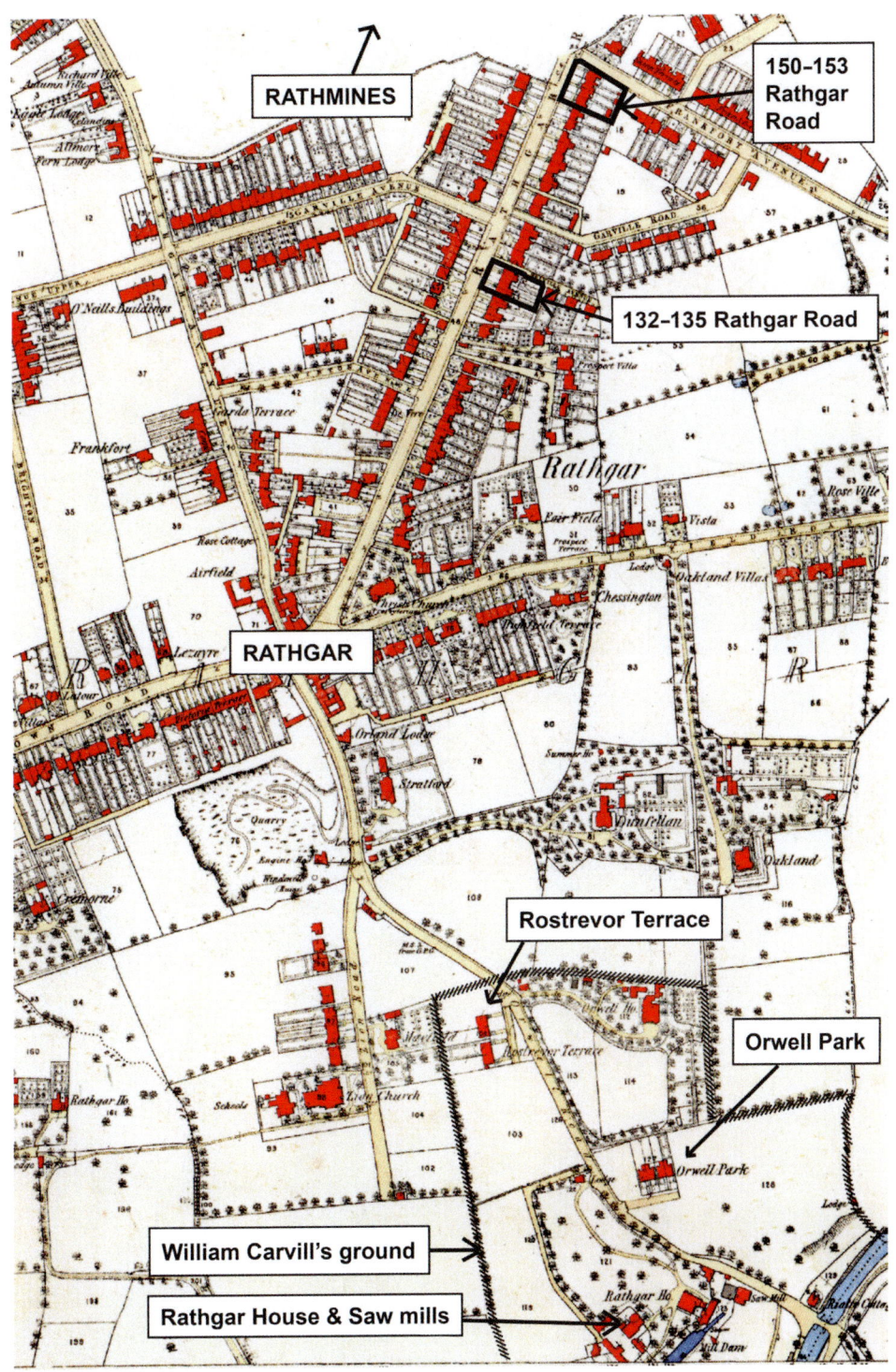

14. Ordnance Survey map of Rathgar, 1865 (Leslie Brown).

15. Numbers 1 and 2 Rostrevor Terrace.

16. Numbers 1–4 Orwell Park.

17. Numbers 1 and 2 Orwell Park, detail of entrance doorcases.

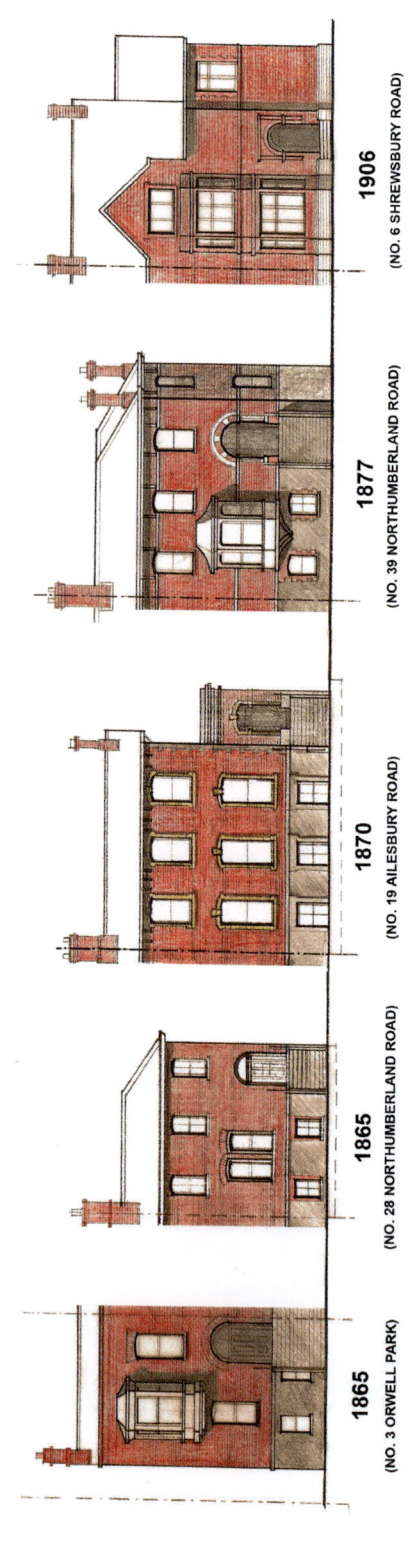

18. The evolution of the semi-detached house form.

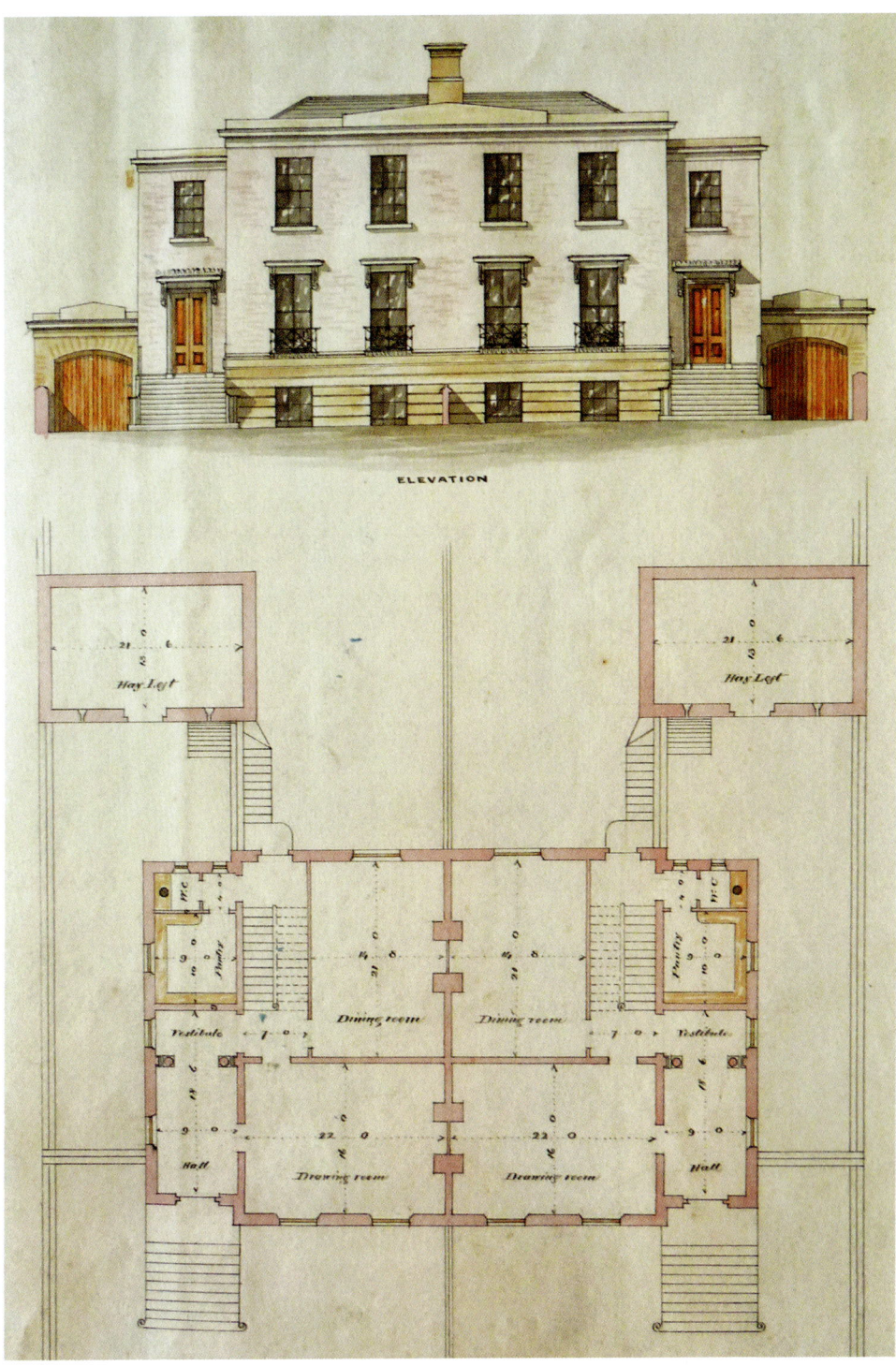

19. Scheme for two semi-detached houses, upper ground-floor plan and front elevation, Rathgar Road, 1851 (RIAI Murray Collection, Irish Architectural Archive).

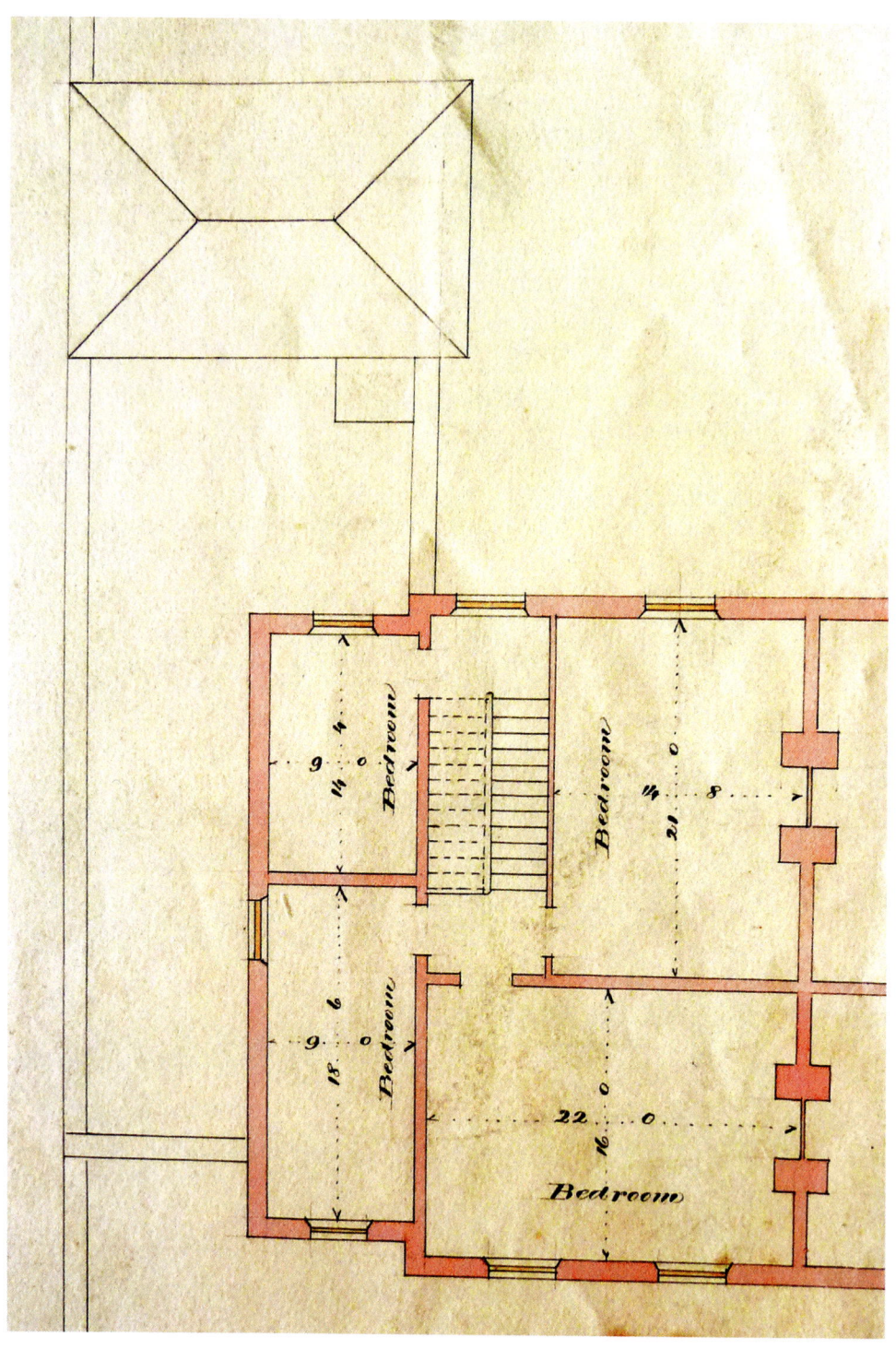

20. Scheme for two semi-detached houses, first-floor plan, Rathgar Road, 1851 (RIAI Murray Collection, Irish Architectural Archive).

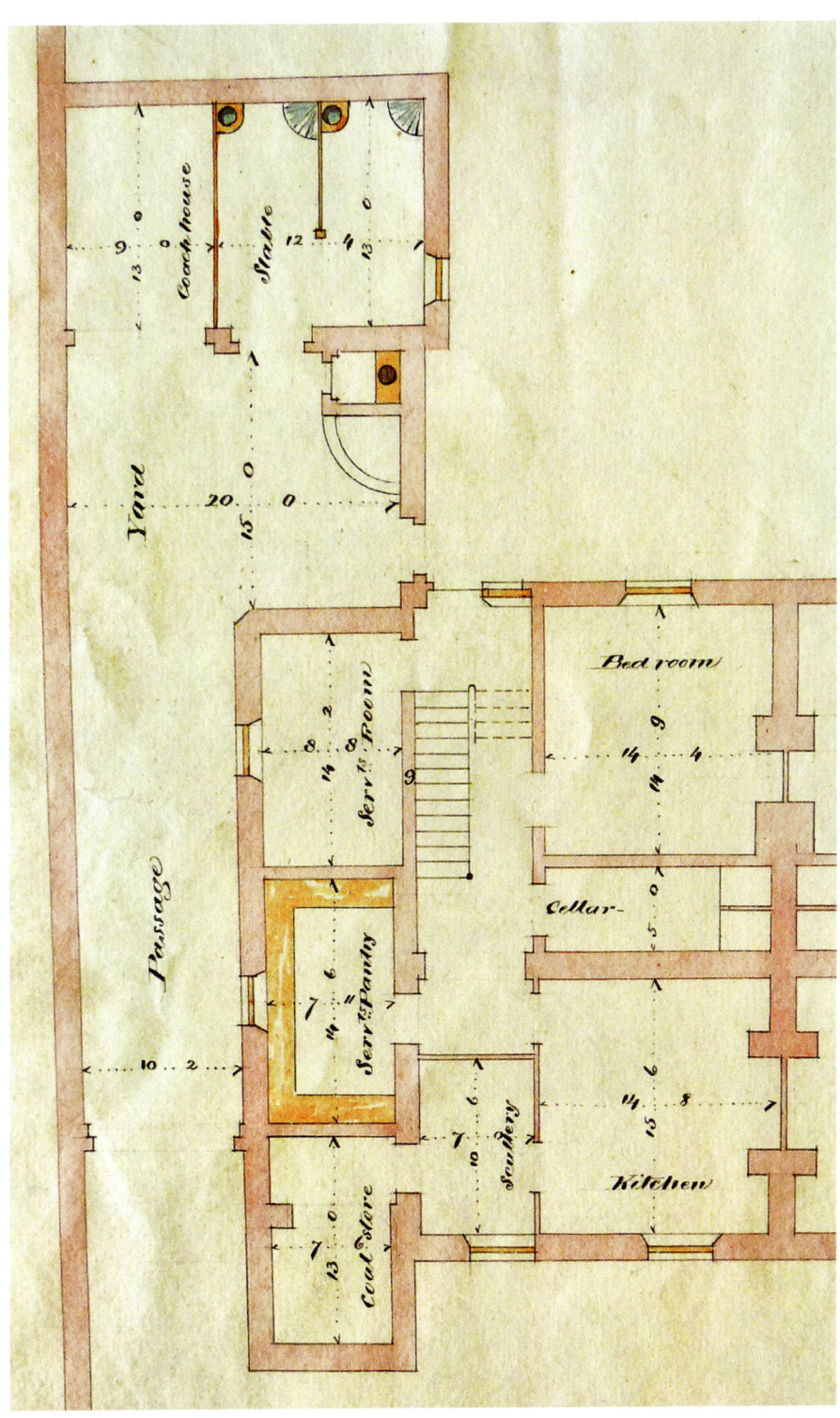

21. Scheme for two semi-detached houses, lower ground-floor plan, Rathgar Road, 1851 (RIAI Murray Collection, Irish Architectural Archive).

22. Numbers 16 and 17 Northbrook Road.

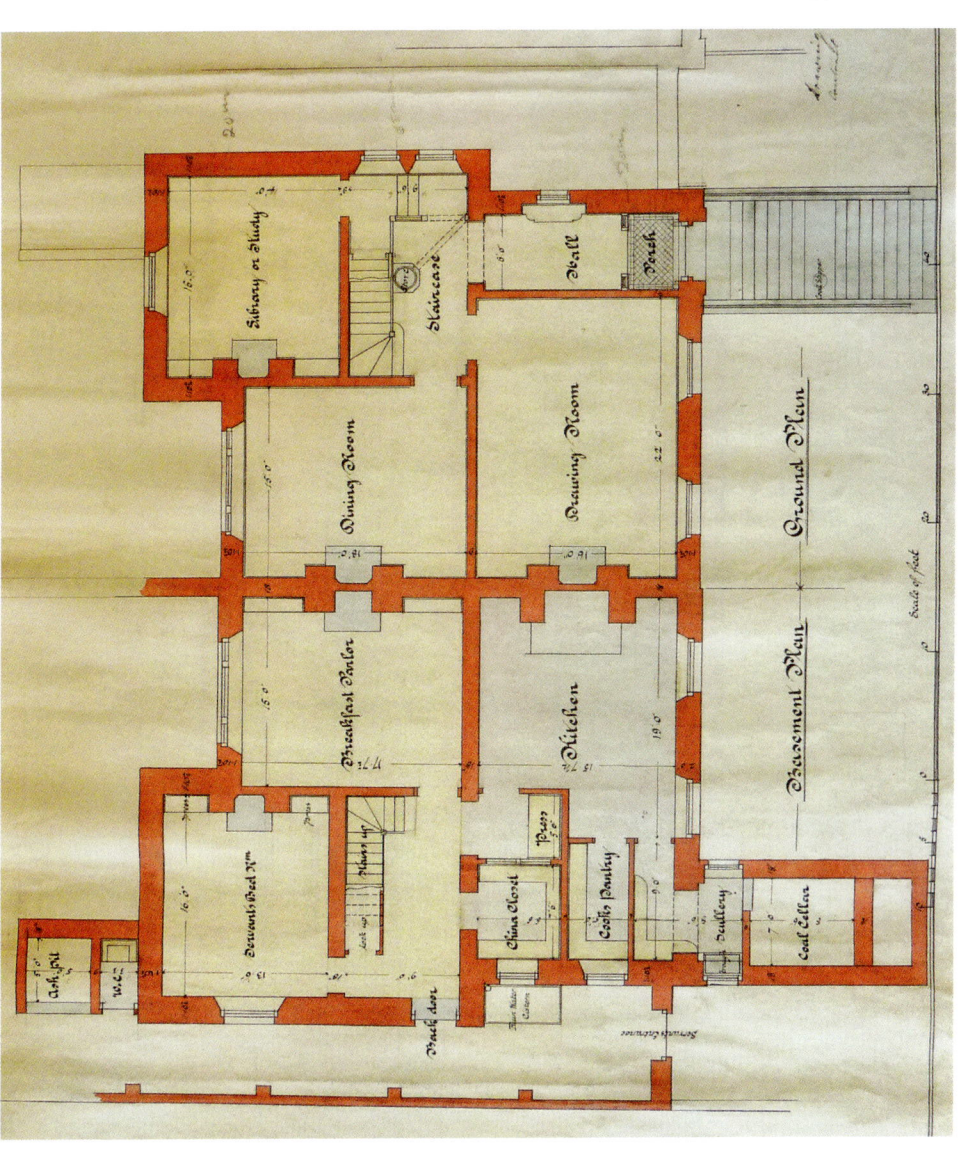

23. Numbers 16 and 17 Northbrook Road, basement and ground-floor plans, 1881 (McCurdy and Mitchell Collection, Irish Architectural Archive).

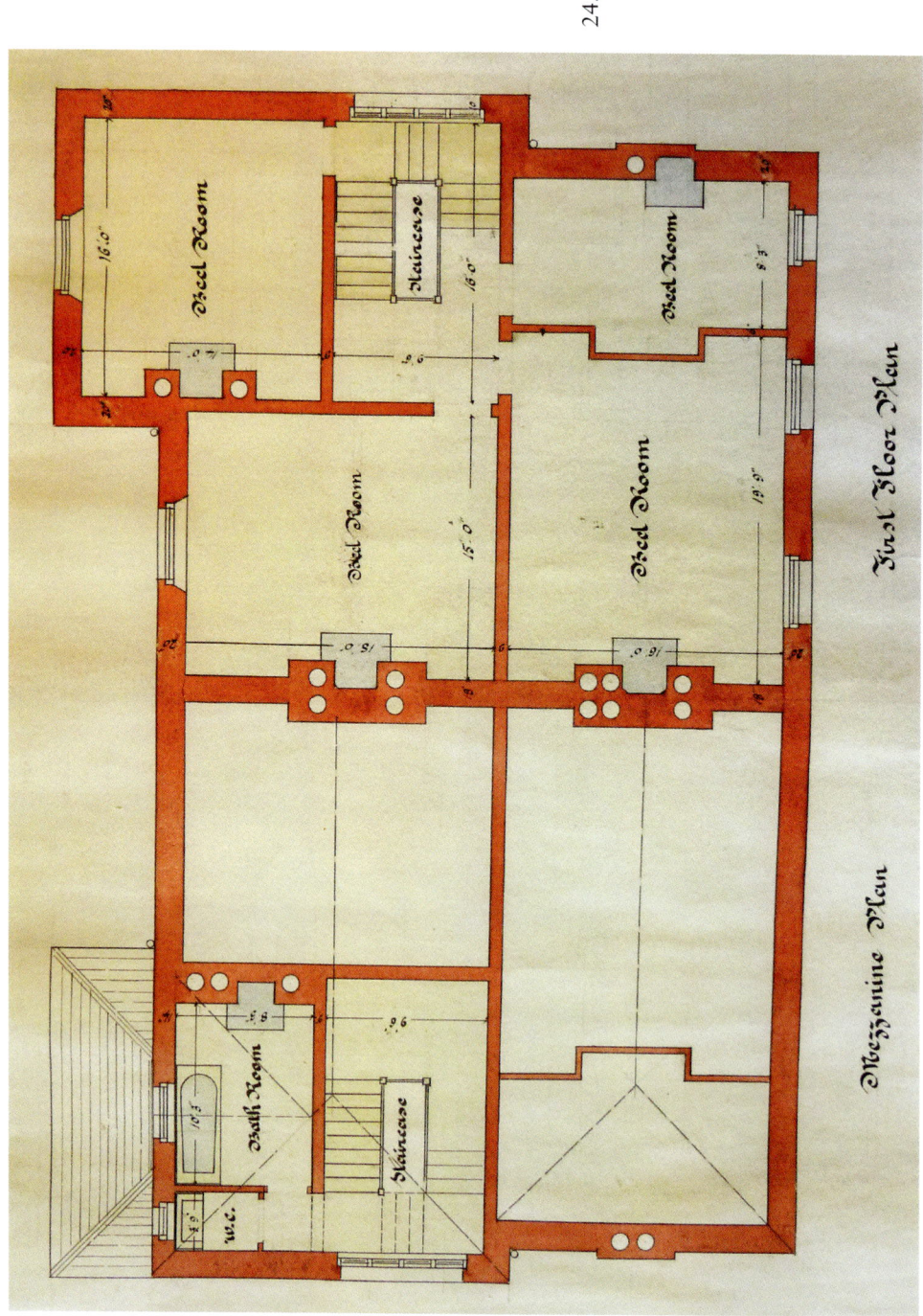

24. Numbers 16 and 17 Northbrook Road, first- and mezzanine-floor plans, 1881 (McCurdy and Mitchell Collection, Irish Architectural Archive).

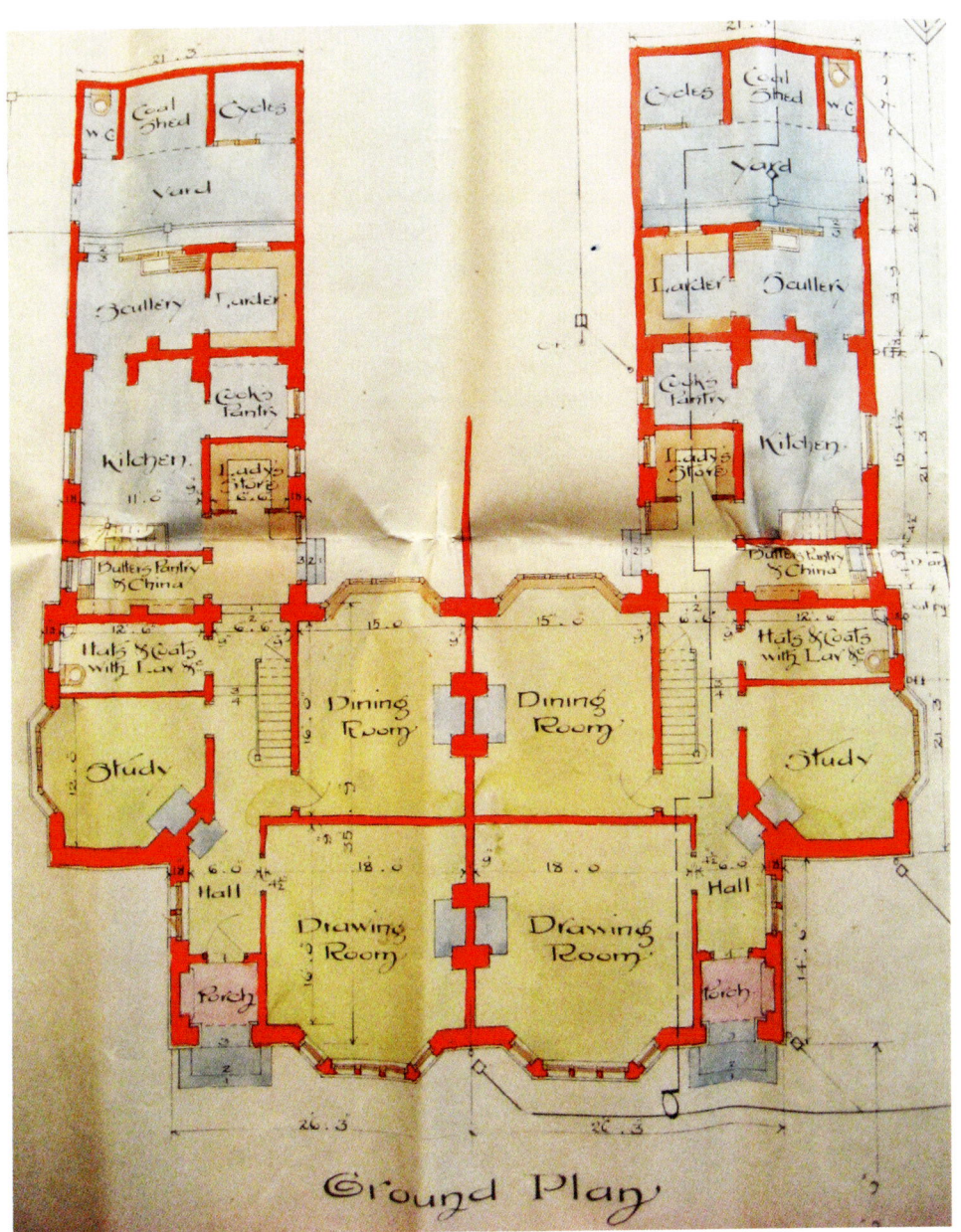

25. Proposed semi-detached houses in Shrewsbury Road, ground-floor plan, 1900 (National Archives of Ireland).

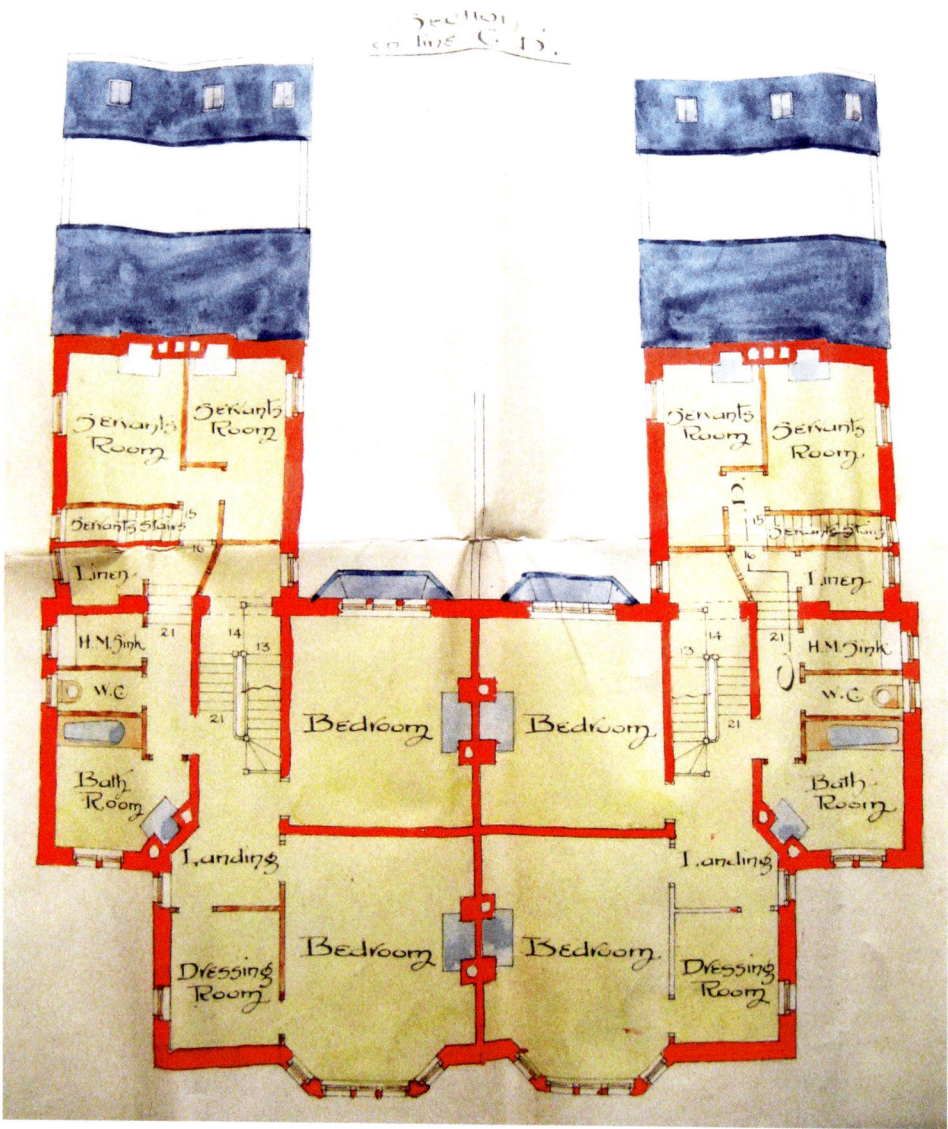

26. Shrewsbury Road, first-floor plan, 1900 (National Archives of Ireland).

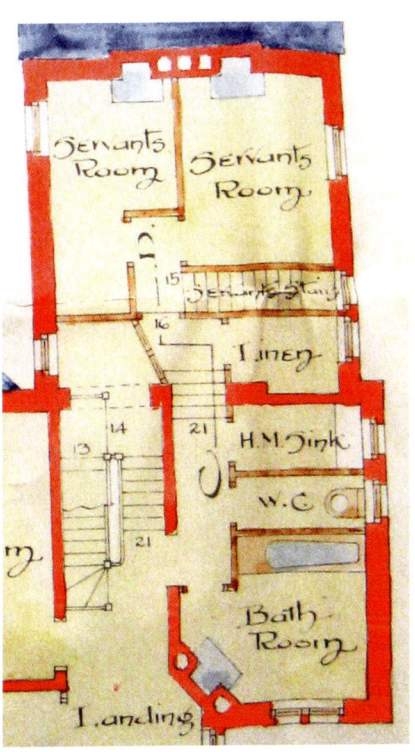 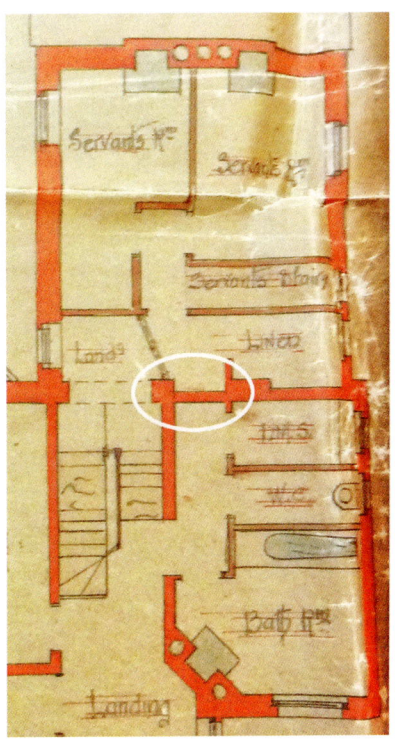

27. Shrewsbury Road, detail of first-floor rear return, 1900 (National Archives of Ireland).

28. Shrewsbury Road, earlier sketch of first-floor rear return, 1900 (National Archives of Ireland).

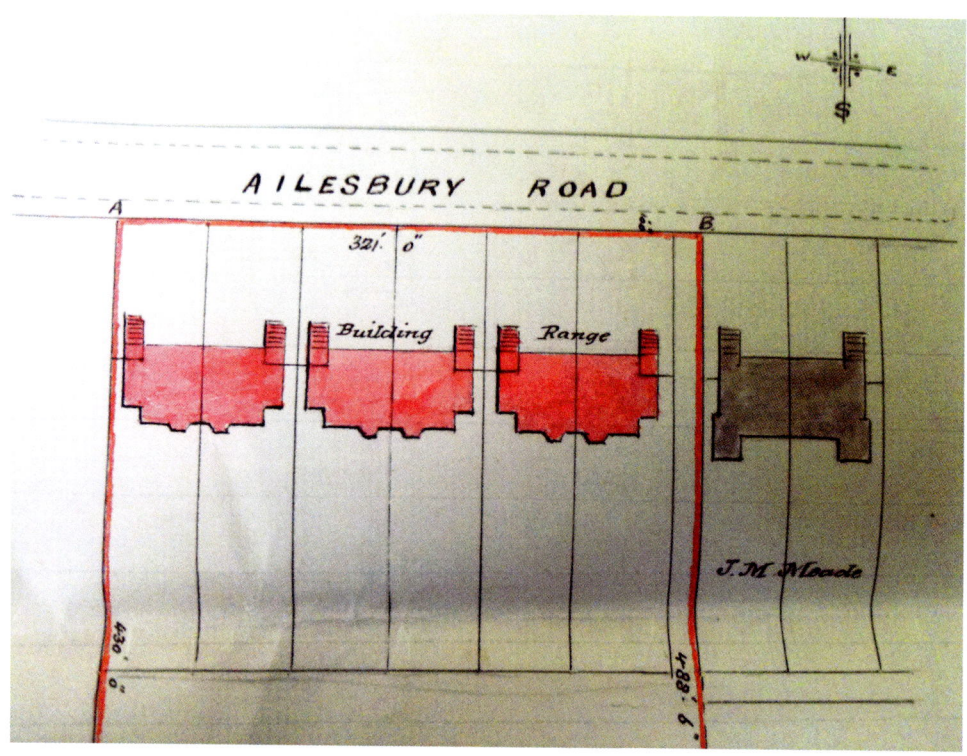

29. Lease map of Ailesbury Road, September 1865, the Earl of Pembroke to Michael Meade (St Michael's College).

3 Control
Land tenure and infrastructure

New streets in green fields

The 1860s saw record growth in the newly emerging suburbs to the southeast of the city, as new roads were cut through the green swathe; the invasion of the country by the town. The two largest areas were Rathmines and Pembroke, both adjoining the city, while six miles along the southern coast was the railway suburb of Kingstown, a major port resplendent in natural beauty. In Pembroke and Kingstown, varying degrees of control were imposed by the landed estate system, in contrast to Rathgar where the private landowner prevailed. How did land ownership and local government contribute to the planning of these new districts, and who was responsible for local services, including the laying of roads and the provision of infrastructure? The chapter reveals the complex relationships between the different vested interests in the Dublin suburbs, an invisible layer of control that had a great impact on its architecture.

Land: the gateway to speculation

By the mid-nineteenth century, most ground in Ireland was controlled by a small minority of property owners. Many of the richest and most extensive lands were located in the province of Leinster, home to the capital city, where estate landlords held almost total control.[1] In Dublin, these large-scale property owners tended to retain the full 'freehold' title, but offered sites for building on leasehold agreements.[2] In doing so, speculators were required to build a house within a specific number of years, and were subject to a range of conditions. In managing their estates in this way, estate landlords transferred most of the profits from building to speculative developers, who could then earn rental income on the property, or sell their leasehold interest to a third party. This was how many of the Georgian streetscapes in Britain and Ireland had been built. An example is the Bedford estate in London, which developed plots in Bloomsbury in the 1720s, by offering leases for sixty-one years.[3] When the lease term was complete, the ground, together with its buildings, reverted to the landlord, which he could then rack-rent to another lessee.[4] Thus, the 'lords of the soil' increased the value of their estate, with minimal investment in building. In Dublin, this form of land tenure had driven much of development during the eighteenth century, primarily by the Gardiner and Fitzwilliam estates to the east of the city.[5]

Each type of landlord had a different approach to speculation. Lord Pembroke, who presided over a large estate southeast of the city, granted relatively short building leases, which strictly regulated the form and finish of building. Meanwhile in the seaside suburb of Kingstown, Lords Longford and de Vesci were the major stakeholders who had a less active role in determining the character of development on their estates. Landlords in Rathmines were the most passive of the three, granting much longer leases with fewer restrictions on development. These varying approaches to land tenure were key factors in influencing the architectural character of each suburban area.

The estate landlord

Land tenure in the Pembroke estate

Of the new suburbs emerging around Dublin during the nineteenth century, the Pembroke estate was the largest single domain to be developed.[6] The eleventh Earl of Pembroke presided over this large territory, which began in the city at Leinster House, extending beyond the boundary along the coast to the Dublin Mountains and as far as Bray in County Wicklow. During the eighteenth century, the estate had played an important role in the city, by laying out some of its most important residential areas, such as Merrion Street and Square. In the opening decades of the nineteenth century, economic decline curbed the growth of the estate until the 1840s, when a network of streets began to emerge to the east of Leinster House. Lord Pembroke continued to expand his estate by buying up large areas of ground outside the city boundary, and by 1860 he controlled a large area to the southeast, from Donnybrook Road, along the coast as far as Merrion.[7] The Earl of Pembroke resided in his country estate in Wiltshire, and rarely visited Dublin, relying on an estate agent to manage his affairs in Ireland. By 1869, *The Dublin Builder* (which had changed its name to *The Irish Builder* in 1867) described its transformation from market gardens to suburban district 'now laid out in every quarter in magnificent roads, all but completely covered with numberless first-class residences'.[8] By 1878, the earl was the owner of 2,301 acres of ground in the County Dublin area.

The Pembroke estate was known for strict regulation, offering tightly controlled leases under relatively short terms of 99 to 150 years. This was the approach of other aristocratic estates in England, where landlords insisted on high standards, to ensure the long-term value of their holdings.[9] In 1853, John Vernon was appointed as agent to the Pembroke estate. His proactive style brought in even stricter regulation: his building leases specified the type of materials, the building form and roof profile to be constructed. However, this rigour was not applied to all parts of the estate, as it depended on whether it was located on the east or west side. The eastern sector ran along the coast, taking in the villages of Ringsend, Irishtown and Sandymount (Figure 0.2), a low-lying area that had been reclaimed from the sea, producing a marshy ground that was prone to flooding. The adjoining western sector lay between Donnybrook and Merrion Roads on higher, better-drained land. Building ground was more attractive here, compared to the waterlogged ground in the eastern sector, constantly under threat from the sea. Consequently, Vernon imposed tighter controls on the more valuable western side, and looser regulation along the coast.[10] These differing levels of control had an impact on the architectural character of the estate.[11]

Chapter 1 discussed the large semi-detached houses built by the Meade family of builders in Ailesbury Road. Located on the western side of the estate, this mile-length thoroughfare cut through a swathe of green fields, three miles to the southeast of the city.[12] The Meades were the first to acquire plots there in 1865, and within five years they had built eleven houses on the south side of the road (Figure 1.21). The original leases survive, showing how the speculative building system worked in practice. Michael Meade leased a large two-acre site on the corner of Merrion Road, where he was required to build 'one good and substantial dwelling house'.[13] The adjoining sites were designated for semi-detached houses, where generous plots had been pegged out, fifty feet wide and 238 feet long. The builders signed leases for ten houses, agreeing to pay an annual ground rent of £3.50 per plot for the first three years, after which rents would double to £7. This was a standard covenant in building leases, enabling speculators to put most of their capital into construction. It also gave them time to build the house and offload their debt by either letting it on to tenants, or selling it on the open market. All of the properties were complete within the three-year period specified in the lease: by 1870, Meade's Italianiate villa stood on the corner, together with ten semi-detached dwellings adjacent.[14]

It was the specifics of the building lease that determined the architectural character of the road. The large plot sizes and generous setbacks (seventy feet) established a scale of grandeur on the street (Plate 30). The lease conditions extended to the treatment of the boundaries: the front was to be finished with iron railings fixed into a cut stone plinth, with iron entrance gates and piers. Neither walls nor wooden fences were permitted to run along the boundaries between the houses, ensuring a clear view of each semi-detached pair. The form of domestic architecture was specified: a detached house for the corner site, and semi-detached dwellings for the adjacent plots. The houses were to be 'no more or less than two storeys high over an elevated basement storey', with 'projecting or cantilever' roofs rather than parapets. A high standard of finish was required for the front façades, consisting of two storeys of brick over a stone base, with slates and lead dressings for the roofs. Two types of bricks were specified: 'the best red bricks' to the front and a cheaper 'red or grey stock bricks' to the side and rear. The leasehold system ensured an illusion of grandeur, presenting the most expensive materials to the street, while economising on the sides and backs (Plate 12). The projecting entrances to Numbers 5 and 7 Ailesbury Road are curious in light of a condition in the building lease that 'no building or projection except steps to the hall door shall be made in front of the said houses'.

Before acquiring a building lease, speculators were required to lodge detailed plans to the estate agent for his approval. An example are the plans submitted by architect Frederick Morley in 1895, for new houses in Londonbridge Road, on the eastern side of the estate. They included a block layout plan, sketch plans and a general specification, which the estate agent approved of, on the condition that a light iron railing was erected to the side boundary, instead of a wall.[15] However, it was not always possible for speculators to submit such detailed plans. In 1860, one speculator explained to Vernon that he had employed a gentleman named 'Gibson' for many years but he 'did not enter so specifically with him into details as I would with a stranger'. In proposing a house on the estate, he outlined the room measurements, ceiling heights and building materials in his letter to Vernon, conceding: '[T]hough it may not be all that either of us could desire will satisfy you that the proposed building will be both substantial & respectable.'[16] Elsewhere, Vernon was found accepting a 'rough tracing' in the absence of completed plans, especially in the eastern sector. Once this was approved by the estate, a 'memorandum of agreement' was signed by the lessee and possession of the ground was given.[17] This was an agreement to grant a lease, but the full leasehold title was not signed until the building was finished to the estate's satisfaction.[18] This had been the practice in other aristocratic estates in eighteenth-century London, to safeguard the landlords' interests. It provided an incentive for a builder to complete a house, as he could not let or sell a property until he was in possession of the lease.[19]

The majority of leaseholders developed just two to four plots at a time. However, larger speculators were given more leeway by the estate, such as the Meade family, who were slow to pay ground rent on their leaseholds. By 1873, Michael Meade was in arrears on a total of six properties: four in Ailesbury Road and two in Sandymount. Nevertheless, Vernon signed a lease with him four years later, to add another house on the north side of Ailesbury Road.[20] By 1880, Meade had spent £30,000 in building on the Pembroke estate, and was owner of one of the largest building firms in the city.[21] John Vernon continued to write to Meade & Son about overdue rents on their holdings, which by 1884 had amounted to what was described by the agent as 'a large sum' of over £459.[22] This continued into the next generation: in 1899, his son Joseph signed leases for sites on Shrewsbury Road, which required him to complete houses there within a year. However, after two years, nothing had been built on the sites. The agent wrote to the builder, asking to take the matter seriously in hand, by completing the development within the current building season. He remained conciliatory in tone however: 'I need not say that Lord Pembroke would not wish to stand too strictly on his rights on this point, especially when dealing with a gentleman whose family have spent, and who is at present spending elsewhere, large sums in building on his lordship's Estate'.[23]

These semi-detached houses were a product of the building lease. At Ailesbury Road, it was estate policy that determined the wide plots, the large setbacks from the street and the treatment of the boundaries. The lease controlled the architectural form of the houses: whether they were paired or detached, as well as their height, roof profiles and building materials. However, within that template the leaseholder could experiment with the design for entrance doorcases, window surrounds and side extensions. While a pitched roof profile was stipulated at Ailesbury Road, the shape of the gable was the choice of the leaseholder: building leases specified 'projecting or cantilever roofs', but the sides could be finished in gables or hips. In time, the speculator could move with the latest fashions, by inserting large bay windows, or polychromatic brick and stone. Thus, the leasehold template brought uniformity and order to the street, but the individuality of the speculator was expressed in other features and details.

These strict controls aimed to ensure the quality, and ultimately the value, of housing in this newly developing suburban ground.[24] However, it was not the case in all areas of the estate, as exemplified in a lease for Belvedere Terrace in Sandymount, located in the less valuable eastern sector beside the sea. When the builder Alexander Graham arrived on the scene in the 1860s, the site already contained a terrace of four houses.[25] He signed a lease to build three adjoining properties, which were to align with the existing buildings. The houses were to be constructed with 'the best materials of their several kinds', with a slate roof finish.

Figure 3.1 Belvedere Terrace, Sandymount.

There were no further specifics, such as a particular type of brick or stone, and there were no references to projecting roofs or elevated basement storeys, as stipulated in the western sector. Instead, Graham was required to spend at least £500 in completing the three houses, equating to a minimum outlay of £166 per house, a minimum form of regulation, resulting in plainly rendered façades (Figure 3.1). This is in marked contrast to terraced houses in the western sector, finished in red brick and granite fronts. Thus, the lease was the principal driver of cost, which, in insisting on the most expensive materials, had a profound impact on development on the east and west sides of the estate. In 1868, the role of the Pembroke estate was praised by *The Irish Builder*, describing it as 'now one of the most important suburbs of Dublin – the many beautiful terraces and villas that have so rapidly sprung up in the district attesting the enterprise and taste of our citizens, and the judicious management of the officials of the Estate'.[26]

Land tenure in the Kingstown estate

In 1865, as ground was being broken at Ailesbury Road, visitors were travelling in their droves to Dublin's International Exhibition. From the deck of their vessels, they were rewarded with their first views of Dublin at the port of Kingstown, six miles along the south shore of the bay:

> Kingstown, . . . seems literally, like Venice, to rise from the sea. Its noble harbour, its piers of which are each about a mile in length, as well as its beautiful terraces and numerous public buildings and villas, are constructed of the white granite of the district. The men-of-war and graceful yachts, which in summer time are ever gliding past, complete a scene not easily forgotten by the tourist.[27]

It was the geography of Kingstown that had transformed this poor fishing village into a major port. Since the eighteenth century, this sheltered cove had been a safe haven for ships travelling to the city. Due to a number of shipping disasters in Dublin Bay in the early nineteenth century, there had been a public outcry for the construction of a harbour to shelter ships in times of distress.[28] Work began on a new harbour in 1815, and thousands of construction workers descended on the area, swelling the population of the town. It was re-named Kingstown in 1821, after the visit of King George IV to Dublin, the first royal visit to the city since 1690.[29] In 1834, the town became the main packet station for Dublin and Ireland's first railway was opened, running from an elegant neoclassical station in Kingstown to Westland Row terminus in Dublin. People flowed into the town after the completion of the railway: between 1841 and 1851, Kingstown's population grew by 43%.[30] By 1846, the seashore was 'girdled by terraces of fine houses',[31] as development began to seep into the hills above the harbour. However, it was the 'genius of steam-that modernizing giant' that transformed Kingstown into 'a great highway between this and the sister kingdom'.[32] Powerful steamships arrived from

Wales in five hours and forty minutes, where trains would convey passengers to Dublin in just fifteen minutes. By 1862, the Kingstown to Dublin railway line was reported to form part of 'the highway between the English and Irish metropolis and provinces', populated by a 'vast and continuous stream of passengers'.[33]

Like the Pembroke estate, the ownership of ground in Kingstown was dominated by the landed family estate. The major landowners in the area were Lords Longford and de Vesci, who together owned 1,280 acres of ground (Figure 0.1).[34] In contrast to Lord Pembroke's ground, which adjoined the municipal boundary, Kingstown was located six miles south of Dublin city and marketed itself as a summer resort. The railway company promoted the attractions of open sea bathing, similar to other seaside resort towns across the United Kingdom.[35] Day trippers could also visit Kingstown by horse-drawn omnibus, with trams running every half an hour and between 6am and 11pm.[36] About one-third of its residents commuted regularly to the city, with about 6,000 holiday makers descending on the town during the summer months.[37] Its villa population was primarily middle class, but there was also a large working class dependent on the building trades, the taverns and domestic service.[38]

Lords Longford and de Vesci granted many ninety-nine-year leases in Kingstown in the opening decades of the nineteenth century. The leases specified a minimum sum to be spent in building, with little control on development.[39] Therefore, these areas were shaped more by the whims of individual developers, resulting in varying house designs, building heights and plot widths. In the 1830s, many of these leases were bought back by the ground landlords, who imposed stricter regulations on building. As a result, the following twenty years saw the emergence of higher-quality housing, such as De Vesci Terrace, Belgrave Square and Longford Terrace. As in the Pembroke estate, developers were required to submit drawings prior to building, to be approved by the landlord's estate agent. Their main concern was the broader impact of a development on the streetscape, in terms of its overall form, and ornamentation.[40] This is reflected in the leases, which stated that each house 'shall maintain, preserve and keep the present lines, levels and elevations'.[41] An example is De Vesci Terrace, which was built in the early 1840s: a series of two-storey rendered houses that would soon crown the hill of Monkstown, capturing 'exquisite views' of the surrounding area.[42] In approving the proposal, the agent was concerned mainly with its external appearance, in particular the articulation of the façade, including the formation of a continuous parapet line.[43] The leases stated that the houses were to be painted a 'Portland stone colour and none other' every two years, ensuring a consistent appearance.[44] De Vesci Terrace is the reflection of estate intervention: it is a homogeneous development, consisting mostly of three-bay terraces, with matching door and window details and repeating bay windows and entrance doorcases. A continuous parapet unites the terrace, and there is an attempt to form a symmetrical façade by projecting out the two central plots and ends by a few feet. It appears to have been a flagship project for the ground landlords: the parapet steps up to form a central pediment, crowned with a statue of Lord de Vesci's coat of arms, who contributed to its cost.[45]

84   *Control: land tenure and infrastructure*

Kingstown's ground landlords were clearly emulating seaside resort towns elsewhere in the United Kingdom, evidenced by their unrealised development for 'New Brighton', laid out in terraces overlooking the sea. Longford Terrace was one of the largest housing developments in the estate, consisting of wide three-storey over basement terraces on the seafront. It was built in two phases: the first fourteen houses were complete by 1842, with the second phase following by 1856.[46] Such was the landlords' concern for uniformity, that they paid to raise the road in front of second phase of houses, to ensure that the two parapet levels aligned (Figure 3.2).[47] A more modest development is nearby Belgrave Square, a development of mainly terraced two-bay houses, which emerged in the 1840s, one block in from the sea (Figure 3.3). The uniformity of the terrace has been attributed to the building lease, which stipulated specific plot widths and setbacks from the street. Developers were also required to build to a particular house design, and a sketch of the door and window detail was usually attached to the agreement.[48] This house type formed a prototype for later developments in the eastern end of the estate.

By 1860, Kingstown was an important and populous town of 21,000 inhabitants, its 'outskirts thickly studded with princely mansions, handsome ecclesiastical, hotel, club, and other buildings'.[49] Despite the acceleration in house building,

Figure 3.2 Longford Terrace.

Figure 3.3 Belgrave Square.

rents had almost doubled over the previous seven years, as the supply struggled to meet the demand.[50] Much of the land along the coast was lined with rendered terraces, vying with each other to capture views of the sea. Developers began to turn to the vacant ground in the hills above the town, where three squares were emerging at the eastern end of the estate on a large elevated site (Figure 3.4). Previously, this had been a rocky outcrop suitable only for the grazing of sheep, but speculators saw potential of the sweeping views over Dublin Bay.[51] Clarinda Park was the first of these squares to appear in 1849, built by a number of developers including P. W. Bryan,[52] a wealthy wine merchant, and James Carson, a civil engineer. The square had a long gestation period: it took over twenty-one years to complete, which was a source of frustration to local residents. In 1863, *The Irish Times* assured readers that 'The project will, no doubt, prove remunerative, owing to the fact that our town is rapidly increasing in wealth and importance'.[53] Two more squares followed in the adjoining fields (Figure 3.4): Royal Terrace was developed by local businessman Francis J. Nugent and Crosthwaite Park was the brainchild of John Crosthwaite, owner and proprietor of the Royal Victoria Baths in Kingstown. Although built by different speculators, the predominant house type is the rendered two-bay terrace, rising two storeys over a basement (Figure 1.14). This house form, combined with the detailing of the paired entrances and the bay

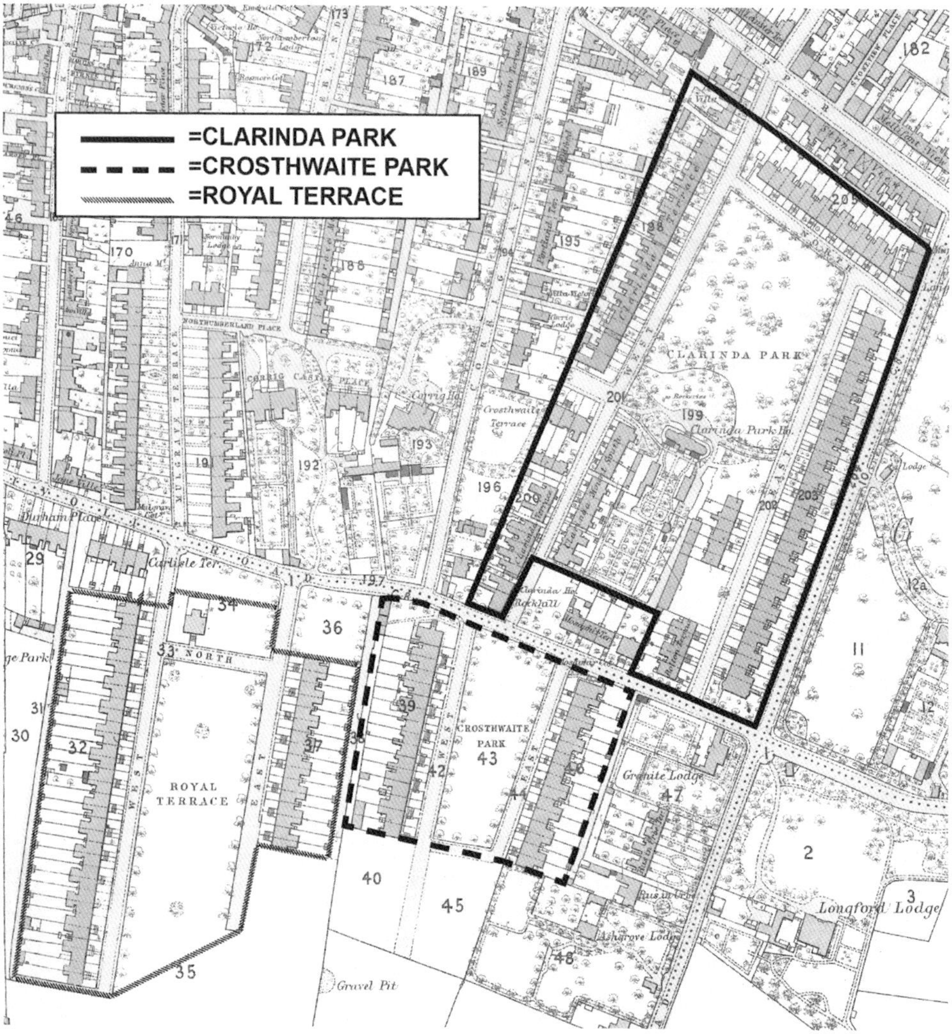

Figure 3.4 Ordnance Survey map of Kingstown, 1867: Clarinda Park, Royal Terrace and Crosthwaite Park (reproduced courtesy Trinity College Dublin).

windows, bears a close resemblance to the architecture of Belgrave Square, which was still under construction a few miles away.

The previous section discussed the original leases granted by the Pembroke estate, showing the impact of regulation on architectural form. No original leases have been found for Crosthwaite Park, so we rely instead on the lease memorials, which are a summary of the agreement.[54] Did the estate agent impose a similar kind of rigour to development here, as appears to have been the case at Belgrave Square? In 1861, Crosthwaite signed two ninety-nine-year leases on the land with the 'lords of the soil', who imposed a minimum spend of £500 per house.[55] In contrast to the houses in Ailesbury Road, John Crosthwaite did not construct his buildings, but instead sub-leased the plots to local developers. On the east terrace, two builders took at least four plots each, while three adjoining houses were developed by the architect and engineer Peter Joseph Moran.[56] In agreeing to sub-lease a plot from John Crosthwaite, speculators were subject to the covenants in his original head lease to the 'lords of the soil'. Thus, they were required to spend at least £500 on each house but 'the style elevation or appearance of the house and premises' was subject to Crosthwaite's permission.[57] This suggests therefore that there was a coherent design behind the development of the terrace. As in other parts of Kingstown, it was most likely submitted by Crosthwaite to the estate agent prior to construction. Once the design was approved, it was then imbedded into a condition in the lease for each house, to ensure a largely uniform façade. Certainly, the ground landlords paid attention to building on their estate. In 1865, as Crosthwaite Park was nearing completion, Lord Longford wrote to his co-owner Viscount de Vesci, informing him that 'Mr Crosthwaite's buildings are progressing most favorably (sic), and himself full of smiles'.[58]

The private landlord

Land tenure in Rathgar

By the time Queen Victoria came to the throne in 1837, Rathgar was a suburban village nestled among country fields, interspersed with the odd quarry and 'several ranges of pleasant houses and numerous detached villas'.[59] Located one-and-a-half miles south of the city, it was not nearly as developed as its neighbour, the 'considerable village and suburb' of Rathmines (Figure 0.2),[60] its main street characterised by 'a continued line of handsome houses, with some pretty detached villas, for about one mile and a half'.[61] To the south was the village of Rathgar, where housing densities were much lower, with terraced houses springing up on a more sporadic basis along Rathgar Road (Figure 3.5). Beyond the village of Rathgar was country proper: the Dodder River marked the southern boundary of the area, and meandered across the landscape, dotted with an assortment of mills, factories and quarries. Since the eighteenth century, this river had been diverted through several millraces to power machinery for the milling of grains, the sawing of timber and the manufacture of fabrics.

Patrick Waldron was the owner of one of the principal villas in Rathgar at this time. On a twenty-five-acre site adjoining the Dodder River, Waldron ran an 'extensive bleaching-green, with printing works' (Figure 3.5).[62] The linen trade was an important industry in Ireland during this time and many families were involved in the bleaching of linen, or the spinning of flax into yarn.[63] Bleaching greens were a common sight, as lands of up to thirty acres were required to spread the fabric out to dry. The Ordnance Survey map of 1843 indicates the presence of 'Rathgar Calico Printing Factory', a large building close to the road and the river. Perched above on an elevated site was his residence Rathgar House, whose main entrance faced away from the factory. The lands below also contained a

88 *Control: land tenure and infrastructure*

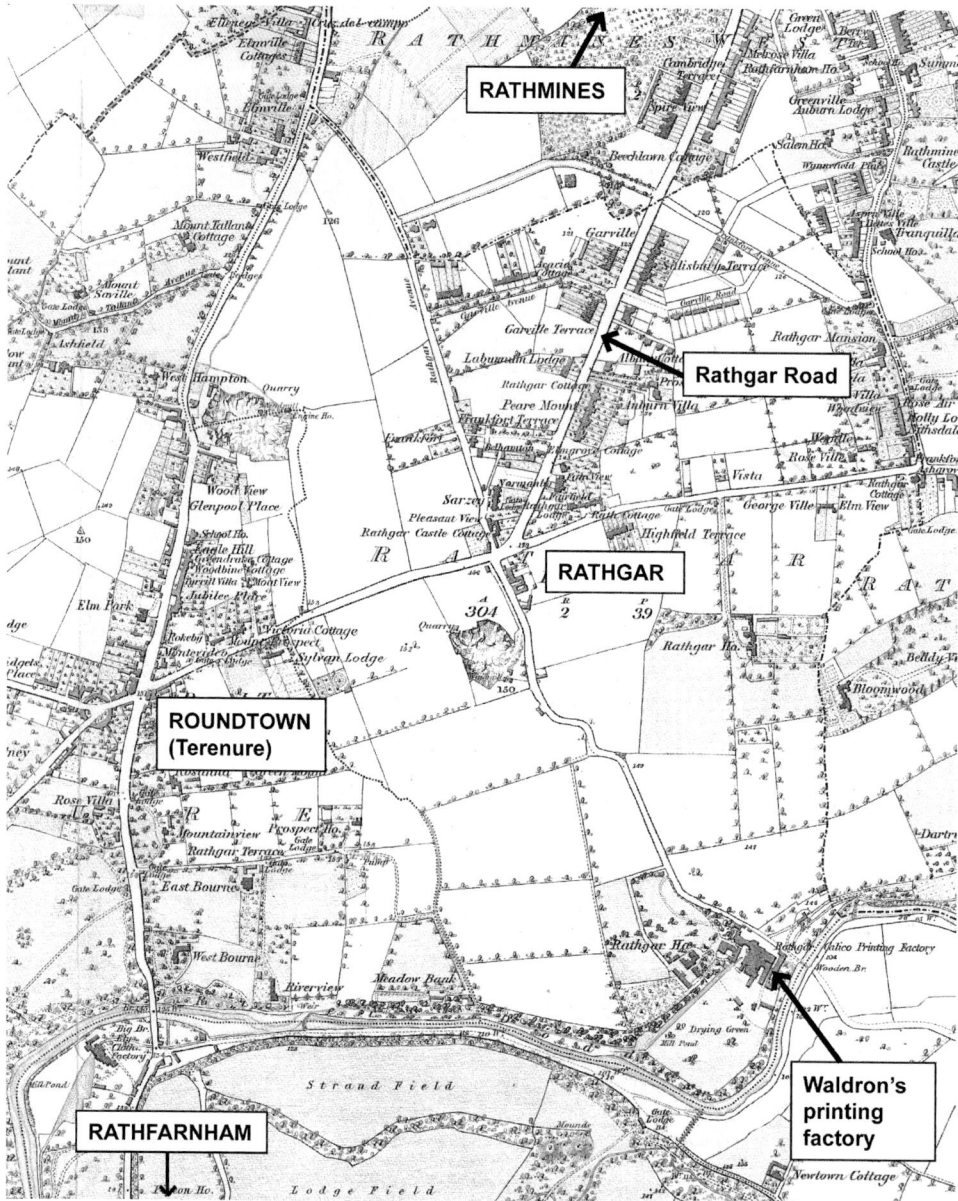

Figure 3.5 Ordnance Survey map of Rathgar, 1843 (reproduced courtesy Trinity College Dublin).

millpond ten metres deep: a body of water used as a reservoir to power the water-powered mill adjacent. It was next to a field marked 'Drying Green', which was protected from flooding by a long dyke.[64] In March 1851, Waldron sold part of his estate to John Crosthwaite of Kingstown, which formed part of the marriage settlement of Crosthwaite's daughter.[65] Patrick Waldron died the following year at the age of eighty, willing that the remaining lands at Rathgar be sold soon after his death.

In contrast to Pembroke and Kingstown, the growing suburbs of Rathmines and Rathgar were not dominated by the estate landlord system. Lord Meath, Lord Palmerston and Lord Longford all held stakes there, but they tended to release ground on long leases of up to 999 years (compared to the leases discussed to date, which lasted an average of 99 to 150 years).[66] Long leases tended to impose little restrictions on building, relinquishing control to smaller speculative developers.[67] Consequently, private developers held more sway here, as they were freer to determine the extent, form and character of their new streets and squares. A major driving force of development in Rathmines was Frederick Stokes, an English property developer, and founder of the township. He was a major house builder both in the city (Portobello) and in Rathmines (Leinster Road, Leeson Park).[68] In neighbouring Rathgar, speculators were enticed to its high, sunny aspect: 'The land rises boldly over the level of the picturesque River Dodder, and presents magnificent sites for building detached or semi-detached Villas, Pleasure-Grounds, and Gardens. The locality is famed for salubrity of air and beauty of scenery.'[69] Carvill was free to build in whatever building form and style he desired, his will stating that he had built valuable houses without 'any formal lease of the building sites from the trustees thereof'.[70] In terms of overall scale and massing, Rostrevor Terrace closely resembles the houses in Ailesbury Road, which were emerging at the same time in the Pembroke estate. However, they are a cheaper, stripped-down version in terms of materials and detailing: the lowest floor is finished in a line render which achieves the appearance of stone, without the associated expense (Plate 15).

The path of improvement: infrastructure

Before the building of tens of thousands of houses, there were only a few primary roads, with no main drains or public lamps in the suburbs.[71] Who would provide the infrastructural framework to support these new districts, such as roads, paths, sewers, water and lighting? Each area was governed by a complex network of local government bodies, with differing levels of control. Some landlords laid out roads and sewers prior to building, but others were more laissez-faire, providing infrastructure on a fragmentary basis.[72] When the Towns Improvement Act was passed in 1828, any area in England or Ireland could establish a local authority to take control of basic local services. Kingstown was the first Dublin suburb to form a township in 1834, followed by Rathmines in 1847 (extended to include Rathgar in 1862), and Pembroke in 1863 (Figure 0.1). Funded by local taxes, these self-governing districts were empowered to lay out new roads and buildings, and provide public services such as lighting, drainage and street cleaning. Many township commissioners had vested interests in local government: when the Rathmines Township was formed in 1847, at least half of the board members were speculative builders, with the remainder mainly businessmen and professionals.[73] Although the township model certainly enabled the growth of these new suburbs, the level of service provision varied between, and within each district. This section will assess the provision of infrastructure in each of the three districts of Pembroke, Rathgar and Kingstown. It will focus on the provision of roads, paths and kerbs, as well as the supply of drainage and water. It will apply the general to the specific, by analysing the provision of infrastructure for houses developed by Meade, Carvill and Crosthwaite, revealing the challenges in transforming green fields to new residential districts.

Infrastructure: the Pembroke estate

Roads, paths and kerbs

The previous section discussed the role of the landowner Lord Pembroke, who controlled development on his estate through the leasehold system. When the Pembroke Township was established in 1863, it took over 1,592 acres of ground adjoining the city (Figure 0.2), including Ringsend, Irishtown, Sandymount, Ballsbridge and Donnybrook. The commissioners were empowered to provide 'lighting, paving, sewerage, draining, cleansing, supply of water and otherwise improving and regulating of the Township'. John Vernon, agent for the Pembroke estate, remained chairman of the township since its foundation, ensuring his hand in protecting his employer's interests, who owned 76% of ground in the township. The district was primarily rural in character, characterised by poorly finished and unsewered roads, with only forty-eight public lamps, and no street crossings.[74]

The next fifteen years saw remarkable changes, as the population increased by 10,000, and over 1,000 new dwellings were built to house new suburban residents.[75] The estate agent continued to undertake many new roads in the area, and between 1863 and 1879, over twenty-six miles of roadway were laid out, at Lord Pembroke's expense.[76] Most of these were located in the prestigious western side of the estate, where speculators were subject to strict leases, ensuring the building of high-quality houses. John L. Robinson, secretary to the township, explained the process as follows: 'Mr Vernon takes fields, he makes roads through them and lets out the plots to the best advantage. He sewers them, paves them, and plants them, and then hands them over to the township commissioners, who maintain them.'[77] These were high-quality roads, 'constructed in the best and most substantial manner',[78] and the paths were surfaced with asphalt, rather than the cheaper tar used elsewhere. These roads, handed over 'fully kerbed', consisted of hard-wearing granite blocks, forming the junction between the road and the path.[79] Landscaping was another important aspect: the estate agent was known for arranging planting 'along the margins of the streets, and converts them into boulevards'.[80] These accounts suggest that the roads, paths and sewers were in place before speculators arrived on the scene, quite an investment, not to mention a gamble, considering the sporadic nature of speculation. However, Vernon required a degree of security before expending large sums on infrastructure, as he explained in 1879: 'If builders will tell me they will build I will lay out the roads, but not until then.'[81] However, it is also clear that in other parts of the estate, roads were laid only after development had occurred, as Vernon explained in 1879: 'All of our footpaths are kerbed where there are buildings ... Some of the rural roads with fields on both sides are not kerbed, nor do they require it till houses are built on it.'[82] Therefore, other parts of the Pembroke estate must have been characterised by many unfinished and unsightly paths, as vacant sites awaited speculators.

John Vernon managed to lure one of the most significant speculators in the estate, when he opened a new boulevard in the mid-1860s at Ailesbury Road. By this time, Michael Meade was running a building firm from his saw mill in Great Brunswick Street, and was involved in a wide variety of projects all over the city and county. In the summer of 1863, he began work on one of many Catholic church projects in Donnybrook, at the western extremity of the Pembroke estate. The site stood at the confluence of four roads, a strategic site from which the clergy intended to draw new suburban residents from 'every quarter of the populous district'. At the same time, plans were already in place to open up another new line of road, cutting through a mile of ground to the east.[83] The route would connect the village of Donnybrook with Sydney Parade Station, which had been recently opened to serve the Sandymount district.[84] Opening up a mile of potential building frontage, the first phase of the road would run across the fields to link with Merrion Road, the main route from Dublin to Kingstown, while the second phase would continue to the railway. In March 1865, *The Dublin Builder* announcing the opening of the first phase of the road:

> The new road leading from the Rock Road to Donnybrook has been thrown open to the public. It is in one direct line, about an English mile in length, and perfectly level. The pathways on each side are wide and well kerbed. The ground adjoining is to be let for building, and should handsome terraces be erected in uniformity, the road will ultimately become a real ornament in Dublin, and form a delightful promenade.[85]

While Meade's men were raising the façade of his parish church at the western end of this new boulevard, he was the first to develop sites at its eastern end. Six months after the road was opened, Meade acquired the first plots there, and built a grandiose Italianate villa for himself on the junction with Merrion Road.

Drainage and water supply in Pembroke

Roads and footpaths continued to be laid down by the estate, but the provision of sewers was more problematic. In 1865, *The Dublin Builder* reported that a 'thorough and effective system of street drainage' had been installed in a large part of the city.[86] However, these drains emptied into the nearest water course, and the River Liffey was reported to be effectively a 'foul and open sewer',[87] emitting an 'intolerable stench' that at one stage threatened the closure of the Four Courts.[88] While these were the difficulties found in municipal areas, greater problems awaited some dwellers in undrained areas, outside the city boundary. Serious health hazards were posed to residents there, where effluent was collected in cess pools, or pits in the ground, located to the rear of houses.[89] These cesspools were commonly built too close to wells, which led to the contamination of the local water supply and outbreaks of disease. As *The Dublin Builder* lamented in 1864: 'We do not exaggerate in stating that we have known whole districts rendered objectionable to live in from this cause alone.'[90] A large open drain ran across a large portion of the district, from Shelbourne Road to the Dodder River.[91]

Infrastructure was an important factor in attracting high-quality builders and well-to-do residents to the suburbs. In the absence of an integrated system of main drainage, Lord Pembroke's agent provided services on an ad-hoc basis. In 1869, Vernon referred to the improvements he had recently completed in Sandymount, to serve the newly laid-out Gilford Road: 'The effect of the drainage upon this low lying land has already become very apparent, and although the work is far from complete, I have already had applications for building plots on that portion of the road which has been widened.'[92] But where a main sewer had been put in place, there could still be problems in disposing of the waste. In the coastal district of Sandymount, a fall of just eighteen inches was not enough to carry the sewage to the outfall at Blackrock.[93] Without a pumped system of drainage, the estate agent admitted that he was 'utterly unable to meet the complaints' of some residents in the area.[94] There were also problems with the pipes installed within the boundaries of properties. The Dublin Improvement Act of 1864 compelled owners to install a 'well-trapped house-drain' to the nearest sewer, but not all house builders were complicit.[95] Reportedly, the 'ignorance of the principles of under-drainage' was the main cause of defective house construction. Due to inadequately sized and incorrectly laid pipework,[96] some sewers were 'constantly stagnant and overflowing'.[97]

This was clearly an untenable situation, in the context of growing rates of disease and a rising population that would only put more pressure on the system. There were urgent calls for a proper system of main drainage; an integrated service that would resolve the issue by pumping the sewerage out to the sea. London had achieved this in 1868, but it remained the subject of much dispute in Dublin for many years, due to various disagreements between the government, Dublin Corporation and the townships. The passing of the Irish Public Health Acts of 1874 and 1878 gave the townships greater responsibility for sanitary services. In 1877, a joint drainage board was formed, enabling both the Pembroke and Rathmines Townships to implement their own system of mains drainage.[98] It was an ambitious undertaking, as these were the most populous of all of the Dublin townships, with a combined population of 41,964. By 1879, the project was complete, involving the drainage of 3,300 acres of land costing about £105,000, transforming what Vernon claimed had previously been 'all a series of cabbage gardens flooded by the Swan stream'.[99]

Also central to public health was the provision of an adequate water supply and in 1871, the Pembroke Township contracted to buy Vartry water from Dublin Corporation. Until then, some areas were supplied by the canal, while the

Sandymount area had to make do with imported barrels of water.[100] The township spent £18,000 on waterworks for the district, laying over twenty-two miles of mains pipes, which would soon transform the public health of the district.[101] By 1879, thirty-three public fountains were in operation, and every road was reported to be fitted with 'numerous' fire hydrants.[102] The Pembroke Township had a paltry thirty-seven men and seven horses at its disposal to repair and scavenge the main roads, while private lanes were the responsibility of building owners.[103] About 18,400 square yards of 'superior asphalt' was applied to the footpaths, and over 300 public lamps and numerous street crossings were installed.[104]

Michael Meade, described as an extensive builder and contractor, appeared before the Municipal Boundaries Commission in 1879. In his capacity as a Pembroke commissioner, he boasted: '[T]here is no township in this or any other country can be better managed.' Despite these claims, it appears that not all parts of the district were finished in such a high standard. Alderman Harris, who lived in Wellington Road, lamented the 'positively dangerous condition' of the street, due to a perilous ridge in the road. It caused a horse to fall and break both his knees, but the road was also unclean, and the footpaths were so bad that Leeson Street was impassable in wet weather.[105] Harris directed his complaints at the township commissioners, who were responsible for the maintenance of roads, pathways and local services. Vernon, in his capacity as chairman, conceded that the roads and sewers in the township were not as perfect as he could wish. However, he argued, they were 'better than the county roads on the one side, and the town roads on the other'.[106] In 1884, Michael Meade was elected vice chairman of the Pembroke Township.[107]

Despite the achievements of the main drainage scheme, there were still problems in the Sandymount area, located in the low-lying eastern sector, where the Dodder River was described as a 'pestilential stench'. The outfall sewer from Londonbridge Road was said to emit a stink that was worse than that from the Liffey in the city. One local resident complained that the higher 'fashionable' end of the township received more attention, but the lower end was abandoned to 'night soil and all kinds of filth'.[108] This was a reference to the Ringsend and Irishtown areas, which were more industrial in character, with a population dependent on boat building, fishing and glassworks. The area was filled with small overcrowded cottages inhabited by 'humble residents', living in wretched conditions that were worse than those on the west coast of Africa. Reportedly, complaints made to the township went unheeded, unless they were made by those 'who happen to have the good fortune to live in the "flash" parts of it'.[109] Thus, the preferential treatment found in the more valuable western sector, discussed previously in relation to land tenure, was also reflected in the provision of infrastructure.

Until the end of the nineteenth century, the County Grand Jury was responsible for the maintenance of roads and bridges outside the city boundary.[110] Part of a large landowning elite, they were some of the most corrupt bodies in the country, tending to serve their own interests, rather than those of the cess-payers. This was further complicated by Dublin Corporation, who shared the cost of maintaining

94   Control: land tenure and infrastructure

some services with the grand jury. Then there were the responsibilities of the estate landlord and the township, resulting in a complex layering of control. Nowhere is this more evident than at Ailesbury Road, where four administrative bodies were responsible for local services in the area: the Pembroke estate, the Pembroke Township, the County Grand Jury and Dublin Corporation. The county/township boundary ran across the middle of the road, leaving one half under control of the township and the other under the grand jury. In 1867, the agent of the estate wrote to the secretary of the Pembroke Township. He confirmed that the estate had maintained the road since it opened two years ago, but now he requested that the commissioners take in charge the first half of Ailesbury Road, from Merrion Road to the township boundary.[111] The other half had been taken up by the grand jury and was being repaired under supervision by the county surveyor. To further complicate matters, the cost of maintaining the adjoining Merrion Road was shared by Dublin Corporation and the grand jury, but 'shoddy work and incomplete repairs' had contributed to its notoriously bad condition.[112] This unequal division of responsibilities impacted on the provision of services: in 1879, Michael Meade confirmed that half of Ailesbury Road was lit by gas lamps, and the other half not at all.[113] Joseph Meade, who inherited the burgeoning building empire, was proposed to the board of the Pembroke Town Commissioners in 1889, since he had 'such a large stake in the township'.[114]

Infrastructure: the Kingstown estate

Roads, paths and kerbs

Compared to Lord Pembroke who financed many of the roads in his estate, Kingstown's ground landlords took a more laissez-faire approach.[115] They laid out some of the main roads in the town at the end of the eighteenth century, to prepare for ground they would lease in 1804. When they bought back large tracts of this ground in 1837, they spent about £12,000 in providing roads for some of their most valuable housing schemes.[116] Many 'gentlemen's residences of an expensive character'[117] were built in the 1840s, to house a surge of wealthy residents at Longford and De Vesci Terraces, Vesey Place, the Hill and Crescent, all in Monkstown at the western end of Kingstown. Over the following twenty years, over a thousand houses were built in Kingstown, but the estate provided only two or three roads to serve these developments.[118] Mr Stewart, agent to the Kingstown estate, claimed that not a single road was made in the district, either by the grand jury or the township since 1804, except for those made by speculators – that is, the 'sub-roads inside the leaseholds'.[119] An example is the ground acquired by John Crosthwaite: in 1861, he leased two fields from Lords Longford and de Vesci. The ground was bound to the north by Tivoli Road, an old medieval route and to the east by Glenageary Road, laid out by the landlords in the early nineteenth century (Figure 3.4). The developer then proceeded to lay out the roads and plots within his site, as the architect John L. Robinson confirmed: 'A man in Crosthwaite Park took a large field, and laid out roads. It was not the lords of the soil did it, he laid out roads, built terraces, and let them, and sold them.'[120] This was in marked contrast to the experience of Michael Meade at Ailesbury Road, where the sites came complete with high-quality roads, paths, sewers and trees. In Kingstown, Crosthwaite prepared the sites himself, and managed the construction of thirty-two houses by different builders, over a five-year period. He was not subject to rent during this time because, as Lord Longford confirmed in 1864, 'it is not usual to charge rent for a while after a building is complete'.[121]

Crosthwaite Park was located in the Kingstown Township, which had been founded thirty years earlier. In 1861, the grand jury relinquished their control of the roads and bridges to the township.[122] Like in other areas, many commissioners were local property developers, who had a vested interest in the success of their suburb. The three squares discussed earlier were all developed by town commissioners, namely: John Crosthwaite (Crosthwaite Park), P. W. Bryan (Clarinda Park) and Francis J. Nugent (Royal Terrace). Crosthwaite was the leading figure of the three, who 'took a leading part in all the affairs of Kingstown'.[123] Over his thirty-year reign, he was elected chairman eight times, and was the instigator of the new town hall, built in the style of a Venetian Gothic palace in 1880. Through a number of different committees, the commissioners were involved in the maintenance of roads, the provision of infrastructure and the regulation of building in the township.[124] In 1867, the 'Roads, Water and Lighting Committee' discussed an order for 200 tons of stone and fifty tons of sand and gravel, for the surfacing of roads in the district.[125] They also provided finishes to footpaths, such as the gravel sanctioned for a pathway at Royal Terrace in 1859.[126] Many of these actions were taken in response to complaints: in 1859, the board reacted to letters from residents of Bombay Terrace, who requested kerbing to the front of their houses.[127] As in Ailesbury Road, blocks of granite were used to form kerbs, but they were also used for road crossings, enabling long skirted ladies to negotiate the muddy streets. It was an issue that vexed Mary Heyden, walking to mass in Rathmines, who lamented: 'The necessity of holding up the tail of my dress out of the mud made the walk tiresome.'[128] The commissioners favoured the use of local stone for this purpose: in 1860, they accepted a tender for 'five Granite Crossings', provided the stones were procured from either the Dalkey or Bullock quarries.[129]

Once a speculator had completed a housing scheme, the commissioners would send out their surveyor to inspect the development. If he was satisfied with the works, he would recommend that they were taken in charge by the commissioners, who would then be responsible for the surfacing and cleaning of the roads and footpaths, and the maintenance of the sewers. At Clarinda Park, progress was remarkably slow, as it took about twenty-one years to complete. In January 1863, *The Irish Times* published a letter from a tenant on the south side, lamenting the bad state of the roads and footpaths on the square.[130] Signing their name 'stuck in the mud', they claimed that very 'little or nothing' had been done to make or repair roads on any side of the development and that the coast road was 'a canal of mud, and the footway but little better, both being made of yellow clay'. By this time, Clarinda Park had been in construction for at least fourteen years, and wouldn't reach full completion until 1870. An appeal was made to the commissioners to surface the roads and paths, but the township defended its position, arguing:

> The Commissioners, however, cannot do everything at once. New houses were being erected, and the roads are probably torn up by the concourse of heavily laden waggons; but the houses are now finished, and a very considerable tax levied from them. Measures should be taken, the moment dry weather sets in, to remedy the evil complained of.

This issue seems to have been at least partially resolved within two months. In March 1863, the board received a letter from a Mr Carson, one of the developers of Clarinda Park, confirming that the road on the east and south sides were now in 'good order' and ready for inspection.[131]

As many of the commissioners were also the builders of houses, this opened up the potential for corruption. This is evidenced by an inquiry held in the town hall in 1877, which alleged that John Crosthwaite, then chairman of the township, had appropriated materials for his own use. The town clerk defended Crosthwaite, arguing that he could not procure materials elsewhere, and so 'took a little of that being used in the township for private use'.[132] The town engineer was also called as a witness, as he was responsible for sanctioning the order. He professed his ignorance on the matter, but accusations of collusion between him and Crosthwaite ensued. Others complained that preferential treatment was given to the streets where commissioners were living. In 1865, *The Irish Times* received a letter from a Mr William Semple, who complained about the lack of watering at Clarinda Park. He lamented: 'Last week we were nearly smothered, and on Saturday the clouds of dust compelled us to close up our windows or the furniture would be destroyed.'[133] The roads required constant maintenance, as they were usually surfaced in macadam, similar to the crushed stone found in Rathmines, which generated mud in winter and dust in summer. Compared to the asphalt finish used in the Pembroke Township, this was an inferior material that was very difficult to clean. Semple lamented that the adjoining Corrig Road was watered twice a day only because a town commissioner lived there. After he went to see one of the commissioners, they sent their men around with a cart, but it gave 'a miserable watering', passing over only one-quarter of the ground. Clearly, the township was struggling to maintain services: by 1864, only five watering carts were serving the whole of the district.[134] Mr Johnston, the township surveyor, reflected on the situation twenty years later, claiming that local taxes had not been high enough to efficiently repair and clean the roads. Many of the commissioners were also owners of houses, and were probably more interested in minimising taxes than in improving local services.[135]

Control: land tenure and infrastructure 97

Drainage and water supply in Kingstown

Kingstown experienced similar difficulties to other Dublin suburbs, where inadequate drainage resulted in the pollution of rivers, and the contamination of the water supply. In 1859, it was reported that raw sewage was being discharged along the foreshore at Sandycove, polluting a four-mile stretch from here to Booterstown.[136] Open sewers were also a feature of the town, which commissioners tried to improve by installing 'proper stench traps' to prevent noxious smells.[137] This was particularly damaging to Kingstown, which was so heavily reliant on tourism for much of its livelihood. In some cases, house drains ran into nearby ditches, where effluent was left 'to soak away as best it can', or to nearby rivers.[138] A particular black spot was the nearby village of Glasthule, an 'Irish Plague Spot' where a 'rudely-constructed sewer' ran into a stream used for drinking and washing.[139] These deficiencies had a detrimental impact on the health of residents: in 1866, an outbreak of cholera led to 127 deaths in the township.[140] By 1872, only about a third of the roads in the township had working sewers, despite the introduction of a series of Public Health Acts.[141] Within seven years, a system of drainage was completed in Pembroke and Rathmines, but residents in Kingstown had to wait until the 1890s, when a joint drainage scheme was finally complete.

In light of these challenges, how were the 200 or so houses at Crosthwaite Park, Royal Terrace and Clarinda Park provided for? Until the arrival of fully integrated system of main drainage, services were provided on an ad-hoc basis. By the time these developments emerged, there were main sewers running along the adjoining Glenageary and Tivoli Roads. The township was responsible for these sewers, and then each speculator then laid the drains from the houses to the main sewer. This is evidenced by Mr Bryan, one of the developers at Clarinda Park, who sought permission from the township in 1864 to run a drain to the main road.[142] He lodged a £1 deposit with the board, 'as a guarantee for the due performance of the work', which would be refunded when he had completed the works.[143] By 1877, John Crosthwaite boasted: 'Every house in Crosthwaite Park is well sewered. All the money that could be had out in Kingstown would not improve the sewerage there.'[144] Sanitary provision improved in the town the following year, with the introduction of the Irish Public Health Act, which compelled house owners to install either a water or earth closet, complete with drains, and sewage was to be purified before being discharged into streams.[145] In 1890, drainage was the main selling point when houses in Crosthwaite Park West were advertised to let. It confirmed that the main drainage in the estate had been reconstructed 'on the newest sanitary principles' under the direction of the engineer W. G. Strype, who would provide leaseholders with a certificate of completion.[146]

A clean water supply was another key factor in improving public health in the townships. For many years, Kingstown had relied on wells for its water supply. By 1879, however, the entire Kingstown Township was served by a supply from the Varty River, supplied by Dublin Corporation.[147] All residents drew water from the system during the day, but the pressure was reduced at night 'in order to check the enormous consumption'. The system did not have the capacity to pump to houses in higher districts during the night, such as in Vesey-place in the hills above Monkstown.[148]

Infrastructure: Rathgar

Roads, paths and kerbs

William Carvill moved into his estate in Rathgar in 1853, which was located just outside the Rathmines Township boundary. Various attempts had been made throughout the 1850s to extend the boundary to include Rathgar, but it took a number of years before the bill was finally passed. In the meantime, the district remained under the control of the grand jury: a notoriously inefficient body, forcing residents to provide services themselves. In some cases, landowners laid out new roads to encourage speculators: in 1859, Sir Robert Shaw of nearby Bushy Park House considered opening a road through his demesne, 'to meet this and present desirable villa lots'.[149] In other cases, developers were required to complete the road that served their plot: when the site for the new Zion church was sold in 1859, the purchaser was bound to lay out a 350-foot stretch of new road fronting the church.[150] Meanwhile, infrastructural deficiencies such as unmaintained roads and lack of services such as lighting, water and drainage continued to remain the norm. Despite these challenges the area continued to grow: in 1860, it was reported that Rathmines and Rathgar had experienced rapid growth in recent years, and it was now 'virtually a wing of the city'.[151]

In 1862, the boundary of the Rathmines Township was expanded to include the neighbouring suburb of Rathgar. As a consequence, land values in Rathgar doubled over the following seventeen years. Three commissioners – who were all wealthy city businessmen living locally – were appointed to the new district. Compared to the relative inactivity of the grand jury, these men were anxious to enjoy the same benefits that Rathmines had experienced due to improved local government.[152] That year, *The Irish Builder* announced that great progress had been made in Rathgar, Rathmines and Harold's-Cross, where: 'Villas detached and semi-detached, cottage residences, and terraces in various designs and styles here stud the soil, and the several roads and approaches seem to have been laid out with much judgement.'[153] As in Kingstown, developers tended to lay out the new roads and paths, which were then adopted and maintained by the township. This is evidenced by the work of commissioner Michael Murphy, who developed seventy acres of land at Kenilworth Square, Rathmines, proclaiming: 'I cut the whole thing out for building, arranged the plots, and laid out the roads.'[154] The township by-laws stated that the roads were to be properly gravelled and sewered and the paths properly constructed, before they could be adopted by the commissioners. However, in many cases, the builders of these roads were also members of the board, which has led to some speculation as to the 'scope for mutually beneficial deals'.[155] Mark Bentley, a major builder in the Rathgar area, laid out about

3,000 feet of building frontage in Rathgar, constructing 'new roads, both main and minor, . . . and an important field for operations is being opened up'.[156] This is most likely a reference to Brighton Square: a triangular shaped plot of land to the northwest of Rathgar village, where two-storey red brick terraces were constructed. Bentley was co-opted onto the Rathmines and Rathgar Township board in 1868, where he remained for five years.

By the time the first four houses at Rostrevor Terrace were built in 1865, the area was developing rapidly, with a population of 1,180:

> RATHGAR, . . . is now one of the most pleasing outlets of the metropolis, studded with handsome terraces or detached villas, and several pretty avenues diverging from the centre, . . . Close to the cross-roads are extensively-worked quarries of calp limestone, which is chiefly raised by blasting.[157]

These changes are reflected in the Ordnance Survey of 1865, as Rathgar Road and its tributaries were now lined in terraces, with uniform setbacks from the street (Plate 14). These districts would soon be aided by developments in transport: within eight years, the area would be served by a horse-drawn tram that would bring commuters from Sackville Street, in the city centre. Trams from Rathmines proceeded through Rathgar village and onwards to Terenure, leaving commuters only a ten minute walk from Rostrevor Terrace. Here, the 1865 Ordnance map shows the road completed only as far as the first four houses, with the adjacent field awaiting development. The first few years saw the greatest spurt in building: by 1868, twelve houses had been built there, but it took another three years to add the last two dwellings.[158] According to the valuation records, the first house enjoyed 'a good prospect',[159] an indication of the views that could be captured from this elevated site (Plate 15). To the southeast was Orwell Park, where a new road had been laid out to serve another scheme of semi-detached houses (Plate 16). Carvill was the likely builder of the road and paths in both schemes, which he would have been required to complete to the township's satisfaction.[160] This is corroborated by Samuel H. Bolton, a builder and Rathmines commissioner for nine years, who reported in 1879: '[I]t is one of the rules of our Board that if any gentleman takes a piece of ground to speculate on it for building purposes, he makes the drains, and makes the roadway, and kerbs it to the satisfaction of our engineer, before we take it off his hands.'[161]

Nevertheless, even when roads were adopted by the township, the commissioners still struggled to fund their continued maintenance. An example is Rathgar Road, the main thoroughfare from Rathmines, which was reportedly used daily by thousands, and especially on Sundays. In 1879, after seventeen years of township control, there were still no raised crossings at the main intersections, forcing walkers to 'wade over the road in mud'.[162] As in Kingstown, most roads in Rathmines were finished in macadam, consisting of crushed stone, which generated mud and dust, being almost impossible to clean.[163] A better finish was found on roads served by trams, as the transport company was required to pave the central portion of the road under the tracks. At the sides, the inferior macadam finish was a source of much complaint in the township, even where stone crossings were introduced. While only a third of the paths were finished in the superior asphalt found in Pembroke, a cheaper tar was used for the remaining fourteen miles.[164]

Drainage and water supply in Rathgar

Before the completion of the main drainage system at the end of the 1870s, residents in Rathgar faced similar challenges as their neighbours in Pembroke. In 1879, six years after the completion of Rostrevor Terrace, the drainage in the area was reported to be 'very bad'.[165] The commissioners had been promising to provide a system of main drainage in the district for a number of years, but in the meantime the main Orwell Road remained unsewered. Effluent from Rostrevor Terrace ran into a private drain at the rear, which discharged into the Dodder River, near William Carvill's saw mill. Rathgar's residents had much in common with their Sandymount neighbours, who were subjected to the 'pestilential stench' of this river. In nearby Zion Road, reports emerged of a 'disgraceful nuisance', where neither a sewer nor a cess pool was provided.[166] Problems with the water supply further compounded the issue: although a new waterworks had been completed in 1863, the system was not sufficiently pressurised to pump to the higher levels at Rathgar.[167] As sanitary facilities were located generally on the upper levels, this had implications for the supply of water closets and cisterns in dwellings.[168] A new pumping station brought water to the district in 1872, but the water was shut off from ten in the evening until six the next morning.[169]

It is clear therefore that great challenges were posed to suburban house builders in the context of sub-standard services. Before the completion of a proper pumped drainage system in 1879, sewage in Rathmines and Pembroke was collected in cess pools, which drained into local rivers. This had obvious implications for the health of suburban dwellers: in Rathmines a 'fearful prevalence of typhus' was attributed to the pollution of the Swan River by effluent exiting from sewer pipes.[170] In 1872, *The Irish Builder* claimed that two-thirds of deaths in the suburban districts, both north and south of the city, were due to a lack of sanitary precautions, including 'foul lanes and alleys, foul water-courses and wells, foul back yards and surroundings, foul dwellings within, impure water in places, no proper house-to-house visitations on the part of sanitary officials and relieving officers, and, finally, the want of proper hospital accommodation'.[171]

Conclusion

Three suburban districts formed the basis of analysis for this chapter, each with their own distinct characteristics. Each district was governed by different forms of land tenure; Kingstown and Pembroke were dominated by the estate landlord system, which granted relatively short leases of 99 to 150 years. In contrast, landlords in Rathmines and Rathgar were more passive, and released ground on longer leases, with fewer restrictions on development. Within the estate system however, there were different approaches to how suburban plots were developed. Landlords in Kingstown stipulated a minimum outlay of £500 per house, but it is also likely that they approved the design for Crosthwaite Park, as they had with previous housing schemes in the 1840s. Of the three suburbs, William Carvill experienced the least restriction in Rathgar, as he speculated without building leases.

The particular geography of each location impacted on development, as exemplified by Crosthwaite Park, which was built on an elevated site, capturing views of the sea and mountains. In the Pembroke estate, higher-quality development was enforced in the elevated, better drained ground on the western side and this is reflected in the strict building leases at Ailesbury Road, which dictated the form, height and roof profile of houses there, and the most expensive materials. Allowances were made for its larger stakeholders such as Michael Meade, a prolific builder who was allowed greater flexibility for non-compliance with the terms of his lease. Lord Pembroke was responsible for laying out the roads and paths, and leasing the plots for building, although the western estate was better served in this regard. When the Pembroke Township was founded in 1863, it took responsibility for maintaining these infrastructural works, and added a range of public services including lighting, water supply and street crossings. Sewers were provided by the estate and the township in an ad-hoc manner, until such time as a system of main drainage was completed in 1879, in cooperation with the suburbs of Rathmines and Rathgar. The fragmentary nature of planning control is reflected in the four administrative bodies that crossed paths at Ailesbury Road: the estate landlord, the Pembroke Township, the County Grand Jury and Dublin Corporation all shared responsibilities for local services.

Compared to the rigidly controlled Pembroke estate, ground landlords in Kingstown took a less active role in the provision of infrastructure on their suburban land, leaving much of it either to the township, or the developer to provide. After signing his lease in 1861, John Crosthwaite prepared the ground for development, by laying out the roads and leasing the plots to local builders. These roads were then taken in charge by the township, which was then responsible for their maintenance, as well as providing other local services such as lighting, drainage and cleansing. Not all areas were properly serviced however, as townships struggled to support development in the ever-expanding suburbs. Prior to the introduction of the main drainage scheme in 1879, houses in Rathmines, Rathgar and Pembroke were drained by the cesspool system, which was wholly inadequate. In light of these adverse conditions, it comes as no surprise therefore that the Dublin suburbs continued to see a recurrence of disease and epidemics during the nineteenth century.

Notes

1 P. J. Duffy, 'Irish landholding structures and population in the mid-nineteenth century', in *The Maynooth Review*, iii, no. 2 (1977), pp. 5 and 15.

2 Leasehold grants were more common in Ireland than in Britain. J. C. W. Wylie, *Irish land law* (West Sussex and Dublin, 2010), p. 24.
3 Dan Cruickshank, *A guide to the Georgian buildings of Britain and Ireland* (London, 1985), p. 22.
4 *The Irish Times*, 14 December 1882.
5 N. T. Burke, 'Dublin 1600–1800: a study in urban morphogenesis' (Ph.D. thesis, Trinity College, Dublin, 1972), pp. 359 and 407.
6 E. McAulay, 'The origins and early development of the Pembroke estate beyond the Grand Canal 1816–1880' (Ph.D. thesis, Trinity College, Dublin, 2003), p. 1.
7 McAulay, 'Pembroke estate', p. 194.
8 *The Irish Builder*, 15 December 1869.
9 M. E. Daly, 'The growth of Victorian Dublin' in Mary E. Daly, Mona Hearn and Peter Pearson (eds), *Dublin's Victorian houses* (Dublin, 1998), p. 28.
10 McAulay, 'Pembroke estate', pp. 12 and 87.
11 Ibid., pp. 87 and 172.
12 Ibid., p. 217.
13 St Michael's House archive, original lease from March 1868, piece of ground on the south side of Ailesbury Road, the Earl of Clanwilliam, Marquis of Ailesbury, Earl of Pembroke, Montgomery and Michael Meade; RD, 1869, vol. 24, mem. 136.
14 *Thom's*, 1868 and 1870.
15 NAI, PEP, Plans elevations etc., plans, specifications and letters regarding houses on Londonbridge Road, 15 June 1895 (Acc. No. 1011/8/12).
16 NAI, PEP, Correspondence, W. M. MacCarty to J. E. Vernon, 10 May 1860 (Acc. No. 1011/2/9).
17 Ibid., Vernon to Thos. Trench, 14 October 1878 (Acc. No. 1011/2/5/ii).
18 *Report from the select committee on town holdings*, H.C. 1886 (213-Sess. 1), evidence of Mr John L. Robinson, p. 30, para. 937 (henceforth cited as *Town holdings, 1886*). 'An agreement to grant a lease under certain conditions is first signed, containing the above and many other stringent provisions, and the leases are not perfected until the houses are completed to the satisfaction of the surveyor.'
19 D. Cruickshank and N. Burton, *Life in the Georgian city* (London, 1990), p. 133.
20 Private collection, copy of original lease from September 1877, piece of ground on the north side of Ailesbury Road, the Earl of Pembroke and Montgomery and Michael Meade Esq.
21 McAulay, 'Pembroke estate', p. 217.
22 NAI, PEP, Letter books, vol. 20, p.795, John E. Vernon to Meade Messrs. M. & Son, 5 January 1884 (Acc. No. 97/46/3/20).
23 Ibid., vol. 24, p. 492, Fane Vernon to The Rt Hon. J. M. Meade, 7 March 1899 (Acc. No. 97/46/3/24).
24 M. E. Daly, *Dublin, the deposed capital* (Cork, 1984), p. 160.
25 Private collection; copy of original lease from March 1859, premises on Sandymount Strand Road, Hannah Bourne and William Eckersley and Alexander Graham; copy of original lease from September 1861, ground and premises at Sandymount, the Earl of Clanwilliam and Marquis of Ailesbury and Lord Herbert and Alexander Graham.
26 *The Irish Builder*, 1 February 1868.
27 W. F. Wakeman, *Tourists' guide through Dublin and its interesting suburbs, specially* (sic.) *suited to the visitors of The International Exhibition* (Dublin, 1865), p. 2.
28 D. Dickson, *Dublin, the making of a capital city* (Dublin, 2014), p. 290.
29 Ibid., p. 300.
30 Daly, *Deposed capital*, p. 176 and *The Dublin Builder*, 15 June 1861.

31 J. R. Joly, *Dublin and its environs: with a map of the city and numerous illustrations* (Dublin, 1846), p. 180.
32 *The Dublin Builder*, 1 June 1860.
33 *Ibid.*, 15 December 1862.
34 *Ibid.*, and Daly, *Deposed capital* p. 194 and *Town holdings, 1886*, Evidence of James Stewart, p. 195, para. 5236.
35 J. K. Walton, *Wonderland by the waves* (Preston, 1992), p. 2.
36 Wakeman, *Tourists' guide through Dublin*, p. 2.
37 *Municipal Boundaries Commission (Ireland), Part I, Evidence, with appendices. Dublin, Rathmines, Pembroke, Kilmainham, Drumcondra, Clontarf, and also Kingstown, Blackrock and Dalkey*, [C.2725], H.C. 1880, evidence of Mr R. J. Ennis, p. 285, para. 70 and Mr John Donnelly (henceforth cited as *Municipal Boundaries, Part I, 1880*) and *Town holdings, 1886*, evidence Mr Donnelly, p. 14, para. 416.
38 Dickson, *Dublin*, p. 325.
39 *Town Holdings, 1886*, Evidence of Mr Stewart, p. 216, para. 5799.
40 L. Johnstone, 'Ground landlords and the development of Sloperton in 19th century suburban Dublin', *2ha*, no. 4, essay 01.
41 P. Pearson, *Between the mountains and the sea* (Dublin, 1999), p. 192.
42 Joly, *Dublin and its environs*, p. 180.
43 *Ex. Info.*, Laura Johnstone, Ph.D. candidate, School of Architecture, University College Dublin, 24 January 2013.
44 S. Cannon and C. Cullen, *Monkstown, a Victorian village* (Dublin, 2014), p. 43.
45 Johnstone, 'Ground landlords and the development of Sloperton', p. 4
46 Pearson, *Between the mountains*, p. 190.
47 Johnstone, 'Ground landlords and the development of Sloperton', p. 4.
48 Daly, 'The growth of Victorian Dublin', p. 32.
49 *The Dublin Builder*, 1 June 1860.
50 Daly, *Deposed capital*, p. 176.
51 Pearson, *Between the mountains*, p. 137.
52 *The Irish Times*, 7 March 1863, and J. J. Gaskin, *Varieties of Irish history from ancient and modern sources and original documents* (Dublin and London, 1869), p. 130.
53 *The Irish Times*, 27 June 1863.
54 Lease memorials were available for twelve out of sixteen houses on the east side, equating to 75% of the properties. On the west side, memorials for only four houses were uncovered, equating to 25% on this side.
55 RD, 1861, vol. 30, mem. 105 and 112.
56 NAI, Card index, corrective affidavit of Ada W. Meade Coffey, 16 October 1922 (Acc. No. T15625).
57 RD, 1864, vol. 11, mem. 287–291.
58 NLI, de Vesci papers, letter from the 4th Earl of Longford to the 3rd Viscount de Vesci, 24 October 1865 (MS 39,014/2/5344).
59 C. Ryan, *Lewis' Dublin, a topographical dictionary of the parishes, towns and villages of Dublin city and county* (Cork, 2001), p. 229.
60 *Ibid.*, p. 232.
61 *Ibid.*
62 *Ibid.*
63 Aghadowey Linen Bleaching Greens, Co. Londonderry, Ireland, excerpts from the book Aghadowey by Rev. Thomas H. Mullin (Belfast, 1972) (www.rootsweb.ancestry.com/~nirldy/aghadowey/ag_linen.htm) (17 December 2012).
64 C. Moriarty, *Down the Dodder* (Dublin, 1991), p. 116.
65 NAI, Family and estate papers, maps and rentals, copy of original lease from 18 August 1863, ground in Rathgar, William Carvill to William Todd (Acc. No. 1146/3/2). Some of

this land was assigned over to merchant James Miley of Eden Quay in 1852 for the use of the trustees and RD, 1852, vol. 12, mem. 75.
66 S. Ó Maithú, *Dublin's suburban towns* (Dublin, 2003), p. 26 and Daly, *Deposed capital*, p. 153.
67 Daly, 'The growth of Victorian Dublin', p. 30.
68 Daly, *Deposed capital*, p. 153.
69 *The Dublin Builder*, 1 July 1867. During 1867, *The Dublin Builder* was renamed *The Irish Builder*.
70 NAI, card index, copy of original grant of probate of William Carvill, Rathgar House, Dublin, dated February 1885 (Acc. No. T6875).
71 S. Jones, 'Dublin reformed: the transformation of the municipal governance of a Victorian city, 1840–1860' (Ph.D. thesis, Trinity College, Dublin, 2001).
72 M. Potter, *The municipal revolution in Ireland* (Dublin, 2011), p. 89.
73 Ó Maithú, *Dublin's suburban towns*, p. 47.
74 *Municipal Boundaries, Part I, 1880*, evidence of Mr A. H. Robinson, p. 184, para. 4873.
75 *Municipal Boundaries Commission (Ireland), Part II, Report. Dublin, Rathmines, Pembroke, Kilmainham, Drumcondra, Clontarf, and also Kingstown, Blackrock and Dalkey*, [C.2827], H.C. 1881, p. 26. (henceforth cited as *Municipal Boundaries, Part II, 1881*), p. 11.
76 *Municipal Boundaries, Part I, 1880*, evidence of John Edward Vernon, p. 178, para. 4655 and evidence of Mr A. H. Robinson, p. 184, para. 4894.
77 *Town holdings, 1886*, evidence of Mr Robinson, pp. 39–40, para. 1145.
78 *Municipal Boundaries, Part II, 1881*, p. 12.
79 *Municipal Boundaries, Part I, 1880*, evidence of John Edward Vernon, p. 180, para. 4731.
80 *Ibid.*, p. 34, para. 989.
81 Daly, *Deposed capital*, p. 160.
82 *Municipal Boundaries, Part I, 1880*, evidence of John Edward Vernon, p. 180. para. 4731.
83 McAulay, 'Pembroke estate', p. 217 and *The Dublin Builder*, 15 June 1863.
84 *Thom's*, 1861 and *Freeman's Journal*, 30 August 1862 and *The Irish Times*, 3 July 1868.
85 *The Dublin Builder*, 15 March 1865.
86 *Ibid.*, 15 August and 1 October 1865.
87 *The Irish Builder*, 1 August 1870.
88 *Municipal Boundaries, Part I, 1880*, evidence of John Edward Vernon, p. 179, para. 4686.
89 Ó Maithú, *Dublin's suburban towns*, p. 97.
90 *Ibid.*, p. 98.
91 *Municipal Boundaries, Part I, 1880*, evidence of Mr A. H. Robinson, p. 184, para. 4881.
92 NAI, PEP, Statements of accounts, Report for the year ended 25 March 1869, pp. 2–3 (Acc. 2011/5/2).
93 *Municipal Boundaries, Part I, 1880*, evidence of John Edward Vernon, p. 180, para. 4724.
94 *Ibid.*, para. 4723.
95 *The Irish Builder*, 15 September 1865.
96 *The Dublin Builder*, 15 March 1864.
97 *The Dublin Builder*, 15 March 1864.
98 Ó Maithú, *Dublin's suburban towns*, p. 101.
99 *Municipal Boundaries, Part I, 1880*, evidence of John Edward Vernon, p. 178, para. 4659.

100 *Ibid.*, para. 4876.
101 *Ibid.*, p. 12 and Ó Maithú, *Dublin's suburban towns*, p. 90.
102 *Municipal Boundaries, Part I, 1880*, evidence of Mr A. H. Robinson, p. 185, para. 4927 and 4937.
103 *Municipal Boundaries, Part II, 1881*, p. 12.
104 *Municipal Boundaries, Part I, 1880*, evidence of Mr A. H. Robinson, p. 184, para. 4897–99.
105 *Ibid.*, evidence of Alderman Harris, p. 72, para. 1786–1787.
106 *Ibid.*, evidence of John Edward Vernon, p. 179, para. 4718.
107 *Freeman's Journal*, 19 June 1884.
108 *Ibid.*, evidence of Mr John Hogan, p. 189, para. 5087–89.
109 *Ibid.*, para. 5100.
110 Ciarán Wallace, 'Local politics and government in Dublin city and suburbs, 1899–1914' (Ph.D. thesis, Trinity College Dublin, 2010), p. 78.
111 NAI, PEP, letter books, vol. 16, p. 635, Carter to John Hill, 7 December 1867 (Acc. No. 97/46/3/16).
112 Wallace, 'Local politics', p. 78.
113 *Municipal Boundaries, Part I, 1880*, evidence of Mr Arthur H. Robinson, p. 279. para. 41–42.
114 *Freeman's Journal*, 22 January 1889.
115 Daly, *Deposed capital*, p. 195.
116 *Town Holdings, 1886*, evidence of Mr Stewart, p. 194, para. 5216, 5225–6 and p. 195, para. 5228 and p. 205, para. 5515.
117 *Ibid.*, evidence of Mr Stewart, p. 195, para. 5250.
118 *Ibid.*, evidence of Mr Robinson, p. 34, p. 991–2 and p. 39, para. 1143.
119 *Town Holdings, 1886*, Evidence of Mr Stewart , p. 200, para. 5372–73.
120 *Ibid.*, evidence of Mr Robinson, p. 50, para. 1443. This evidence is corroborated by Mr Stewart, who confirmed that it was Mr Crosthwaite who leased the ground and laid out the roads at Crosthwaite Park. *Ibid.*, evidence of Mr Stewart, p. 201, para. 5405–5406.
121 NLI, de Vesci papers, Letter from the Lord Longford to the 3rd Viscount de Vesci, 21 March 1864 (MS 39,014/1).
122 Ó Maithú, *Dublin's suburban towns*, p. 38.
123 *Freeman's Journal*, 19 July 1884.
124 Ó Maithú, *Dublin's suburban towns*, p. 77.
125 KT, LA4/119, 5 February 1867.
126 *Ibid.*, LA4/5, 19 December 1862.
127 *Ibid.*, LA4/4, 29 July 1859.
128 C. Kennedy, *The diaries of Mary Hayden 1878–1903*, vol. 1 (1878–83) (Killala, 2005), p. 309.
129 *Ibid.*, LA4/4, 24 August 1860.
130 *The Irish Times*, 15 January 1863.
131 *Ibid.*, LA4/5, 13 March 1863.
132 *The Irish Times*, 7 April 1877.
133 *Ibid.*, 15 June 1865.
134 Glenageary Road (near Crosthwaite Park) appears to have been particularly bad in this regard. KT, LA4/120, 19 July 1864.
135 *Municipal Boundaries, Part II, 1881*, p. 22.
136 *Ibid.*, 2 September 1859 and Ó Maithú, *Dublin's suburban towns*, p. 102.
137 KT, LA4/4, 10 June 1859.
138 *Ibid.*, LA4/120, 25 May 1866.
139 *The Dublin Builder*, 1 September 1862.

140 Ó Maithú, *Dublin's suburban towns*, p. 97.
141 M. Corcoran, *Our good health: a history of Dublin's water and drainage* (Dublin, 2005), p. 82.
142 KT, LA4/119, 30 September 1864.
143 *Ibid.*, 25 August 1864.
144 *The Irish Times*, 9 April 1877.
145 Ó Maithú, *Dublin's suburban towns*, p. 82.
146 *The Irish Times*, 3 September 1890.
147 *Municipal Boundaries, Part I, 1880*, evidence of Mr R. J. Ennis, p. 284, para. 24.
148 *Ibid.*, para. 28, 30 and 34.
149 *The Dublin Builder*, 1 December 1859.
150 P. H. Browne and D. R. C. Hilliard, *Zion Church Rathgar: a brief account of its history, 1861–1961* (Dublin, 1961), p. 8.
151 *The Dublin Builder*, 1 December 1860.
152 *Municipal Boundaries, Part I, 1880*, evidence of Mr John H. Evans, p. 112, para. 2427.
153 *The Irish Builder*, 1 January 1862.
154 *Municipal Boundaries, Part I, 1880*, evidence of Mr Michael Murphy, p. 133, para. 3208.
155 Ó Maithú, *Dublin's suburban towns*, p. 78.
156 *The Dublin Builder*, 1 April 1860.
157 *Thom's*, 1865.
158 *Ibid.*, 1865–1875.
159 Griffith Valuation, Rathfarnham, 1864–1875, vol. 1, p. 210.
160 Ó Maithú, *Dublin's suburban towns*, p. 79.
161 *Municipal Boundaries, Part I, 1880*, evidence of Mr Samuel H. Bolton, p. 131, para. 3116.
162 *Ibid.*, evidence Mr John Beveridge, p. 11, para. 223.
163 Ó Maithú, *Dublin's suburban towns*, p. 81.
164 *Municipal Boundaries, Part I, 1880*, evidence of Mr Henry Johnston, p. 145, para. 3614, 3619 and 3737. According to the city engineer Parke Neville, there were also private roads in the townships which did not require as much maintenance, as they were used only by residents. *Ibid.*, evidence of Mr Parke Neville, p. 27, para. 631.
165 *Municipal Boundaries, Part I, 1880*, evidence of Mr Mark Bentley, p. 167, paras. 4418–4419.
166 *Ibid.*, para. 4437.
167 Ó Maithú, *Dublin's suburban towns*, p. 88.
168 *Municipal Boundaries, Part I, 1880*, evidence of Mr Charles Dawson, p. 60, para. 1523. *Ibid.*, evidence of Mr John H. Evans, p. 116, para. 2633.
169 *Municipal Boundaries, Part I, 1880*, evidence of Mr Henry Johnston, p. 146, para. 3653.
170 *Municipal Boundaries Commission (Ireland), Part I, Evidence, with appendices. Dublin, Rathmines, Pembroke, Kilmainham, Drumcondra, Clontarf, and also Kingstown, Blackrock and Dalkey*, [C.2725], H.C. 1880, evidence of Mr James Boyle, p. 69, para. 1692–4.
171 *The Irish Builder*, 15 October 1872.

4 Builders, speculators and labourers

Introduction

In 1909, *The Irish Builder* published a special golden jubilee edition of the trade journal. Looking back on fifty years of development in Dublin, it pointed to the city's open spaces, adorned with many statues commemorating its eminent citizens and social reformers. However, there were none to recognise the role of the builder, described as: 'the capable and energetic men who for years burrowed like moles beneath our city . . . but alas! Alas! They were only contractors and their lot, and who thinks of thanking or lauding them?'[1] This chapter aims to begin to address this imbalance by focusing on those responsible for developing some of Dublin's Victorian streetscapes. It begins with a brief overview of the speculator and then focuses on the work of three builder/developers, who erected high-quality houses in different sectors. Part of a rising Catholic middle class, it follows their careers through the Victorian age, as they engaged in business and wider industrial markets. To what extent was house speculation profitable for these entrepreneurs? Where did they source the labour force who physically constructed these streetscapes? This chapter opens up the world of Dublin's nineteenth-century builders, revealing their creative impact on the Victorian city and suburbs.

Who was the house speculator?

From builders to architects, city merchants to grocers, a wide range of speculators invested in Dublin's Victorian suburbs. Naturally, many came from the building industry, who used their skills and networks to profit directly from their trade. With a ready supply of labour and materials sourced at cost, builders could engage in domestic construction as an extension of their normal operations. An example is Cockburn & Sons, one of the city's main firms who completed their flagship project – the museum at Trinity College in 1857. Within two years, they had acquired leases for plots to the south of the city, in the prestigious Wellington Road, and built four houses there, following on with another five properties in Elgin Road in 1863.[2] Like many builders, Cockburn & Sons were also timber merchants, who operated a saw mill in Great Brunswick Street (present-day Pearse Street). Timber accounted for almost a third of the material cost of a house, making domestic building an obvious by-product for these merchants, who were receiving shipments of lumber at the quays. Cockburn's competitor was Joseph Kelly who, after extending his City Saw Mills in 1860, was building houses in the seaside suburb of Bray later that year. Kelly also operated as general builders' suppliers at his mills in Thomas Street, offering a variety of materials such as slate, stone, roof tiles and sewer pipes.[3] It is likely that most carpenter speculators carried out the joinery themselves and commissioned the brickwork and masonry from other sub-contractors. This saved on the employment of a general contractor, whose services could add as much as 15% to the cost of a house.[4]

Architects were also prominent speculators. Chapter 3 discussed the role of the architect and engineer Peter Moran, who built on at least three plots at Crosthwaite Park. Other examples are John McCurdy, Trinity College's official architect, and E. H. Carson, who both speculated in different parts of the southern suburbs.[5] To what extent were architects involved in the design of Dublin's suburban houses? Certainly, most of the city's prominent architects were involved in domestic projects, from large mansions to speculative suburban houses.[6] Compared to Georgian Dublin, which was built mostly by builders and craftsmen, architects were increasingly involved in domestic design in the Victorian age. However, in 1864, *The Irish Builder* conceded that although there were 'many splendid specimens of their skill in Rathmines, Rathgar, Dundrum, and some few even in Kingstown', the majority were built without an architect, or even a master builder.[7] Instead, the works were entrusted to a journeyman mason and carpenter, or even worse 'to the still more inadequate supervision of some pretentious charlatan'.[8] A suburban house in Dublin could be built by a few journeymen for £300, but the employment of an architect could double the price. The standard architects' fee added 5% to the overall building cost: 2.5% for the preparation of documents and 2.5% to supervise the works. Clearly, this was too much for some speculators, as they chose to forego design services to maximise profits. This, the journal claimed, produced a cheaper 'jerry' class of house, where substandard building materials and inadequate drainage was patched up with 'gandy (*sic*) papering and painting'.[9] It advised against this cheaper form of speculative development, lamenting: 'Can proprietors conscientiously consent to the erection of their buildings by the timber merchant, the brick maker, the ironmonger, or any of the numerous wholesale merchants in connexion (*sic*) with building? We think not.'[10]

This view is reflected in the archival data, which shows the range of speculators involved in house building. In the Pembroke estate, a wide variety of developers leased house plots in Waterloo and Wellington Roads in the 1840s: many were builders but there were also turners, plumbers, and dairy owners, as well as members of the political classes and the upper professionals.[11] In Northumberland Road, a group of eight houses emerged at the junction with Haddington Road by 1865 (Plate 2). The leaseholders were James Farrell and Patrick O'Toole who were both Dublin builders, but Thomas Walker was a grocer with an address in Bath Avenue.[12] Walker probably engaged a contractor to construct his four houses, but Farrell and O'Toole were the likely builders of their properties. Other, smaller investors such as clergymen, army officers and businessmen were also involved in leasing plots in Dublin's city and suburbs.[13] Some were involved directly in building, but others engaged contractors to carry out the works. As a builder, Michael Meade most likely constructed his own houses in Ailesbury Road, but John Crosthwaite was a businessman who subcontracted the work to local men. In 1861, *The Dublin Builder* confirmed that a stucco plasterer was building four houses on ground in Rathmines, complete with brick fronts and granite cornices.[14] Female speculators were also prevalent: in 1861, it was reported in Rathmines that: 'very many of those erecting new houses in the district belong to the gentler sex'.[15] Uniting this wide pool of speculators was a common drive for profit, as *The Dublin Builder* remarked in 1860: 'Finding such a sudden rage for cheap houses, surveyors, valuers, auctioneers, have entered the field: and now what is the result? . . . "Get money honestly if you can, but get it," seems to be the maxim generally followed.'[16]

Three Catholic speculators

From the seventeenth century, a series of penal laws were passed in Ireland, which limited the capacity of Catholics to hold public office, to practise law, or to buy and inherit property.[17] There was nothing to prevent them trading however, and gradually Catholics began to accumulate wealth through the mercantile trades. By the end of the seventeenth century, these merchants controlled much of the wealth of towns like Limerick, Galway and Cork.[18] This enabled them to loan money on discount, but the penal code still prohibited them from acquiring leases for longer than thirty-one years, or holding public office. However, the tide began to turn during the last quarter of the eighteenth century, as a number of Catholic Relief Acts were passed. The most significant change was the lifting of the property restrictions in 1782, allowing Catholics to purchase land, while further reforms in the 1790s admitted Catholics to the legal professions. Further reforms lifted the ban on parliamentary voting, as was the right to vote and to hold positions in municipal corporations, the ultimate barrier to self-government. Through the work of Henry Grattan and Daniel O'Connell amongst others, the Catholic Emancipation Act was passed in 1829, granting freedom for Catholics in Britain and Ireland, including the right to hold public office.

Michael Meade, William Carvill and John Crosthwaite were born into this new era of freedom for Irish Catholics. Their generation would soon reap the rewards of religious freedom, enabling them to forge new opportunities in a rapidly advancing city. They joined the ranks of increasing numbers of affluent Catholic professionals, who had populated Dublin since the turn of the nineteenth century.[19] After the English and Welsh municipal reforms of 1835, legislation was introduced into Irish cities in 1841, marking a gradual shift in power from a Protestant minority to a Catholic majority.[20] These three men were some of the merchants, the lord mayors and the town commissioners, who helped shape the Victorian city. John Crosthwaite took a leading part in the affairs of the Kingstown Township, located six miles south of the city where he was elected chairman eight times. His son-in-law William Carvill was active in a suburb closer to the city at Rathgar, after forging his earlier career in the timber and iron trades in Canada. Most prominent of the three was Michael Meade, who came from humble beginnings to build up the largest building firm in the city. By the time of the house building boom of the 1860s, all three men were perfectly positioned to begin carving out new streetscapes in empty fields beyond the canals. The rows of houses that they built next to their homes were a means of amassing wealth and financial security.

Precursor to boom

Born in Dublin to a Catholic family in 1814, Michael Meade first appeared in the records in the 1840s, as a carpenter and builder in Townsend Street, to the north of Trinity College (Figure 4.1).[21] By 1843, he was insolvent, but he must have recouped his losses fairly quickly, as within two years he was back in business at the same address. During the years of the Famine that followed (1845–1850), Meade was active politically, campaigning for Catholic rights and a repeal of the Union. Dublin experienced a surge in population during these years, as Famine survivors were drawn to the city, where 'vast numbers of country beggars mingled in the traffic'.[22] After the economic downturn of 1847–1848, Meade moved his premises to nearby Great Brunswick Street, the centre of the building trade. Meanwhile, six miles further south along the coast, John Crosthwaite had built the Royal Victoria Baths in Kingstown, offering open-sea bathing and hot and cold baths of salt and fresh water (Figure 4.2).[23] He remained proprietor there for many years, but in 1849 he acquired the Woodpark estate, in the hills above the town.

The same year, William Carvill arrived home from Canada, where he had spent his early career in the iron and shipping trades (Figure 4.3). Carvill was originally from Rostrevor in County Down, where his older brother Francis was one of the foremost self-made entrepreneurs in Newry, having introduced shipbuilding to the town.[24] In 1836, William Carvill had emigrated to Saint John in New Brunswick, one of three maritime provinces located on Canada's eastern seaboard. William's younger brother George followed four years later; as young men they were engaged in the iron and timber trades in Saint John, but it wasn't long before they began to launch ships from there.[25] The first of these was named after William's future wife. *Eliza*, a barque of 120 tons, was launched with a crew of five in 1838. Four years later, his vessel 'New Zealand' was carrying over five times the tonnage, manned by twenty-four men.[26] Since the early 1800s, timber merchants had been turning to the abundant Canadian forests as a source of lumber for European markets. A major centre for the trade was New Brunswick, where most villages and towns could boast of at least one saw mill manufacturing boards, planks and shingles. European merchants capitalised on this market demand: ships carrying lumber eastwards across the Atlantic could return with passengers bound for North America.[27] By the time William Carvill arrived in Saint John in the 1830s, Ireland and New Brunswick had been linked commercially for at least forty years, due to the transatlantic timber and emigrant

Builders, speculators and labourers 111

Figure 4.1 Cartouche of Michael Meade, Meade monument, Glasnevin Cemetery (Glasnevin Trust).

Figure 4.2 Portrait of Mr John Crosthwaite (John Carvill).

trade. Back in Newry, Francis Carvill built the town's first ship *The Mary Anne* in 1845. During the worst years of the Famine, he remained the main emigration agent in Newry, sailing numerous vessels between Ireland and North America. As Laxton maintains, the trans-Atlantic voyage was often perilous, and many ships made the journey only once during the Famine period. However Francis Carvill's ship, aptly named *The Brothers*, made a voyage every year from Newry to New

Figure 4.3 Portrait of William Carvill (John Carvill).

York, a total of ten Atlantic crossings during the Famine years.[28] He was engaged in trade with his brothers William and George, who also operated as timber and shipping merchants on the Canadian side.[29] However, William Carvill did not have his sights set on remaining in British North America and in 1849 he returned to Ireland.[30] Although separated by great distances, he remained in partnership with his brother George, who became one of Saint John's wealthiest citizens, residing in a large detached house in the city.[31]

Not until the 1850s is there evidence of a connection between the Crosthwaite and Carvill families. Shortly after William Carvill's return to Ireland in 1850, he married John Crosthwaite's only daughter Eliza Maria in Kingstown.[32] As part of the marriage settlement, Crosthwaite entrusted over twenty-eight acres of his estate in Kingstown, and another twenty-one acres nearer the city in Rathgar.[33] Soon after the marriage, Crosthwaite became a town commissioner for Kingstown, a position that he would hold for almost thirty years.[34] By this time, Michael Meade, as yet unrelated to the Carvills and Crosthwaites, was operating a building firm from his premises in Great Brunswick Street, beside his competitors, the builders Cockburn & Sons.[35] In 1853, Meade moved to Number 17 Westland Row, which he shared with the architect John J. Lyons, who had been involved in drawing the streetscapes for Shaw's Dublin guide.[36] Lyons had just set up office and would prove an important contact for Meade, as founder of the building trade journal *The Dublin Builder*. Meade's earliest recorded project was the Turkish Baths at Lincoln Place in 1858, followed by two houses in Rathgar, designed by the architect James Rawson Carroll, a young architect who had recently set up practice in Great Brunswick Street. Meade began to benefit from a golden age of church building, as the lifting of anti-Catholic legislation enabled the clergy to commission major works to cater for a burgeoning laity.[37] Gradually, he built up an ecclesiastical clientele, commencing with the Passionist Monastery at Mount Argus for the renowned architect James Joseph McCarthy. Meade also began work on the first of many public works contracts: in 1858, he broke ground for a new building to the rear of the Four Courts, designed by James Higgins Owen, architect to the Board of Works.

As Meade's firm continued to expand, William Carvill was busy setting up a business of his own. During the early 1850s, he established himself in the city as a corn merchant at Number 38 Sir John Rogerson's Quay.[38] Commuting from Kingstown in 1853, he and his wife Eliza were residing in a house at lower Clarinda Terrace. Carvill also began work on the property in Rathgar, which stood on an elevated site above the meandering Dodder River. It consisted of an assembly of structures, including a mill-race, a calico mill and a medium-sized early-Victorian house. He replaced the existing industrial structures with a saw mill and began to adapt the house as his own residence.[39] As Carvill pursued business interests in Dublin, he continued to work in partnership with his brother George in Canada. In 1853, they were among those campaigning for the extension of the port of Saint John in New Brunswick, to facilitate the shipping of lumber from their saw mill. In the summer of 1857, *The Belfast News-Letter* proudly announced the launch of a new ship from Saint John: '... a splendid ship, of about 1,000 tons burthen, called the *William Carvill*, after one of our enterprising merchants, who at present resides in the mother country.'[40]

Throughout 1859, William Carvill and Michael Meade published advertisements side-by-side in Dublin, auctioning off a wide range of timbers arriving on separate ships from Canada. Due to a post-Famine rise in construction activity, timber imports had been rising in recent years, and by this time Dublin was importing almost twice as much lumber as Belfast.[41] Meade was in the process of building a saw mill of his own at Numbers 152–162 Great Brunswick Street that year, on a large plot adjoining the terminus of the Dublin and Kingstown railway. A carpenter by trade, it was a natural choice for Meade, but it would also provide him with an important material resource for his growing building empire. The extensive sawing, planing and moulding mills were built to house 'powerful machinery' to process timber for building.[42] The saw mill must have been a conspicuous sight in the city – its 150-foot-high chimney was reported to be 'the tallest structure of its class in Dublin' (Figure 4.4).[43]

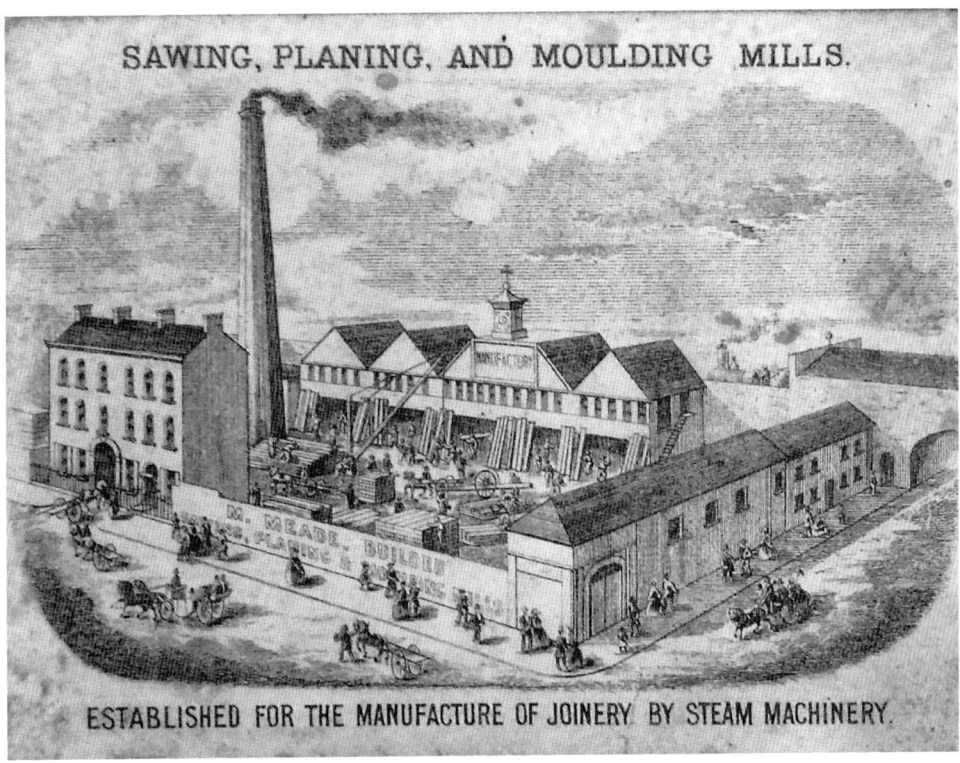

Figure 4.4 Meade's Saw Mills (National Library of Ireland).

Dublin's Victorian housing boom

During the 1860s, Dublin's building trade flourished, benefitting from Britain's mid-Victorian boom and its own post-Famine economic upturn. Throughout the decade, Meade's business continued to prosper. His contracts were wide ranging, which brought him into contact with some of the leading architects of the day. In 1862, he was working on a number of projects in the city designed by the architect William Caldbeck: two houses in Eustace Street and a new Italianate premises in Grafton Street.[44] Ecclesiastical work continued to thrive, and during this period Meade worked with the architects Pugin and Ashlin on St Colman's Cathedral in Cork, their largest commission in Ireland. Ashlin, the son of a Cork merchant, had been in partnership with the London architect Edward Welby Pugin since 1860, when he opened a Dublin office to run the Irish side of the practice.[45] With a predominately Roman Catholic clientele, Ashlin soon became the leading ecclesiastical architect in Ireland. One of his most important Dublin projects was the Church of Saints Augustine and John on Thomas Street, which Meade began work on in 1866. Other collaborations included parish church commissions in the expanding Dublin suburbs, such as the churches of St Patrick in Monkstown (1861–1866) and the Sacred Heart in Donnybrook (1863–1866). Meade won the contract for the city's cattle market in 1862, soon to be the biggest of its kind in Europe, serving the needs of the ever-growing populations in the United Kingdom.[46] He also began work on Ireland's largest public works contract during this time: Ennis Lunatic Asylum (1863–1866) designed by the Limerick architect William Fogerty. This enormous complex of buildings, constructed on a forty-acre site, was said to be so large that 'one would imagine this establishment could accommodate all the indoor and outdoor idiots, madmen, women, and children in the whole kingdom of Ireland'.[47]

Operations continued unabated at Meade's Saw Mills in Great Brunswick Street, providing many of the raw materials for his building contracts. Advertisements boasted of 'First class Workmen, selected from the Regular Carpenters of the City' who manufactured doors and windows, staircases, shutters and green houses (Figure 4.4). Reportedly, only the best-seasoned timber was used and goods were 'forwarded to all parts of the Kingdom'.[48] Nearby was William Carvill's timber yard in the Custom House Docks, where he continued to receive shipments from around the world.[49] The majority of cargo came from Canada, but increasingly trade extended to new colonies in Central America and East Prussia.[50] Some of the lumber was auctioned off on its arrival in his dockland premises, but the remainder went for processing at his mill in Rathgar, three miles south of the city.[51] By 1870, William Carvill had involved himself in a variety of businesses in Ireland and abroad. The partnership with his brother George had dissolved in 1869, but he continued to receive shipments of timber from Canada. In May of that year, he prepared to auction off over 31,084 pieces of spruce deals and 12,000 sawn laths arriving from Saint John in New Brunswick.[52] Throughout the 1870s, Carvill continued to acquire more property in the Dublin area, as well as in his home county of Down.[53]

Much of this timber provided the raw material for the city's busiest period of domestic construction during the 1860s. This is reflected in a report from *The Dublin Builder* that predicted a busy building season in 1860, boasting: 'Our suburbs are extending, green fields are metamorphosed into populous districts, . . . "bustle" is the word in every quarter, and the welcome sounds of the hammer and trowel are met at each step.'[54] Michael Meade was just one of many builders involved in domestic construction: the previous summer he had finished eight houses in Rathgar: four for himself (150–156 Rathgar Road, described in Chapter 1) and another four nearby for various clients.[55] By 1862, he was in the process of building eight houses and a villa in Bray for William Dargan, the railway entrepreneur.[56] This seaside town, located thirteen miles south of the city was envisaged as the 'Brighton of Ireland', where in recent years development there had been 'literally gigantic; houses here, there, everywhere' with 'hotels of monster form' catering for the crowds arriving during the summer season.[57] In 1863, buoyed by his burgeoning business, Michael Meade moved his family from the city into a terraced house in Sandymount, overlooking the sea (Figure 3.1). It was just one mile away from the site for the future Ailesbury Road, which the Pembroke estate was intending to lay out from Donnybrook to Sydney Parade. Perhaps this was a more convenient base for him to make plans for his grandiose Italianate villa, which he would build on the corner with Merrion Road by 1865 (Figure 4.5). A testimony to his growing success, the villa is characterised by a seven-storey tower, said to be modelled on Osborne House, Queen Victoria's country retreat on the Isle of Wight. A spiral staircase rises through the campanile, affording views from the city to the sea and the Wicklow mountains. Suburban houses of this scale were a rare sight in Ireland, where there was always a good selection of Georgian properties on the market.[58] Meade was determined to put his stamp on the new suburbs and moved into the property in 1865.

By the mid-1860s, the three men were carving out new streetscapes in the fields around their homes. The first of these developments emerged in the seaside suburb of Kingstown in 1860, where it was noted that 'six houses of a very superior class, with handsome oriel windows carried up two storeys in height, and filled with plate glass, are being erected by Mr Crosthwaite'.[59] These were the first of two terraces to be complete here, which faced each other across a common green space (Figures 1.8 and 3.4).[60] These were not the only properties that Crosthwaite developed: Lord de Vesci, one of the main landowners in Kingstown, confirmed that he had 'speculated very largely in property'[61] in the area. At the same time, his son-in-law William Carvill had begun to develop ground in Rathgar, located over seven miles to the northwest.[62] By 1870, he had constructed eighteen semi-detached houses on his forty-six-acre estate (Plates 14–16). Meanwhile, a few miles to the east was the prestigious Pembroke estate, where the Meade builders had just completed ten houses on the newly laid Ailesbury Road (Figures 1.21 and 1.22).[63] The houses catered to an elite class and were let to high-ranking professionals, or those in the upper levels of the public service.[64] Characterised by granite and red bricks fronts, the high-quality materials used here have ensured that Ailesbury Road remains one of the most valuable streets in Dublin today.

Figure 4.5 St Michael's House, Ailesbury Road.

Making money on speculative housing

These houses played an important role in providing security for this rising Catholic merchant class. In the absence of occupational pensions, a home could provide a regular income for a widow, a spinster or a retiree. Michael Meade sold only one of the twelve houses that he built in Ailesbury Road: Number 2 was bought by Henry Richard Pim, a former British army captain who paid £2,000 for the house in 1879, commanding a large corner site adjoining Merrion Road (Plate 13).[65] The remaining eleven houses were let directly to tenants, providing Meade with an approximate gross annual rent of £1,250 by 1881. This was a substantial income, considering that the most a medical doctor could earn at the height of his career was £1,000 a year.[66] It does not account for other properties owned by the Meades at this time, consisting of at least twelve houses in the suburbs and a number of properties in Dublin city.[67] William Carvill sold only two of his houses at Rostrevor Terrace: Number 6 to Mr Thomas Daniel in 1866, and Number 2 to Michael P. Dunne in 1871.[68] The remainder, consisting of twelve semi-detached homes, were rented out to tenants. This provided an annual gross rental income of over £889, equivalent to over eleven years' salary for a skilled carpenter at the time.[69] He owned other properties in Dublin city and suburbs, and in his home county of Down.[70]

Housing was also an important commodity in entering a marriage. In December 1870, William Carvill's daughter Catherine (grand-daughter of John Crosthwaite) married Michael Meade's son. Catherine was the eldest child of a Crosthwaite/Carvill union, and her marriage to Joseph Meade marked the convergence of the three families. Each side brought two properties to the marriage: The Meades entrusted two of their houses on Ailesbury Road and the Carvills conveyed Numbers 13 and 14 Rostrevor Terrace in Rathgar.[71] These marriage settlements were an almost universal practice in the wealthier sector of society, providing an income for a wife and her children, should she be widowed later in life. Joseph and Catherine Meade did not live in any of these properties; but instead let them out to the city's upper middle class. Ailesbury Road was one of the most expensive streets in the Dublin suburbs, home to solicitors, army colonels, land agents and judges.[72] By 1873, Number 7 Ailesbury Road was let to a Mrs Jane Murphy and Number 5 to William Stephen Snow, a Lieutenant-Colonel in the British army. The newlyweds moved into Number 153 Rathgar Road (Plate 4), which Joseph's father had built in the late 1850s.[73] They spent the first nine years of their marriage in this house, where Catherine bore five children, three of whom died between 1876 and 1879. The first was Elizabeth, a 'dearly beloved daughter' who died of bronchitis at fourteen months, followed by two boys: Michael (infant) and Joseph (aged three and a half). In addition, two of Joseph's brothers and two of Catherine's siblings died during these years. Premature deaths such as this were not unusual during the period; Sir Charles Cameron, Dublin's chief health and medical officer, lost five of his eight children early in life.[74] Frequent outbreaks of disease transcended class divides and were often related to poor sanitary provision. The couple moved

120 *Builders, speculators and labourers*

to Number 19 Ailesbury Road in 1880, also built by Joseph's father, where their daughter Eva was born within two years (Figure 4.6).

In contrast to Meade and Carvill, who were most likely involved directly in building, John Crosthwaite acted as a middleman, who sub-contracted the work out to local builders. This was common practice in London, where the leaseholder

Figure 4.6 Joseph M. Meade and family, c.1883 (John Carvill).

'very often does not build; he finds a lot of little builders, old foremen, and men of that sort, to whom he advances bricks and other things, and they find the labour'.[75] At least three builders were involved in constructing the sixteen houses on the east side of Crosthwaite Park. Of the eleven lease memorials found, almost half of these were sold immediately after completion, while the remainder were held as security for future loans.[76] One of the builders was Edward Roche, who sold one of four houses that he built there in 1864, but mortgaged the remainder to various parties. In contrast to wealthier speculators like Meade and Carvill, who could afford to retain their properties for rent, these small-time operators appear to have been offloading some of their debt, while using the rest as leverage for the next venture. Roche tapped into an informal lending market, traditionally dominated by solicitors and moneylenders, with widows, professionals and merchants also reaping the rewards. This was not a new phenomenon, and has precedent in the building of Dublin's eighteenth-century townhouses.

Private mortgages were also used to facilitate the completion of partly built structures. In 1834, the architect and builder John Gibson mortgaged two houses he was building in Northumberland Road to a Henry Butler of College Green. Butler lent him £500 to 'complete and finish' the properties at an interest rate of 6%.[77] A reflection of the piecemeal nature of speculation, developers might only have enough credit to finance the partial construction of a house, relying on investors to fund the remainder. This was also a familiar practice in the streets of London, as observed by Charles Manby Smith in 1857:

> Whole miles of streets in London are built upon speculation, somewhat in the following way: by men who have little to lose, and everything to hope for. Chips the carpenter joins with Hod the bricklayer in renting a piece of ground for a term of eighty or ninety years. Neither of them, perhaps, has money enough to erect a single house; but between them they contrive to get up a couple of carcasses as high as the second or third story, and there they stop. They can go no further; but at this stage of the proceeding the houses are mortgageable; and if the situation be a good one, holding out the prospect of a speedy tenancy, capitalists are readily to be found who will advance money upon mortgage for their completion.[78]

Although Crosthwaite delegated the building of his houses to speculative developers, he retained the original leasehold interest on all forty-two properties at Crosthwaite Park. When he sub-leased the plots to builders and other parties, they in turn paid him ground rents sufficient to make him a substantial profit.[79] By the turn of the century, the sixteen houses on the east side were earning his estate a net annual profit of £191 per year, or approximately £570 for the whole development, equivalent to half a year's salary for a lawyer. This was a significant return on an investment that did not subject Crosthwaite to any of the costs, and associated risks in building. Added to this were the profits from his other speculative ventures. According to Mr Stewart, agent to the Kingstown estate, John

Crosthwaite built extensively in the township and made 'a large fortune' from speculation.[80]

An analysis of sale prices for houses in Crosthwaite Park reveals why Victorian speculators were incentivised more by rental income. There were only modest increases in house prices during the Victorian age, a reflection of the wider economic fluctuations of the period.[81] Patrick Kelly, a builder from nearby Glasthule, sold one of his houses for £788 in 1863, but he received only £675 a year later for a similar house on the Park, a drop in price of over 14%.[82] Yet when the latter house was sold again in 1874, it secured £800, a full recovery over the ten-year period, but a modest enough result in an era of mild inflation. Residential buyers had of course limited access to bank credit to finance house purchase in Victorian Dublin, such as became the norm a century later, helping to fuel the property booms of the modern era. In contrast to London, where the building society was a major backer of suburban development, financial institutions do not appear in the records for these suburban houses. Therefore, in such an environment of restricted credit, speculative house building tended to occur on a modest scale, with an average of two to four plots being developed at a time.

Despite these challenges, speculation was clearly a lucrative activity for some developers. It provided an income for the families during the lifetime of the lease, but it also offered security for the next generation. On his wife's death in 1884, Joseph Meade inherited the entire east side of Crosthwaite Park in Kingstown, consisting of the sixteen houses built almost twenty years earlier. Developed by John Crosthwaite, they were probably inherited by his only daughter, mother to Joseph Meade's wife. That year saw the passing of the older generation, with the deaths of John Crosthwaite in July and William Carvill in December. Carvill died with assets worth in excess of £44,687, a substantial fortune for the time, and similar to that of his father-in-law John Crosthwaite.[83] A 'considerable portion' consisted of shares in ships, but these assets had fallen in value by the time of his death. In addition to his business premises, he owned houses and lands in Dublin city and county, and in his home county of Down. After his death, the timber business in Rathgar was gradually wound down. Domestic property remained at the core of Michael Meade's estate when he died two years later. As head of an 'extensive and important' building firm in the city, he had earned a 'handsome fortune'[84] over his thirty years in business. He left his family with assets worth over £32,442, quite an achievement considering his humble beginnings as a carpenter.[85] He bequeathed the family villa in Ailesbury Road to Joseph, his eldest son, who was also made executor of the will. His leasehold properties were distributed amongst his family, such as Number 17 Ailesbury Road, which was left to his son Daniel 'to receive rents and profits from these premises for his life'.[86] The next generation owned property in Kingstown, Rathgar and Pembroke, a legacy that they would build on in years to come.

The second generation

On his father's death in 1886, Joseph Meade inherited the building firm. There was a reduction in output at Meade & Son during the 1880s, reflecting the general economic depression in the country, since the agricultural recession of 1879.[87] Joseph moved into his father's villa, St Michael's on Ailesbury Road (Figure 4.5). By this stage, he had become an important political figure in the city, having been elected a member of Dublin Corporation in 1884, as alderman for the Trinity Ward.[88] Within two years, he had been appointed High Sheriff for Dublin City,[89] a position favoured by high-ranking nationalists, marking his rise through the hierarchy of local government. He continued to speculate in the suburbs, acquiring a property portfolio that would outstrip that of his father. He signed leases for two plots at Northumberland Road, in the prestigious Pembroke estate.[90] The first scheme was finished by 1885, displaying a high degree of architectural sophistication (Figure 1.12 and Plate 8),[91] and the second formed part of his daughter's marriage settlement two years later.[92] By the turn of the century, Joseph Meade's property empire was worth a substantial fortune, equating to £60,000 in Pembroke and Rathmines, and £50,000 in Dublin city.[93] The properties were located in major city streets such as Lower Mount Street, Lower Merrion Street and South William Street, and around his saw mills at Great Brunswick Street. He also acquired thirty-five houses in the Dublin suburbs, including seven properties in Rathmines and seventeen in the Pembroke estate. Bray was also represented, including four 'newly-built houses' and 'a large and handsome residence' on Bray seafront.[94]

In 1891, Joseph Meade began the first of his two years as Dublin's Lord Mayor. He was praised as 'a large employer, a merchant prince, respected by the citizens of all classes' (Figure 4.7).[95] During his first year in office, he presided over many important developments in the city, such as the introduction of electric lighting and improvements in drainage. He was awarded with an honorary degree of Doctor of Laws at Trinity College Dublin and contested Stephen's Green in the Parnellite interest. He was narrowly defeated by Mr Justice Kenny, a Catholic unionist lawyer who later went on to serve as solicitor-general for Ireland.[96] In 1893, he was honoured with the ultimate distinction, when he was appointed to her majesty's most honourable privy council in Ireland[97] Meade's commercial expertise kept him eagerly sought after as an advisor on various boards: among his many roles he was chairman of the Hibernian Bank and the Dublin Master Builders' Association, as well as a director of Boland's Mills and numerous other public companies.[98]

While building villas for Dublin's upper middle class, the Meades were also producing housing for the poorer sectors of society. Since the 1870s, they had been connected with The Dublin Artisans Dwellings Company, the 'only sizeable semi-philanthropic housing body in Ireland', which aimed to build homes for the working classes.[99] Meade & Son had been the first contractors to get involved, and constructed a scheme in Buckingham Street in 1877, designed by the Belfast-born architect Sir Thomas Drew as a 'model tenement block'.[100] After his father's

124 *Builders, speculators and labourers*

Figure 4.7 'The Right Honble. Joseph M. Meade, LL.D., P.C.' (Dublin City Library and Archive).

death, Joseph Meade completed a number of similar housing projects, including eighty-three homes in Rialto (1895–1899) and three Guinness Trust blocks in Bride Street (1893–1901). However, compared to other major UK cities, Dublin was not successful in providing adequate, urban working-class housing, when there was a plentiful supply of tenement properties. By 1892, Joseph Meade had purchased ten houses on Henrietta Street, one of the city's most important Georgian thoroughfares.[101] Built for the elite in the early eighteenth century, these mansions are generally double the width of a standard Georgian townhouse in Dublin (Figure 4.8). Meade's purchases equated to the whole of the north side of the street, and two houses on the southern side, earning him a substantial annual rent of £1,500 by the turn of the century. Previously, he has been referred to as 'one of the most notorious slum landlords of the late nineteenth century', as he is said to have stripped out many original features in the houses, specifically the woodwork, the staircases and the mantelpieces, and subdivided them into tenements.[102]

However, new research reveals that Meade's central role in philanthropic associations, and his criticism of the tenement middleman, makes him an unlikely slum landlord. Furthermore, it appears that the majority of the properties had already deteriorated by the time he bought them between 1887 and 1892. He then proceeded to refurbish and remodel the properties – works that were remembered twenty years later as an exemplar of tenement improvement. Mr Delany, a local government inspector, confirmed in 1914 that Meade had 'practically reconstructed these houses inside and formed them into flats, and provided them generally with sanitary accommodation'.[103] These findings have provided the opportunity to reshape our perception of Meade: a successful builder, politician and businessman who also worked to improve the housing conditions of the poor. After all, his fellow city councilors described him in 1890 as 'one of those men who, having

Figure 4.8 Henrietta Street, Dublin.

sprung from the people, had made for himself a commercial position second to none in the city'.[104]

Meade died at home suddenly in July 1900 at the age of sixty-one. Expressions of sorrow were heard from all quarters and he was hailed as one of the city's 'leading merchants and noblest citizens'.[105] The funeral was reported to be one of the largest in living memory in the city, attended by the highest ranks of the professional and commercial classes. Rows of carriages lined the streets around his villa on Ailesbury Road, as gentlemen queued to pay their respects.[106] From here the hearse proceeded to Glasnevin Cemetery, where thousands of people lined the route. He died as a new century dawned, leaving behind a large fortune, with the capital value of his assets worth over £89,000, including over 122 properties in the city and surrounding county.[107] His son William completed any outstanding contracts and gradually wound down the timber and building empire. With some 900 employees, the closing of the firm led to a dramatic increase in unemployment among building workers in the city.[108] In 1905, the family villa in Ailesbury Road and its business premises in Great Brunswick Street were finally sold off, ending sixty years of the Meade building legacy.

Labourers

Thus far, this book has focused mainly on the landlords, builders and town commissioners, and their role in shaping Dublin's Victorian streetscapes. For the most part, these were men of an elite class, who also inhabited suburban bourgeois houses. However, the hands that physically shaped these structures did not return home to such comfortable surroundings. Only about a quarter of general labourers lived in the suburbs;[109] the majority were recruited from the army of poor casual labourers, many of whom lived in the city tenements. Frequent articles appeared in *The Irish Builder,* lamenting the plight of the builders' labourer, who inhabited 'filthy lanes and bye-ways of sickening odour, and ascend some of their dilapidated stairways into tottering, overcrowded attics ... where his family endure in constant privation a miserable existence'.[110] Dublin had some of the worst slums in the British Isles, filled with a plentiful supply of tradesmen, who travelled to suburban building sites in the morning.[111] They worked an average of ten-and-a-quarter hours a day, six days a week[112] in the busy season between early spring and late autumn. By 1871, approximately 6,500 men and 3,000 women were employed in the building trades in Dublin, equating to 5% of the city workforce.[113]

Adverse working conditions led to frequent labour disputes in the building trades in Dublin. A particular bone of contention was the disproportionate earning potential within the industry. At the top of the scale were the skilled construction workers – that is, masons, bricklayers, carpenters or other craftsmen, who could earn up to three times the wage of a builders' labourer.[114] The latter formed the largest group in the industry, and carried out general building work such as the clearing of rubble, the digging of foundations, or the demolition of structures.[115] By 1865, a carpenter earned an average wage of thirty shillings a week, similar to that in England and Scotland, but the cost of unskilled labour in Ireland was relatively cheap. A builders' labourer earned a mere ten shillings a week, out of which he had to pay rent, and feed and clothe his family.[116] Furthermore, these wages were not guaranteed throughout the year, with reduced pay during the dark winter months, and no income during bad weather. Both skilled and unskilled labourers began forming trade associations and societies, to campaign for better rights for their workers. By 1869, although all of the larger building firms in the city had agreed to increase the builders' labourer's wage, *The Irish Builder* called for the provision of suitable homes for this class, maintaining that 'one half of the world do not know how the other half exist'.[117]

In 1859, it was reported that there was a scarcity of building labour in the city due to 'famine, pestilence, and emigration'. A union of Dublin carpenters took advantage of this dearth in the market, announcing their intention to strike for an increase in wages. Calling for stonelayers, bricklayers and slaters to follow suit, they warned that the strike would have an adverse effect on speculative suburban building, 'which for some years has afforded a vast amount of employment to a number of hands'.[118] In contrast to the master builders, who owned luxurious homes and private vehicles, the carpenter had little to look forward to, a mere slave living a 'precarious existence'.[119] Furthermore, employers were known to source cheaper labour from outside the city: in 1861, a large Dublin saw mill brought in a contingent of carpenters and joiners from England and Scotland who worked for less than the average Irish wage.[120] Echoes of this could be found in other trades: the following year, an association of stucco plasterers complained that despite the large sums spent in building, Dublin Corporation had overlooked local tradesmen for those mere 'birds of passage'.[121] Inspired by ongoing disputes in England, workers continued to appeal for increased pay and reduced working hours throughout the 1870s. By 1876, despite artisans' wages having increased in Dublin, their families were still housed in the 'same wretched tenement houses, renting two rooms at most, in some instances only one'.[122]

In 1890, as president of the Builders' Association, Joseph Meade signed an agreement with the brick and stone laying trades, for improved working conditions, including reduced hours and better rates of pay.[123] Six years later, a similar agreement was reached with the carpenters and joiners of the city. All carpenters and joiners were entitled to overtime pay and were allocated set times for breakfast and dinner. During the busy summer months, the men would work a fifty-four-hour week, from 6.30am to 5.30pm on a weekday, and until 1.45pm on a Saturday. These 'city hours' applied to building sites located within a one-mile limit from the municipal boundary. Beyond this point, a walking time of three miles an hour was given to workers travelling within another three-mile radius. In other words, a bricklayer travelling to a site in Shrewsbury Road, located 1.7 miles from the city boundary, would be allowed a thirty-four-minute walking time, arriving on site at 7.04 am. Clearly, the main mode of transport for the labourer was by foot, as cab, train or tram fares were prohibitive for such low-paid workers.[124] Outside the four-mile limit, the employer was to pay 'country money' for its workers, amounting to 8d per day for lodgings.[125] By 1909, *The Irish Builder* conceded that life had improved for the builders' labourer in the previous fifty years. The average working day had been reduced, wages had increased by 60%, although they were still substantially lower than in London.[126] Nevertheless, the plight of the construction worker was certainly not over: by 1911, over 24,000 men, equating to a quarter of the male population in Dublin, worked as unskilled general labourers, who mostly lived in overcrowded, insanitary accommodation.[127]

Conclusion

In summary, a strong work ethic and an entrepreneurial spirit brought success and wealth to the Meades, Carvills and Crosthwaites. Emerging in the post-Famine period, Michael Meade began in the carpentry trade, forging new opportunities in a rapidly advancing city. William Carvill worked in the iron and shipping trades in Canada, before returning to Dublin to set up a timber business of his own. Meanwhile, John Crosthwaite was in business in the port of Kingstown, and remained town commissioner there for over thirty years. The wealth and influence amassed by the Meades, Carvills and Crosthwaites are reflected in the high-quality buildings they constructed in Dublin's Victorian suburbs. Of the three families, the Meades were the most successful, forming one of the largest building empires in the city. Joseph Meade's life spanned the Victorian age: he was born two years after Queen Victoria came to the throne, and died six months before her demise. He is representative of the kinds of achievement that were possible for this rising Catholic middle class, as he built on the success of his father, while forging a formidable political career of his own. Nevertheless, he presided over a city of two halves, as *The Dublin Builder* noted in 1859:

> Look at the builders, when a few years at their vocation, they have a range of houses, a luxurious home, private vehicles, and more than all this, the consolation that, in their old age, the comforts they enjoyed through life cannot be abridged. Then turn to the working man – What has he, or what has he to look forward to – a poor slave, subject to every whim and caprice of those over him – an unfortunate toiler, whose precarious existence depends as much upon a looked – for obsequiousness as upon the talents that God has given him?[128]

Notes

1 *The Irish Builder and Engineer Jubilee Number, 1859–1909* (Dublin, 1909), p. 34.
2 E. McAulay, 'The origins and early development of the Pembroke estate beyond the Grand Canal 1816–1880' (Ph.D. thesis, Trinity College, Dublin, 2003), pp. 100, 243 and 262.
3 *General Advertiser*, 14 January 1860.
4 D. Smith, *Architectural builders' memoranda book of prices* (Belfast, 1863), pp 21 and 23.
5 M. E. Daly, 'The growth of Victorian Dublin', in M. E. Daly, M. Hearn and P. Pearson (eds), *Dublin's Victorian houses* (Dublin, 1998), pp 32–33 and RD, 1869, vol. 24, mem. 137–140.

6   IAA, Dictionary of Irish Architects 1720–1940.
7   *The Dublin Builder*, 15 March 1864 and 15 February 1868. Note that in 1867 *The Dublin Builder* became known as *The Irish Builder*.
8   *Ibid.*, 15 March 1864.
9   *Ibid.*, 1 December 1866.
10 *Ibid.*, 15 January 1861.
11 McAulay, 'Pembroke estate', p. 151.
12 RD, 1863, vol. 19, mem. 182; 1865, vol. 21, mem. 299; vol. 22, mem. 2.
13 Daly, 'The growth of Victorian Dublin', p. 33.
14 *The Dublin Builder*, 15 August 1861.
15 *Ibid.*, 15 March 1861.
16 *Ibid.*, 1 July 1860.
17 D. Dickson, *Dublin, the making of a capital city* (Dublin, 2014), p. 107.
18 M. Wall, 'The rise of a Catholic middle class in eighteenth-century Ireland' in *Irish Historical Studies*, xi, (1958), p. 97.
19 Dickson, *Dublin*, p. 297.
20 S. Jones, 'Dublin reformed: the transformation of a municipal governance of a Victorian city, 1840–1860' (Ph.D. thesis, Trinity College, Dublin, 2001).
21 *Freeman's Journal*, 28 October 1843.
22 Dickson, *Dublin*, p. 317.
23 P. Pearson, *Between the mountains and the sea* (Dublin, 2001), p. 127.
24 Old Newry Society, *The book of Newry* (Newry, 2008), p. 118.
25 *Ex. Info.*, Deirdre McEvoy, genealogist: *Saint John Globe*, 18 December 1884 and *The Daily Telegraph* (Saint John), 25 July 1884.
26 *Journal of the House of Assembly of the province of New Brunswick*, [p. cxcviii], January–March 1839 and [p.cxxiv], January–April 1843 (http://.eco.canadiana.ca) (28 August 2012).
27 R. S. Harrison, *Merchants, mystics and philanthropists: 350 years of Cork Quakers* (Cork, 2006), p. 193.
28 E. Laxton, *The famine ships: The Irish exodus to America 1846–51* (London, 1997), p. 23.
29 *Ex. Info*, Deirdre McEvoy, genealogist: *Freeman's Journal*, 1 October 1857.
30 *Ibid.*, *Saint John Globe*, 18 December 1884 and *The Daily Telegraph* (Saint John), 25 July 1884.
31 *Ibid.*, *The Daily Telegraph* (Saint John), 24 September 1883 and 25 July 1884.
32 *Belfast News-Letter*, 12 February 1850.
33 RD, 1850, vol. 15, mem. 236 and NAI, Family and estate papers, maps and rentals, Copy of original lease from 18 August 1863, ground in Rathgar, William Carvill to William Todd (Acc. No. 1146/3/2).
34 *Thom's*, 1851–1880.
35 H. Shaw, *The Dublin pictorial guide and directory of 1850* (repr. Belfast, 1988).
36 IAA, Dictionary of Irish Architects 1720–1940, Michael Meade.
37 B. Grimes, *Majestic shrines and graceful sanctuaries, the church architecture of Patrick Byrne, 1783–1864* (Dublin, 2009), p. 2.
38 *Thom's*, 1853.
39 Dublin City Council, Planning records, conservation report by Thomas C. McGimsey Architect, November 2007, p. 4 (planning application ref. 1020/08).
40 *Ex. Info.*, Deirdre McEvoy, genealogist: *Belfast News-Letter*, 22 May 1857 and *Canadian News and British American Intelligence*, 10 June 1857.
41 A. Bielenberg, *Ireland and the industrial revolution: the impact of the industrial revolution on Irish industry, 1801–1922* (London and New York, 2009), p. 197.
42 *Freeman's Journal*, 13 July 1859.

130   *Builders, speculators and labourers*

43 *The Dublin Builder*, 1 June 1862.
44 *Ibid.*, 15 January 1862.
45 IAA, Dictionary of Irish Architects 1720–1940, Pugin and Ashlin.
46 L. Clare, 'The Dublin Cattle Market', in *Dublin Historical Record*, lv, no. 2 (2002), p. 180.
47 Quoted in B. O'Donoghue, *The Irish county surveyors, 1834–1944* (Dublin, 2007), p. 89.
48 *Freeman's Journal*, 28 April 1862.
49 *Thom's*, 1861–1870.
50 *Freeman's Journal*, 6 and 7 May 1862.
51 *Thom's*, 1860–1865. He also continued to operate as a corn merchant at 38 Sir John Rogerson's Quay until at least 1865.
52 *Freeman's Journal*, 4 May 1870.
53 RD, 1870–1879, William Carvill. Out of a total of twenty-one deeds registered by him throughout the 1870s, eight relate to land in Dublin.
54 *The Dublin Builder*, 1 May 1860.
55 *Ibid.*, 1 June 1859.
56 IAA, Dictionary of Irish Architects 1720–1940, Michael Meade.
57 *The Dublin Builder*, 1 January 1862.
58 B. De Breffny and R. Ffolliott, *The houses of Ireland: domestic architecture from the medieval castle to the Edwardian villa* (London, 1975), p. 216.
59 P. Pearson, *Dun Laoghaire, Kingstown* (Dublin, 1981), p. 100.
60 OS 1865, Kingstown and *Thom's*, 1865.
61 Mary E. Daly, *Dublin: the deposed capital, a social and economic history 1860–1914* (Cork, 1984), p. 195.
62 OS, 1865, Rathgar and RD, 1866, vol. 32, mem. 270.
63 *Thom's*, 1870.
64 *Thom's*, 1875–1885. Most of the occupants were solicitors, but other residents included an army colonel, a land agent and a county court judge.
65 RD, 1879, vol. 16, mem. 193.
66 G. Jones, '"Strike out boldly the prizes that are available to you": medical emigration from Ireland', in *Medical History*, liv (2010), p. 62.
67 St Michael's House Archive, copy of will and three codicils of Michael Meade, dated 11 January 1883.
68 Private collection, copy of sale catalogue dated 6 July 1894, rentals and particulars of the estate of William Hamilton Carvill and The Right Honourable Joseph Michael Meade and RD, 1866, vol. 32, mem. 270.
69 F. D'Arcy, 'Wages of skilled workers in the Dublin building industry, 1667–1918', in *Saothar*, xv (1990), p. 33.
70 NAI, Card index, copy of original grant of probate of William Carvill, Rathgar House, Dublin, dated February 1885. (Acc. No. T6875).
71 RD, 1871, vol. 1, mem. 140.
72 *Thom's*, 1875–1885.
73 *Ibid.*, 1873–1878.
74 Daly, 'The growth of Victorian Dublin', p. 10.
75 *Report from the select committee on town holdings*, H.C. 1886 (213-Sess. 1), p. 362, para. 8954 (henceforth cited as *Town holdings, 1886*).
76 RD, 1865, vol. 17, mem. 129 and 1867, vol. 32, mem. 225.
77 RD, 1834, vol. 10, mem. 41 and *Thom's*, 1840-61.
78 C. M. Smith, *Curiosities of London life* (London, 1857), p. 346.
79 NAI, Card index, Corrective affidavit of Ada W. Meade Coffey, 16 October 1922 (Acc. No. T15625).

80 *Town Holdings, 1886*, evidence of Mr Stewart, p. 201, para. 5397 and 5398.
81 Daly, *Deposed capital*, p. 55.
82 RD, 1863, vol. 16, mem. 75 and 1864, vol. 11, mem. 288 and 1864, vol. 20, mem. 87.
83 NAI, Card index, copy of original grant of probate of William Carvill, Rathgar House, Dublin, dated February 1885. (Acc. No. T6875).
84 *Freeman's Journal*, 26 May 1886.
85 NAI, Calendar of all grants of probate, 1887, Michael Meade.
86 St Michael's House archive, Copy of original will and three codicils of Michael Meade with probate attached, 11 January 1883.
87 Daly, *Deposed capital*, p. 61 and Bielenberg, *Ireland and the industrial revolution*, p. 161.
88 Dublin City Archives, Lord Mayors Biographies, Joseph Michael Meade (Acc. No. R1/01/07).
89 *Freeman's Journal*, 15 February 1887 and RD, 1889, vol. 50, mem. 6.
90 RD, 1882, vol. 6, mem. 76.
91 *Thom's*, 1885, Northumberland Road.
92 RD, 1887, vol. 7, mem. 199.
93 *The Irish Times*, 26 June 1900.
94 *Ibid.*, 14 November 1900.
95 *Ibid.*, 8 July 1890.
96 *Freeman's Journal*, 6 July 1892.
97 *Ibid.*, 28 January 1893.
98 *The Irish Times*, 16 July 1900 and *The Times*, 4 June 1888.
99 M. Fraser, *John Bull's other homes, state housing and British policy in Ireland, 1883–1922* (Liverpool, 1996), p. 71.
100 Daly, 'The growth of Victorian Dublin', p. 45.
101 Numbers 3–10 Henrietta Street were registered in the Registry of Deeds in 1894, but the properties were bought by Meade in an auction in November 1892. *Irish Times*, 30 November 1892.
102 P. Pearson, *The heart of Dublin* (Dublin, 2000), p. 361; and M. Craig, *Dublin 1660–1860* (Dublin, 1980), p. 103.
103 T. Murtagh, 'Henrietta Street in the nineteenth century' (unpublished research paper, Dublin City Council), p. 77.
104 *Freeman's Journal*, 8 July 1890.
105 *The Irish Times*, 18 July 1900.
106 *Ibid.*
107 *Ibid.*, 14 November 1900.
108 *Ibid.*, 16 July 1900 and Daly, *Deposed capital*, p. 63.
109 Dickson, *Dublin*, p. 311.
110 *The Irish Builder*, 1 January 1869.
111 L. M. Cullen, *An economic history or Ireland since 1660* (London, 1972) p. 166; and S. Ó Maithú, *Dublin's suburban towns* (Dublin, 2003), p. 112.
112 *The Irish Builder and Engineer Jubilee Number, 1859–1909* (Dublin, 1909), p. 33.
113 Dickson, *Dublin*, p. 366.
114 O'Grada, p. 395 and *The Irish Builder and Engineer Jubilee Number, 1859–1909* (Dublin, 1909), p. 33.
115 F. A. D'Arcy, 'Wages of labourers in the Dublin building industry, 1667–1918', *Saothar 14*, 1989, p. 18.
116 *The Dublin Builder*, 15 February 1865 and 1 April 1866.
117 *The Irish Builder* (formerly *The Dublin Builder*), 1 January 1869.
118 *Ibid.*, 1 September 1859.

119 *Ibid.*
120 *Ibid.*, 15 August 1861.
121 *Ibid.*, 15 December 1862.
122 *The Irish Builder*, 15 January 1876.
123 *The Irish Builder*, 1 March 1890.
124 C. Callan, 'The regular operative house painters' trade union', *Saothar*, vii (1981) p. 33.
125 *The Irish Builder*, 15 August 1896.
126 M. E. Daly, 'Social structure of the Dublin working class', in *Irish Historical Studies*, vol. 23, no. 90 (November 1982), p. 130.
127 T. Murtagh, *Henrietta Street in the nineteenth century* (unpublished research paper for Dublin City Council, September 2015), p. 92.
128 *The Dublin Builder*, 1 September 1859.

5 Process
Building materials

Introduction

The nineteenth century was a period of great technological advancement. The industrial revolution transformed the building site, where machine-made bricks, previously moved by hand, were now hoisted up the façade by steam crane. The railway age brought materials from far and wide and this, combined with the ideals of the Gothic Revival, introduced polychromatic brick to house façades. This chapter will examine the detailed construction of a number of Victorian houses in Dublin, which vary in their use of materials, from the uniformly rendered façades of Crosthwaite Park, to the red brick and cut granite fronts of Ailesbury Road. Drawing on current conservation practice, it focuses on the three main building materials of brick, stone and timber, showing their role in forming the suburban house form. It also investigates the sources of these materials and how they were transported to site. Were these houses products of their locations, or did speculators turn to foreign markets for their supply? Revealing the wider supply routes that supported the building of Dublin's Victorian suburbs, this chapter unlocks some of the complex processes that brought the city's polychromatic façades to life.

Brickwork

Next to calp limestone, brick has been described as the 'quintessential Dublin walling material', having characterised much of the city's domestic architecture since at least the seventeenth century.[1] It was used mostly as a facing material, but it was also used to build foundations, internal walls, chimneys, boundary walls and drains. The quality of a brick wall depends on the type of clay selected, and the method of manufacture. The best-quality brick was a 'marl' or 'malm', which was yellow in colour and used mainly for facings.[2] Next in quality was the grey stock brick, the standard brick in England, known for its strength and durability, used for external walls, arches or piers, or to form 'a very good front'.[3] Lowest in quality were 'place bricks', which came from the worst burned portions of the kiln, used for internal partitions, or for lining the inside of walls. In 1861, *The Dublin Builder* reported them to be 'of a very perishable character', and advised against using them at all.⁴ Improvements in manufacturing techniques brought machine-made brick from England: a harder, more durable and more consistent product. Mechanisation was slow in coming to Ireland, and much brick-making still continued to be carried out by hand until at least the middle of the nineteenth century.⁵ The Hibernian Brick and Tile Company were manufacturing machine-made bricks in Wicklow town by 1862, claiming their materials are 'fully equal, if not superior, to anything imported from England'.⁶ Despite these improvements, the majority of brick continued to come from abroad, as *The Irish Builder* (formerly *The Dublin Builder*) observed in 1872: 'If we want good facing bricks, we import them.'⁷

The strength of a brick wall is reliant on the quality of the brick, the pattern of bond employed and the mortar that binds it together. The red brick elevations of Ailesbury Road are finished in a Flemish bond, but the stock brick sides are constructed in an English garden wall bond (Plate 12). Both bond types are formed by arranging a series of headers (end facing) and stretchers (side facing), laid in different directions. While stretchers bind a wall across its length, headers tie it along its depth, and the strongest wall provides a good combination of these cross and longitudinal ties. Of the two bond types, English garden wall bond is the stronger, as it employs a greater number of headers, providing a better cross bond. Although Flemish bond is weaker structurally, it had been favoured in Ireland since the seventeenth century, due to its more attractive appearance. It is commonly found in eighteenth-century terraces in both London and Dublin.⁸

To maximise the strength of a brick wall, a bonding pattern should extend unbroken across the depth of a wall, with full headers bonded into the bricks behind. However, it appears that this preferred method of construction was the exception rather than the rule. At Number 7 Ailesbury Road, the outer face of the front wall was built in red brick, but the inner face was constructed with an inferior 'place' or 'common' brick, made up of only half-burnt clay. Economy was the major impetus here: in the early 1860s, County Dublin stocks cost from twenty-six to thirty shillings per thousand, but inferior place bricks were much cheaper.⁹ Red bricks were the most expensive kind of stock brick, about one-and-a-half times the price of a County Dublin stock.¹⁰ Thus, savings were made even in the building of boundary walls: in alterations to a house in Terenure in 1876, the outside face of the garden walls was finished in red brick, but the inside was faced in 'Athy selected stocks'.¹¹ While minimising the cost of more expensive materials, speculators could also save on labour costs, as the inside face could be laid faster and cheaper than the carefully composed Flemish bond outside.¹²

This deceptive practice had implications for the strength of brick wall construction. In order to minimise the use of the expensive red brick front, one brick was often cut in half to form two 'false' headers. Full headers might only be introduced periodically, reducing the strength of the cross bond while rendering the red brick front: 'only a half-brick thin veneer, infrequently tied-in to the backing brickwork'.¹³ If this backing was constructed in an inferior place brick, the structure was compromised further, as this 'weaker and more brittle' material was carrying the main loads.¹⁴ Not surprisingly, contemporary writers were critical of the practice: in 1823, the architect Peter Nicholson lamented: 'The outer appearance is all that can be urged in favour of Flemish Bond.'[15] Nevertheless, the practice seems to have continued during the nineteenth century, as it was specified for houses in Northbrook Road in 1881. In forming a Flemish bond to the front, the architect stipulated full headers at every fourth course, but only 'where practicable' in intermediate courses. It is this inferior workmanship that has led to some of the structural problems inherent in some of these houses today.

Having established some of the different types of bricks used in Ailesbury Road, we now turn to the source of these materials. In the nineteenth century, brickmaking was carried out in the most remote areas of every county in Ireland.[16] By 1863, as many as eighty-four different areas of brick manufacture were recorded. Since 1771, however, the practice had been banned within a two-mile radius of Dublin, due to the health risks associated with the practice.[17] In contrast to London where brick-making was carried out close to suburban building sites, the practice was banned in Dublin, compelling developers to source the material from further afield. As *The Irish Builder* lamented in 1887: 'Here, in Dublin, we have no such thing as bricks manufactured in its immediate vicinity, and we have to pay for several miles of land cartage.'[18] Even where brickmaking was permitted in outlying districts, it continued to remain a contentious issue, particularly in densely populated areas. In 1861, an injunction was granted against a Mr Alexander Edie, preventing him from erecting a kiln on a plot of ground near the Dublin suburb of Blackrock. Edie's employees had been burning tens of thousands of bricks close to a National School and residents were concerned about the emission of ammonia from the operation.[19] It seemed that the process formed large quantities of white smoke and a 'peculiar smell', which permeated the countryside for miles around.[20]

In 1861, it was reported that local stock bricks were made in the traditional manner in County Dublin, in Clondalkin, Newlands and Ashfield.[21] It was the amount of iron oxide in the clay that gave brick its colour, ranging from a light yellow hue to a dark red.[22] County Dublin stocks were yellowish brown and could be used as facing bricks, as recorded in a scheme of four houses at Ranelagh in 1866, designed by the architect William Fogerty. They were also used to face the gable walls of the houses in Ailesbury Road (Plate 12). Other types of stock bricks were grey in colour, such as those manufactured in Athy, which were said to be of good quality. With the development of the canals, bricks were the main cargo transported to Dublin and brickfields sprung up close to the canals, particularly at Athy and Tullamore.[23] Michael Meade was certainly sourcing Athy brick for some of his projects: they were used in a premises on Grafton Street in 1862 and for the enlargement of Westland Row railway station in 1878.[24] In 1888, it was reported that large quantities of Athy stock were being sent to Dublin to build suburban houses in Rathgar and Rathmines.[25]

Although red brick went out of fashion in London after 1730, it continued to be used for a longer time in Dublin's eighteenth-century townhouses.[26] However, by 1871, red brick was rarely manufactured in Dublin, as *The Irish Builder* confirmed: 'Again, all the old houses in Dublin, without an exception, are built of red brick; now, except the solitary sample which I alluded to before, not a red brick has been produced in the county within the memory of man.'[27] The effect was often achieved by colour washing local grey stock brick, giving it the appearance of a red brick front.[28] This does not seem to be the case at Ailesbury Road, as the red brick shows no unevenness of colour. It is also clearly superior in quality to its grey stock neighbour, with its smooth finish and straight edges, suggesting a machine-made product.

In 1845, architect George Wilkinson reported that most red bricks used in Dublin came from Bridgewater or Staffordshire in England, and were 'of good quality'.[29] However they cost sixty shillings per thousand: more than twice the cost of an Irish yellow stock brick. By 1861, red bricks were also sourced in the growing industrial city of Belfast, where they were considered to be of 'excellent quality', exuding a reddish warm colour. This was the effect sought by architect E. H. Carson in 1862, when he specified red stock bricks from Belfast to the façade of Warwick Terrace in Rathmines.[30] They had been manufactured by the Hayfield Brickworks, the first Irish brick manufacturers to install a Hoffmann kiln. By the end of the 1860s, *The Irish Builder* reported that these bricks were superior to 'the best Bridgewater', and were much used in Dublin.[31] Bridgewater bricks continued to be imported in significant quantities, and were used for the building of many nineteenth-century suburban houses there.[32] The 'best pressed machine made red Bridgewater brick' was specified for the façades of Numbers 16 and 17 Northbrook Road in 1881, including the chimneys and the boundary walls (Plate 22).[33] By this time, Dublin had a local supply of high-quality red brick, with the opening of Kingscourt Brickworks in 1875 and Portmarnock Brick and Terracotta Works in 1881. However, it appears that Irish brick companies could not keep up with demand, and large quantities of imported brick continued to be used in Dublin houses. Michael Meade, was supplying 'Bridgwater goods' from his timber mill in the city, while building houses in Ailesbury Road.

Bricks were used to build external walls, but they were also required for internal walls and chimneys, and to form window openings. At Northbrook Road, the rear façades were to be constructed entirely in rubble stone, but the openings were to be formed in 'picked Co. Dublin or Youghal stock brick'. Today, this detail is hidden behind a lime render, but in other houses it was retained as a facing, as can be seen at Northumberland Road (front cover). These houses are also characterised by curved window lintels, which required special 'rubbed and gauged' bricks for this purpose. The nineteenth century marked a dramatic change in this regard, as square window heads and reveals gave way to curved profiles.[34]

Brick is a fire resisting material, making it particularly suitable for the construction of chimneys. The removal of the parapet detail made Victorian chimneys more visible, opening up the opportunity to use them as decorative set pieces (front cover). At Number 13 Ailesbury Road, the chimney stack was constructed mainly of stock bricks, from the firm 'PATENT R. BROWN & SON PAISLEY'. This was the enterprise of Robert Brown, founder of Ferguslie Fireclay Works, outside Glasgow in Scotland. The seemingly unending supplies of suitable clay in the Paisley area spawned the manufacture of a wide range of fireclay goods, such as ornamental fireclay bricks, glazed sewerage pipes and floor tiles.[35] From the 1850s, auxiliary branches of the company were opened in cities throughout the United Kingdom, including Glasgow (1856) and Belfast (1858). By the time Michael Meade signed the leases for plots on Ailesbury Road, a branch had been opened in Dublin, at a premises in the North Wall. In 1868, *The Irish Builder* reported on the success of this 'highly-important depot', where a variety of clay materials were offered, including paving bricks, pig troughs and ornamental quoins.[36] The chimney stacks to Number 4 Ailesbury Road, built nine years later, is a reflection of the increasing amount of decoration on suburban houses. The base is constructed of stock bricks, but the more visible central section is faced with bands of red and yellow brick, with a series of corbelled bricks supporting the chimney cap. Supporting the eaves of Number 4 is a yellow brick corbel also sourced from overseas, from a manufacturer near the town of Irvine in Scotland. For the chimneys at Northbrook Road, the architect specified 'good hard Tullamore brick' for the chimney breasts, but above roof level they were to emerge entirely in red Bridgewater brick, matching the front and rear façades (Plate 22).

The architect specified granite rubble for the internal walls at basement level in Northbrook Road. On the upper levels, most of the internal walls were to be constructed in solid 'good hard Tullamore brick', nine inches wide. In addition, two thinner walls were inserted, six inches wide: one at ground-floor level (Plate 23: between the hall and dining room) and another at first-floor level (Plate 24: between the two front bedrooms). These are the only two walls in the house that are not supported from below, demanding a lighter form of construction. According to Allen, timber partitions were used for this purpose, as he explained in 1900: 'The principal advantages which partitions possess are, that they save space, and being light in weight, can be raised upon a floor; whereas a brick partition wall must either rest on another wall beneath, or be built on girders, which entails additional expense.'[37] Two types of internal walls were specified by the architect in Northbrook Road: 'Studd partitions' (*sic*) and 'bricknogging partitions'. Both types were constructed in timber, and were suitable for use above the ground floor. Bricknogging partitions are timber-framed walls infilled with brick and plastered over, commonly found in Irish buildings since at least the eighteenth century. This type of construction flanks the stairwell on both of the upper levels at Number 7 Ailesbury Road, and was most likely used to build the wall between the hall and dining room at Northbrook Road. A 'Studd partition' was constructed entirely of timber and finished in lath and plaster. The most likely location of this was on the bedroom floor, where a 'trussed' stud partition was specified: a braced structure spanning from one wall to another, designed, as the architect explained, 'so as to throw the weight off the floor'.[38]

It is clear therefore that a wide variety of bricks were used to build Dublin's suburban houses. Red brick tended to be sourced in Belfast or England, yellow brick in County Dublin and grey brick in the Irish midlands, near Athy and Tullamore. How then were these materials transported to site? By 1880, County Dublin stock brick was brought by cart from the Rathfarnham area (near Rathgar) to supply sites in the city and suburbs.[39] In 1860, the landowners Bentley & Son were advertising bricks 'at half price' with building plots in Rathgar, and promised prospective tenants in Foxrock 'a first-rate quality of hard-burned stock brick' made on site.[40] However, it appears that most brick travelled large distances. This made speculative development more expensive than London, where bricks tended to be made close to suburban sites. By 1887, *The Irish Builder* lamented that most brick was 'delivered by the canals from some fifty or sixty miles distance, with land cartage afterwards of a mile or more. In this we do not include English imported bricks, which, of course, have to bear the cost of sea-borne carriage in addition.'[41] Imported brick arrived at the quay in Dublin, and then travelled by cart through the city to the townships. However, speculators could also turn to local builder providers in the city, such as the timber merchants John Martin & Sons who were selling imported brick from their lumber yard on the North Wall, and builder George Moyers, who was promoting 'Bridgewater red fronting brick' at his slate and tile yard on the quays in the 1870s.[42]

Stone

The juxtaposition of stone and brick differentiates Dublin's nineteenth-century suburban houses from their English equivalents. Cut stone is particularly characteristic of high-quality domestic architecture, such as in the western side of the Pembroke estate, which was subject to strict building control. Michael Meade's leases in Ailesbury Road specified different grades of brick to the upper storeys, and cut stone to the lower level. Specifically, a 'punched or chiselled granite' finish was required at Ailesbury Road and this runs along the lower level, across the side of the entrance steps, with a granite string course and quoins marking the transition to the brick facing (Figure 1.22).[43] This lease ensured that this template was repeated in new streets across the western side of the estate, including Lansdowne, Raglan and Northumberland Roads. In the less valuable eastern sector where building controls were looser, cut stone façades are less common. When William Carvill began constructing houses in Rathgar, he did so without a building lease, and was free to build in whatever materials he chose. He limited the use of granite to the parts most prone to weathering: in the string courses, window cills, external steps and copings. He was following traditional building practice: in Dublin's Georgian townhouses, granite was also used in a minimal way for the parts that were most exposed to weathering. Instead of cladding the lower storey of Rostrevor Terrace in expensive cut stone, Carvill mimicked the effect by finishing the walls in a lime render, to resemble an ashlar finish (Plate 15). Similarly, the quoins that define the corner of the main volume are made of patent pre-cast stone, rather than granite.

A stone finish was an expensive choice, as it had to be cut from the rock face by quarrymen, and carved into shape by a stonecutter nearby. Most of the cost went to transporting this heavy and cumbersome material, often across large distances from mountains over twenty miles away. In addition, there were expenses relating to the supervision of the works: in 1866, *The Dublin Builder* advised architects to double or triple their site visits, where cut stone was used.[44] A lime render finish was a much cheaper option, as the material could be sourced close by and mixed on site by a plasterer. By 1863, the net labour cost of a chiselled granite finish was fourteen times that of a 'Stone-finishing ashlar imitation', executed in lime and sand.[45] It was this that incentivised an architect to specify a mixture of 'red stone dust' and Portland cement, to the porch walls of a house in Terenure, to imitate the stone dressings of the entrance.[46] The practice was not without its critics: Charles Cameron, chief medical officer to Dublin spoke to the Royal Institute of the Architects of Ireland in 1870, lamenting: 'Of course I have not a word to say in favour of the common process of painting plaster in imitation of stone; the practice is about as commendable as that of palming off pinchbeck for gold, or paste for diamonds.'[47]

Much of the granite used in Dublin in the eighteenth century had been quarried in the mountains to the south and southwest of the city. This unbroken 'granite-chain' of hills, was the largest granite district in Ireland, stretching through the counties of Wicklow and Carlow to Kilkenny.[48] The stone varied in colour, from 'speckled grey' to white, and differed in quality depending on location.[49] At Kingstown, it was coarse and hard, making it useful mainly for plain and heavy work, while County Wicklow granite was finer and easier to cut, making it more suitable for ornament. Although less durable than Kingstown granite, it had a 'lighter and more uniform and handsome colour', and had reportedly been used to clad many of Dublin's most important public buildings in the eighteenth century, such as the Four Courts and the G.P.O.[50] In the nineteenth century, Wicklow granite was used to clad many of the city's churches and railway stations. By 1866, *The Dublin Builder* reported that 'every building in Dublin is built of granite – our streets are paved with it – we use it for every purpose.'[51] However, it was an expensive choice: a builders' price book dating from 1863 listed three different types of granite in Dublin. The cheapest came from Kilgobbin quarries in south County Dublin, next in price was 'Kingston granite', but the most expensive was quarried in the area of Ballyknockan in County Wicklow.[52] Stonecutters had been working in the Ballyknockan area since 1824, and by the time of Dublin's Victorian housing boom, there were at least ten quarries in operation there.[53] The largest belonged to John Brady who first advertised in *The Dublin Builder* in 1866, promoting the availability of stone in lengths of up to sixteen feet and eight tons in weight.[54]

It appears that Ballyknockan granite was used widely in speculative house building in Dublin. When Warwick Terrace was constructed in 1862, *The Dublin Builder* reported that each house was accessed by a 'spacious flight of steps, of Ballyknockin granite'.[55] The development was located in the Rathmines Township, which was not subject to the same kinds of strict covenants as the Pembroke estate. However, this did not preclude the use of expensive materials. Instead, the speculator made their own choice of finish, depending on budget, trends and target market.[56] They also used the material sparingly: in 1881, the architect William M. Mitchell was specifying 'the best chiselled granite from Ballyknocken' to two semi-detached houses in Northbrook Road, also in Rathmines (Plate 22). It was used to clad the front of the lower storey, and form the entrance steps and window cills to the street elevation. A cheaper stone was chosen for the less public faces: the window cills to the rear and side and the coping to the west flank wall were built with 'good Co. Dublin granite'. The difference between these two stones is still evident today, with the brighter Ballyknocken stone to the front and the more weathered County Dublin granite to the side and rear. In 1863, a cill from a Ballyknockan quarry was more than twice the price of one from Kilgobbin (present-day Stepaside in County Dublin).[57]

In 1879, Samuel H. Bolton, a major builder-developer and Rathmines commissioner, confirmed that about 20,000 tons of sand, gravel and granite travelled through his township every year. It was destined for use in the city, and was transported in heavily laden carts.[58] This would have included the stone coming from the Ballyknockan area, where special long horse-drawn carts left the quarry in the evening, laden with heavy stone. They travelled the twenty-mile distance overnight, on mountain roads, arriving in time for the morning off-loading at building sites.[59] This was the route taken when the vast amounts of stone were being delivered for the various additions to the Four Courts, which Michael Meade completed over a twenty-year period from c.1858. Meade reported that about half a million tons of Ballyknockan granite had been used for the Police Courts building, which passed through the townships of Rathmines and Pembroke to the city.[60] This was only one of a number of extensions Meade built at the Four Courts, the second of which was completed in 1866, just as his houses in Ailesbury Road were under construction. With Meade dealing in such large quantities of Ballyknockan granite, with deliveries passing his suburban housing sites, it seems likely that this material was also used to face his houses in Ailesbury Road. Today, only one quarry still operates in the Ballyknockan area, run by the firm of C. McEvoy & Sons, established in 1865. Based on repair works carried out on houses in Ailesbury Road, they confirm that the facing originates from a County Wicklow quarry, rather than one in south County Dublin.[61]

Cut stone façades came from a 'dimension stone quarry', which produces top-quality stone, especially for facing work. The granite was cut to size by stonecutters in the quarry before final adjustments were made by a stone mason on site.[62] This finely worked stone was relatively thin, but it was backed and bonded into a rougher material sourced in a 'rubble stone quarry'.[63] Rubble stone could also form a backing for brick façades, as specified in the Northbrook Road houses.[64] In 1866, *The Dublin Builder* reported that 'ordinary mountain stone' was used mainly for rubble work, flagging, cills and quoins in the city, despite it being 'of the most rubbishy description, both as regards materials and workmanship'.[65] Much of this 'mountain stone' was quarried in south County Dublin, as distinct from the better-quality granite from County Wicklow.[66]

An even cheaper form of rubble stone was 'Dublin Calp': a black or grey limestone in plentiful supply and quarried in the Dublin area since medieval times.[67] This is the underlying bedrock of most of the city area, running in a southerly direction as far as Donnybrook and Rathgar.[68] It had been the most dominant walling stone in Dublin up to the 1730s, and was hidden behind the ashlar stone façades of many of the city's most important buildings.[69] By 1845, calp limestone was still the main material used in rubble walls in Dublin, but granite was more readily employed for facing work.[70] Calp varied in quality, 'from rottenness to extreme hardness', but some varieties had the capacity to produce hydraulic limes, making them suitable for building below ground level.[71] This is reflected in the specifications for houses in Northbrook Road, where the architect selected granite rubble for the external walls and 'rubble blackstone masonry' (calp) for the footings. When calp was used above ground level, damp problems could be counteracted by lining the internal face of walls with brick, as specified for a house in Terenure in 1876. According to *The Dublin Builder*, brick lining was 'indispensable' in habitable walls built of calp, but it was not required if a high-quality granite rubble was used, as it was relatively dry.[72] Calp was also used for the construction of many streets in the city, giving its nickname 'Dear Dirty Dublin', as reported in 1875: 'On the roads of the County Dublin, and in the city also, some wretched limestone metalling has been used, the stone being from the worst beds of the calp formation – the results, of course, being constant mud and slush in wet weather, and clouds of blinding dust in summer time.'[73]

Calp limestone is also the underlying bedrock of the suburb of Rathgar, where by Carvill's time there was a large quarry to the north of his estate (Plate 14). It had been in use since at least 1800, and had been the source for the building of the nearby Zion church and the Church of the Three Patrons on Rathgar Road.[74] However, by the time Rostrevor Terrace was under construction in the mid-1860s, another quarry had taken shape on Carvill's land, just south of his saw mills. It was located on the lower field next to the Dodder River, with a lime kiln and pump nearby, and this was most likely used to supply rubble walls for Rostrevor Terrace. As the ground was low-lying and prone to flooding, the pump was probably used to extract ground water to the Dodder River.[75] Limestone was also used to produce quicklime, which, when mixed with sand and water, produced mortars, renders and plasters, essential materials for building.[76] This is corroborated by the sale notice for Rathgar Saw Mills in 1900, which reported: 'There is a lime stone quarry upon these lands, and a lime kiln, which is being worked, and there is a large and very profitable output, which could be increased.'[77] This lime kiln is still in existence today. With rubble stone, lime and timber available close by, William Carvill was equipped with the majority of raw materials for house building.

The availability of building materials was key to attracting speculators to the suburbs. In 1862, a landowner in Foxrock advertised sites for villa building, adding that 'an excellent quality of rubble masonry can be executed for about 5s. a perch, owing to stone being close to hand, lime and sand available'.[78] Lime was an essential raw material for building, but could also be used as a damp proofing measure: for the semi-detached houses in Northbrook Road, a 'thick layer of lime riddlings' was specified on top of the ground floor. While the availability of lime depended on the geology of the district, sand was often dredged from the nearest river or sea bed.⁷⁹ When Meade & Son built Artane Industrial Schools in the 1870s, they sourced rubble limestone masonry from a nearby quarry, but as there was no sand in the area, they turned to the sea for supplies.⁸⁰ Most lime and sand in the Pembroke Township was sourced locally, as the secretary reported in 1879: 'The sand is raised in the township; the lime is burned in the township.'⁸¹

Calp limestone is the dominant subsoil rock in Dublin, but this changes to granite at the southern end of Booterstown, which continues south to the Wicklow mountains.⁸² It was on this rocky outcrop overlooking the sea that the district of Kingstown developed in the early nineteenth century (Figure 0.1). Much of the town was built with this local stone, as reported in 1865: '[I]ts beautiful terraces and numerous public buildings and villas, are constructed of the white granite of the district.'⁸³ However, Kingstown stone was quite different in character to other forms of granite, being 'very hard, the quartz predominating, and . . . seldom used for any but plain and heavy work',⁸⁴ and was used to construct the rubble walls of many buildings in the town. George Smith, the stone contractor for Kingstown harbour, built a large granite dwelling named 'Stone View' in 1820 for his son, towards the eastern end of the town. It was on this elevated site overlooking the sea that Clarinda Park developed thirty years later. Smith ran a quarry on lands now occupied by the People's Park, located to the northeast of Crosthwaite Park, Royal Terrace and Clarinda Park.⁸⁵ These developments are all finished in a lime render, and constructed in eighteen-inch rubble walls, making this quarry a likely source for these schemes. In 1868, *The Irish Builder* reported that this large granite quarry exposed a stone of 'different mineral structure from that of its neighbourhood', giving it a particular mottled look.⁸⁶

As Kingstown granite was a particularly hard stone, many of the town's most important buildings were faced with a softer granite from Dalkey quarry, located just over two miles east of Kingstown. This quarry had been opened in 1815 to provide stone for the construction of Kingstown Harbour, but it had also been used to supply material for Howth harbour and the bridge over the Menai Straits.⁸⁷ In 1865, John Cunningham, the proprietor of the quarry, confirmed that he had been supplying a high-quality granite for many years to the principal builders of Dublin, as well as for contracts abroad. He had recently supplied a large cargo of cut stone for the Thames embankment in London and for the Corporation Works in Liverpool.⁸⁸ Large quantities were extracted for improvements to Dublin port, and Michael Meade used it to face a new commercial building on the corner of Sackville and Abbey Street in 1872. It continued to be used to clad local buildings in Kingstown: when a new hospital was constructed by Meade in the 1870s, it was finished mainly in Dalkey granite.⁸⁹ Where the budget allowed, granite was also sourced from Ballyknockan, such as Kingstown train station where the local stone was considered too hard for facing work.⁹⁰

Timber

In 1857, Charles Manby Smith described the transformations occurring on the outskirts of London, pointing to the central role of the carpenter:

> Pending the making of the bricks, foundations have been dug, and now a crop of handsome houses, arranged as streets, crescents, squares, or detached villas, springs out of the ground with a celerity hardly intelligible to the casual visitor. Simultaneously with the building, the carpenters' work has been going on in a huge temporary workshop erected on the spot. No sooner are the carcasses completed, than the interior fittings are ready to be adjusted . . .[91]

Timber was crucial to the provision of housing, equating to on average about 30% of the total cost of domestic construction.[92] Behind every brick façade was a supporting structure made from timber, including floor and ceiling joists, roofing, and internal partitions. It also formed the basis for staircases, doors, windows, moulded archways, skirtings and furniture; and plaster finishes were laid on a framework of timber lath. A standard Dublin house required different kinds of timber: at Northbrook Road, white American oak was specified for the structural members, red pine for the windows and external doors, and 'Norway boards' for the floors. An essential but often hidden part of suburban house design, domestic architecture was influenced by the limitation of the materials employed. Taking Meade's houses in Ailesbury Road as an example, the floor joists span from front to back on the entrance floor, from the street façade to the spine wall (Figure 1.23). This span is almost identical in the six houses that were surveyed, varying from sixteen feet two inches to sixteen feet four inches. It is also sixteen feet in the architects' plans for Rathgar Road in 1851 (Plate 19), Northbrook Road in 1881 (Plate 23) and Shrewsbury Road in 1900 (Plate 25). This is the maximum span of the simplest form of timber floor construction, called the 'single floor', using the common nine-inch-by-two-inch joist. It consists of a series of common joists spanning from wall to wall, carrying the flooring above and ceiling beneath, without the requirement for intermediate support.[93] Where the span is greater, double floors are recommended, comprising large beams placed underneath the joists at ten-foot intervals. According to a structural engineer with forty years' experience of working with these types of houses in Dublin, this is a well-known carpenter's rule of thumb.[94]

By the beginning of the eighteenth century, most home grown forests in Britain and Ireland had been depleted. This led to a reliance on foreign sources of lumber from Norway, Sweden and the Baltic coasts of Germany, Poland and Russia.[95] As the industrial revolution took hold in Britain, demand for timber grew exponentially. The arrival of the railway saw an unprecedented demand, with over 1,700 sleepers required to lay each mile of track, and large quantities to furnish carriages and build new railway stations. By 1861, red and yellow fir was reported to be the most common timber used in Britain, which was sourced mainly in Northern Europe.[96] However, an increasing amount of stock came from Canada and America: particularly Douglas fir and pitch pine, which had been used both structurally and decoratively for some time.[97] By 1862, Great Britain and Ireland were importing annually some 540,000 loads of Canadian pine timber; most of it was manufactured on the Ottawa River, extending over an area of over 11,000 square miles, giving employment to over 40,000 men.[98] By this time, there were eight saw mills in Dublin, most of them operating from a wholesale yard on the quays. Timber merchants advertised in local newspapers, announcing the arrival of red deals from Norway, and white American oak and red pine from Canada, Mexico and Russia, much of which went to fuel the housing boom.[99] In April 1863, there was a rise in employment in the timber trades, due to '[t]he increase of buildings in Rathgar, Rathmines, Ball's-bridge, and in Bray, and other immediate places on the Wicklow line'.[100]

Michael Meade was one of these timber merchants, who announced the opening of a new 'Planing, Sawing, and Moulding Mill' in Great Brunswick Street in 1859. New steam-powered machinery manufactured doors, sashes and mouldings faster and cheaper than ever before. Meade was the first to introduce steam power to the timber trade, boasting that his was 'the only Manufactory of the kind in Dublin'.[101] Where previously a number of men cut logs by hand, new stone saws had transformed timber fabrication. The premises was located on a large site adjoining the terminus of the Dublin and Wicklow Railway, built to house 'powerful machinery' to manufacture timber for building (Figure 4.4), while competing with the large amounts of ready-prepared carpenters' work imported from England and Scotland. Meade prided himself on his 'long practical experience in the working of all descriptions of Timber', producing flooring, skirtings and mouldings 'of all Sizes and Patterns', as well as doors, sash frames and shutters, staircases and mouldings.[102] The saw mill contained a number of workshops, where machines made by eminent firms in Britain were used for log-cutting, mortising, tenoning, sawing, boring and grooving. Machine-made carpentry was manufactured here for the home grown market, but products were also being exported 'to all parts of the Kingdom'.[103] The orders included furniture for the Oriental Baths in London and two new Catholic churches in Dublin, timber for a mansion for the Countess of Glengall, and nine houses in Bray and Kingstown, plus 'a Gothic screen of elaborate design' for Clondalkin Catholic church.

Clearly, Meade's Saw Mills were providing much of the raw material for his increasing number of building contracts. In 1863, a smithy was added to the enterprise, supplying a large quantity of ironwork for the Corporation Cattle Market, soon to become the biggest of its kind in Europe.[104] The manufacture of other materials followed suit, including slates, sewer pipes, tiles, plastering and slating laths,[105] and later a stone mason's workshop was added.[106] However, in September 1868, after the completion of his first four houses on Ailesbury Road, the saw mill was destroyed by fire, including '[t]he immense quantities of timbers that were stored in the concerns, together with the workshops and sawing department . . . and a large number of carts, wagons, derricks, hoists, and building appliances'. Only the office buildings, engine-house and smithies remained, but Meade soon began clearing out the site, preparing for the erection of new fireproof buildings in their place.[107]

Michael Meade usually auctioned off lumber at his site in Great Brunswick Street, but the majority of timber merchants in Dublin operated a wholesale yard on the quays. There they sold shiploads of raw timber, often operating a saw mill nearby. Lumber arriving on the quays travelled through the city before being delivered to the suburbs: 'A resident in Rathmines, or Pembroke, orders his goods in Dublin, and they are delivered in the townships; and coal, timber, merchandise, groceries, and matters of that sort are brought out.'[108] Martin & Son were Meade's competitors: they advertised alongside each other in February 1859, promoting 'several Cargoes of North American and Baltic WOOD GOODS (*sic*)' at the Custom House Docks.[109] These 'prince merchants' had recently erected extensive saw mills at North Wall Quay, illustrated in *The Dublin Builder* the following year (Figure 5.1). The drawing demonstrates the potential scale of such an operation, with a labyrinth of yards storing a wide variety of raw and sawn timber. Central to the operation was the saw mill, where planing and moulding machines manufactured sawn timber, including railway wagons and furniture. In the bottom right-hand corner, a timber wharf was being extended on a continuous basis to cope with the increasing loads of lumber arriving mainly from Canada and the Baltic.[110] Such

Figure 5.1 John Martin & Son timber merchants, North Wall, Dublin (from *The Dublin Builder*, 1 February 1860, reproduced courtesy Trinity College Dublin).

was the extent of Martin & Son's trade, the company commissioned its own fleet of ships: in the 1830s, they sent its senior captain to New Brunswick in Canada to build and buy new vessels, which were then registered in Dublin port.[111] William Carvill was also in the business of launching ships from Canada, having spent his early life in the port of Saint John in New Brunswick, a major centre of shipbuilding. Along with his brothers he was engaged in the iron, shipping and timber trades there from 1838, but on his return to Ireland in 1849 he established a saw mill in Rathgar.[112] From a premises in the North Wall in the city, he auctioned off shipments of lumber from as far as Canada, Central America and East Prussia, while the remainder went for processing at Rathgar.

Conclusion

Many factors influenced the choice of building material in the Dublin suburbs. The first related to building control: the high-quality finishes imposed by Lord Pembroke are evident in the expensive cut stone and red brick façades of Ailesbury Road. Most of these materials travelled long distances: the granite facing was quarried twenty miles away in the Wicklow mountains, while the yellow stock brick was most likely sourced in County Dublin. Speculators also turned to foreign markets: red machine-made brick was sourced in Bridgewater or Belfast, while firebricks and corbels for Ailesbury Road travelled from Scotland. In the seaside district of Kingstown, an abundance of local granite ensured that the houses were usually constructed in rendered granite rubble, while a nearby quarry was the probable source for the building of Crosthwaite Park. William Carvill was equipped with most of the materials to build houses in Rathgar, with a limestone quarry and a saw mill on his estate. He was not subject to stringent regulation, and so built a cheaper, stripped-down version of the Pembroke estate houses, rendering the lower level to mimic the effect of stone. Nevertheless, he still opted to build semi-detached houses clad in expensive red brick, which indicates that fashion and the housing market had a role to play in his choice of building materials. One of the most significant findings of this study was the relationship of the speculative housing market to the broader international trade in lumber. William Carvill's business interests extended far beyond the confines of the Dublin suburbs, as he was engaged in the shipping and timber trades on both sides of the Atlantic. Carvill and Meade received shipments of lumber on the Dublin quays, which they then fabricated in their saw mills, forming the skeletal timber structure behind their masonry façades.

Notes

1. C. Casey, *Dublin, the city within the grand and royal canals and the circular road with the Phoenix Park* (New Haven & London, 2005), p. 3.
2. Jack Bowyer (ed.), *Handbook of building crafts in conservation, a commentary on Peter Nicholson's The New Practical and Workman's Companion* (London, 1981), p. 69.
3. *The Dublin Builder*, 15 April 1861.
4. Ibid., 15 April and 15 June 1861.
5. S. Roundtree, 'A history of clay brick as a building material in Ireland' (M.Litt. thesis, Trinity College Dublin, 1999), p. 88.
6. *The Dublin Builder*, 1 June 1862.
7. *The Irish Builder*, 1 December 1872. Until 1867, *The Irish Builder* was known as *The Dublin Builder*.
8. Roundtree, 'A history of clay brick', p. 47.
9. *The Dublin Builder*, 15 June 1861 and 1 June 1862.
10. G. Wilkinson, *Practical geology and ancient architecture of Ireland* (Dublin, 1845), p. 249.
11. IAA, PKS, notes and queries, Mr Jackson's house, Roundtown Road, Terenure, 1876 (Acc. No. 77/1/B06a/25).
12. J. Marshall and I. Willox, *The Victorian house* (London, 1986), p. 43.
13. Department of the Environment, 'Bricks: a guide to the repair of historic brickwork' (Dublin, 2009), p. 29 (www.dublincity.ie/sites//Planning/HeritageConservation/Conservation/Brickwork.pdf; accessed 15 August 2015).
14. Bowyer, *Handbook of building crafts*, p. 71.
15. Ibid., p. 83.
16. Roundtree, 'A history of clay brick', p. 94; and David Smith, *Architectural builders' memoranda book of prices* (Belfast, 1863), pp. 34–35.
17. S. Roundtree, 'Dublin bricks and brickmakers', in *Dublin Historical Record*, lx, no. 1 (2007), p. 65.
18. *The Irish Builder*, 1 September 1887.
19. *The Dublin Builder*, 1 June 1861.
20. Roundtree, 'A history of clay brick', p. 92.
21. *The Dublin Builder*, 15 June 1861; and Roundtree, 'Dublin bricks and brickmakers', p. 66.
22. J. P. Allen, *Practical building construction* (London, 1900), p. 2.
23. Roundtree, 'A history of clay brick', p. 92.
24. IAA, PKS, Bill of measurement, Numbers 24 & 25 Grafton St., 1864 (Acc. No. 77/1/B02/30); and Bill of quantity, Westland Row railway station, 1878 (Acc. No. 77/1/B08/12).
25. Roundtree, 'A history of clay brick', p. 92.
26. Casey, *Dublin*, p. 4.
27. *The Irish Builder*, 1 May 1871.
28. Roundtree, 'A history of clay brick', pp. 52–53.
29. Wilkinson, *Practical geology*, p. 249.
30. *The Dublin Builder*, 15 October 1862.
31. Roundtree, 'A history of clay brick', p. 109.
32. Ibid., p. 80.
33. IAA, McCurdy & Mitchell Collection, Northbrook Road, pair of semi-detached houses, specification for the committee of Adelaide Road Presbyterian Church by W. M. Mitchell, 1881 (Acc. No. 82/49.83).
34. Roundtree, 'A history of clay brick', p. 49.

35 F. G. Hay, 'The Enterprise of Mr Brown: Robert Brown and the Ferguslie Fireclay Works' in Stuart James and Gordon McCrae (eds), *Renfrewshire Studies* (Paisley, 1997), p. 39.
36 *The Irish Builder*, 1 October 1868.
37 Allen, *Practical building construction*, p. 123.
38 IAA, McCurdy & Mitchell Collection, Northbrook Road, pair of semi-detached houses, specification for the committee of Adelaide Road Presbyterian Church by W. M. Mitchell, 1881 (Acc. No. 82/49.83).
39 *Municipal Boundaries Commission (Ireland), Part I, Evidence, with appendices. Dublin, Rathmines, Pembroke, Kilmainham, Drumcondra, Clontarf, and also Kingstown, Blackrock and Dalkey*, [C.2725], H.C. 1880, evidence of Mr Parke Neville, p. 26, para. 590 (henceforth cited as *Municipal Boundaries, Part I, 1880*),
40 *General Advertiser*, 21 January and 18 February 1860.
41 *The Irish Builder*, 1 September 1887.
42 Ibid., 1 September 1877.
43 St Michael's House archive, original lease from March 1868, piece of ground on the south side of Ailesbury Road, the Earl of Pembroke to Michael Meade.
44 *The Dublin Builder*, 1 December 1866.
45 Smith, *Architectural book of prices*, pp. 40 and 77.
46 IAA, PKS, Notes and queries, Mr Jackson's house, Roundtown Road, Terenure, 1876 (Acc. No. 77/1/B06a/25).
47 *The Irish Builder*, 1 June 1870. Pinchbeck was an alloy of zinc and copper used as a cheap imitation of gold.
48 The Rev. Samuel Haughton, 'Experimental researches on the granites of Ireland', in *Quarterly Journal of the Geological Society of London* (August 1856), p. 171; Patrick McAfee, *Irish stone walls* (Dublin, 1997), p. 32; and *The Dublin Builder*, 1 September 1860 and 15 March 1865.
49 Wilkinson, *Practical geology*, p. 14.
50 *The Dublin Builder*, 15 March 1865 and 15 March 1866.
51 Ibid., 15 October 1866.
52 Smith, *Architectural book of prices*, p. 104.
53 S. Ó Maithú and B. O'Reilly, *Ballyknockan, a Wicklow stonecutters' village* (Dublin, 1997), pp. 3 and 10.
54 *The Dublin Builder*, 1 October 1866.
55 Ibid., 15 October 1862.
56 M. E. Daly, 'The growth of Victorian Dublin', in Mary E. Daly, Mona Hearn and Peter Pearson (eds), *Dublin's Victorian houses* (Dublin, 1998), p. 30.
57 Smith, *Architectural book of prices*, p. 104.
58 Municipal Boundaries, Part I, 1880, evidence of Mr Samuel H. Bolton, p. 126, para. 2949.
59 Ó Maithú and O'Reilly, *Ballyknockan*, p. 19.
60 Municipal Boundaries, Part I, 1880, evidence of Mr Michael Meade, p. 188, para. 5061–5062.
61 Ex. Info., C. McEvoy & Sons Ltd., Stone masons, Ballyknockan, Co. Wicklow, 7 August 2012.
62 T. Hand, 'Supplying stone for the Dublin house', in C. Casey (ed.), *The eighteenth-century Dublin town house* (Dublin, 2010), p. 87.
63 McAfee, *Irish stone walls*, p. 52.
64 By substituting twenty-one-inch rubble walls for eighteen-inch brick, a nett saving of £42.11.9 was proposed at Palmerstown House. IAA, PKS, Estimate of proposed reductions, Palmerstown House, undated (Acc. No. 77/1/B06a).
65 *The Dublin Builder*, 15 October 1866.

66 Municipal Boundaries, Part I, 1880, evidence of Mr A. H. Robinson, p. 185, para. 4942.
67 Wilkinson, *Practical geology*, p. 247.
68 *The Irish Builder*, 15 November 1868.
69 Frank Keohane, *Period houses: a conservation guidance manual* (Dublin, 2001), p. 56; and Hand, 'Supplying stone for the Dublin house', p. 84.
70 Wilkinson, *Practical geology*, p. 245.
71 McAfee, *Irish stone walls*, p. 40.
72 *The Dublin Builder*, 1 June 1861.
73 *The Irish Builder*, 11 November 1875.
74 P. H. Browne and D. R. C. Hilliard, *Zion Church Rathgar: a brief account of its history, 1861–1961* (Dublin, 1961), p. 7; B. Grimes, *Majestic shrines and graceful sanctuaries, the church architecture of Patrick Byrne, 1783–1864* (Dublin, 2009), p. 129; and Angela O'Connell, *The servants' church, history of the Church of the Three Patrons in the parish of Rathgar* (Dublin, 2004), pp. 21–22.
75 Wilkinson, *Practical geology*, p. 244.
76 McAfee, *Irish stone walls*, p. 47.
77 *The Irish Times*, 5 December 1900.
78 *The Dublin Builder*, 1 June 1862.
79 Wilkinson, *Practical geology*, pp. 199 and 249.
80 *The Irish Builder*, 15 July 1879.
81 *Municipal Boundaries, Part I, 1880*, evidence of Mr A. H. Robinson, p. 185, para. 4942.
82 *The Irish Builder*, 15 November 1868.
83 W. F. Wakeman, *Tourists' guide through Dublin and its interesting suburbs* (Dublin, 1865), p. 2.
84 Wilkinson, *Practical geology*, p. 14.
85 Dun Laoghaire-Rathdown County Council, Conservation Division, report on architectural conservation areas in Dun Laoghaire, pp. 3–4 (www.dlrcoco.ie/conservation) (10 October 2011), p. 3.
86 *The Irish Builder*, 15 November 1868.
87 C. Ryan, Lewis' *Dublin, a topographical dictionary of the parishes, towns and villages of Dublin city and county* (Cork, 2001), p. 201.
88 *The Dublin Builder*, 1 April 1865.
89 *The Irish Builder*, 15 September 1872.
90 K. A. Murray, *Ireland's first railway* (Dublin, 1981), p. 168.
91 C. M. Smith, *Curiosities of London life* (London, 1857), p. 363.
92 Calculated by the following priced estimates: PRONI, Young and MacKenzie Architects, estimate for the erection of a house in Fitzwilliam Park, Belfast, 1896 (Acc. No. D2194/76/6); *Ibid.*, estimate for the erection and completion of a villa at Adelaide Park, Belfast, 1891 (Acc. No. D2194/37/9). The section allocated to the carpentry and joinery is second only to the masonry and brickwork, ranging from between 28% and over 34% of the overall cost.
93 Ex. Info., Tom O'Neill, structural engineer and owner of Number 13 Crosthwaite Park, 11 February 2012 and Allen, *Practical building construction*, pp. 99 and 110.
94 Ex. info Thomas J. O'Neill.
95 A. Gibney, 'Studies in eighteenth-century building history' (Ph.D. thesis, Trinity College Dublin, 1998), p. 126.
96 *The Dublin Builder*, 15 June 1861.
97 Bowyer, *Handbook of building crafts*, p. 83.
98 *The Dublin Builder*, 1 January 1862.
99 *Ibid.*, 1 February 1859.

100 *Ibid.*, 15 April 1863.
101 *Ibid.*, 1 November 1859.
102 *Ibid.*, 1 May 1860.
103 *Ibid.*, 1 February 1862.
104 *Ibid.*, 1 April 1863.
105 *Ibid.*, 15 July 1863.
106 *The Irish Times*, 17 April 1905.
107 *The Irish Builder*, 15 January 1869.
108 *Municipal Boundaries, Part I, 1880*, evidence of Mr Walker, p. 105, para. 2356.
109 *The Dublin Builder*, 1 February 1859.
110 *Ibid.*, 1 May 1859.
111 E. B. Anderson, *Sailing ships of Ireland* (Dublin, 1951), p. 67.
112 *Freeman's Journal*, 6 and 7 May 1862 and *Thom's*, 1860–1865. He also continued to operate as a corn merchant at 38 Sir John Rogerson's Quay until at least 1865.

Conclusion

> 'The individual dwelling offers one of the best means
> of studying the city and vice versa.'[1]

The house is the most enduring building form in any city, a material representation of a way of life, reflecting the habits, tastes and needs of its citizens. The houses analysed here are a potted story of Dublin's expansion during the Victorian age, made possible with the cooperation of landowners and new urban authorities. A wide range of speculators placed themselves at the centre of opportunity by exploiting the home, a basic social need, for financial gain. The houses might have been built for the wealthy middle class in their long crinoline dresses, but their façades were assembled by the skilled and unskilled labourers from the tenements. It was the casual labourer who dug the foundations, the bricklayer who pressed the lime mortar into the joint, and the stonemason who chiselled the granite facing on site. Today, the occupants of these houses live in 'an environment which they have not made and which was unknowingly prepared for them by the dead skulls and finger-bones in the cemeteries'.[2] Thus, these homes are as much a product of the city's labourers as they are of the speculators and landowners who appear more frequently in the records.

* * *

Maurice Craig's seminal *Dublin 1660–1860* appeared in 1952 and charted the social and architectural evolution of the city. Written in the post-war era when modernism prevailed, Craig lamented the end of the city's classical tradition sometime between 1860 and 1870, 'a time when nothing particular was happening'.[3] This view places an emphasis on Dublin's eighteenth-century development, while ignoring its far larger nineteenth-century expansion, both inside and outside the canals. The great era of building occurred during the second half of the Victorian age, where Dublin's principal streets were gradually lined with 'new and handsome buildings', from banks to insurance offices and libraries. It was a golden age of church building, where the clergy commissioned major works to cater for a burgeoning laity. The 1901 Ordnance Survey is a testimony to that progress, showing that an estimated 35,000 homes were built to house a rising middle class. *The Irish Builder* recognised the city's great strides of progress in 1909, where changes in science, art and handicraft had transformed life in Victorian cities; electricity had been largely unknown fifty years earlier, but now it had permeated all forms of industry, from lighting to mechanical power, telegraphy to transport. It was the great era of engineering; steam power transformed communication, linking the city to the outside world through railways and steamships. Dublin was well paved and well lit, with an abundant supply of pure water and an integrated system of main drainage, while the new suburban townships were a 'remarkable' improvement of the age.[4]

Like other cities on these islands, Dublin's historic urban fabric is characterised by a medieval core, a Georgian heart, and a Victorian periphery. However, by the turn of the twentieth century, it was no longer the second city of the empire, and was outstripped by Belfast in 1891 as Ireland's pre-eminent industrial city. As a result, it has little of the gritty industrialisation of cities like Birmingham or Manchester: few factories were built in Dublin, and it does not contain large numbers of villa mansions built for wealthy industrialists. Nor does it match the multiplicity of the 'two-up, two-down' working man's house so prevalent in other cities in Britain. It also contrasts sharply with Belfast, which made a remarkable transformation from a small merchant town (one-third of Dublin's size in 1841), to a major centre for linen manufacturing, shipbuilding and heavy engineering. Belfast's housing catered for a wide range of citizens; handsome villas for the wealthy middle classes were constructed, but the majority of accommodation catered for all kinds of working-class families.[5] A large proportion of Belfast's labour force was employed in manufacturing, with regular and dependable wages. In Dublin, casual work and under-employment were common and the increasing numbers of professionals, white collar and government workers created a markedly different housing market. More homes were required for the wealthier 'middling' sort in Dublin, who sought refuge in new districts outside the city boundaries. Inside the canals, the city's many unskilled labourers were crammed into narrow back lanes, or subdivided tenement buildings. By 1911, 63% of citizens living in the city were working class; only one-fifth was employed in manufacturing and half of the workforce was engaged in unskilled occupations. Today, Dublin's historic urban fabric is characterised mainly by houses of the genteel sort, its eighteenth-century townhouses, Victorian terraces and semi-detached homes, while those of the working classes have been largely swept away, or gentrified.

Dubliners' lives were transformed by the physical form of these new residential districts. In contrast to the city's Georgian streets, which were lined with 'cliff-like' terraces close to the street, wide boulevards were characteristic of the upper middle-class suburbs, with houses reduced in scale and more space in front and between the buildings. In 1869, *The Irish Builder* remarked on this metamorphosis in the Pembroke Township, which only a few years previously had been occupied by market gardens, but was 'now laid out in every quarter in magnificent roads, all but completely covered with numberless first-class residences'.[6] Michael Meade made the transition from city to suburb: in the 1840s, he was living over his business in Westland Row, but within twenty years he had built a large Italianate villa three miles from the city, in an area that would soon mutate into the most prestigious suburb in Dublin. Before the Victorian age, all classes lived cheek by jowl in a much smaller urban area. The technological age provided the opportunity to concentrate a growing bourgeoisie, who enjoyed lower taxes, better air and beauty of scenery, all within reach of the omnibus. These areas were the breeding ground for a new kind of social exclusivity, where church and home were populated by the 'right' sort of people. Behind this phenomenon was the desire to have it all: access to the commercial heart of the city without having to pay for, or live with, its increasing poverty and overcrowding, combined with the advantages of living in a semi-rural environment. These prosperous new suburbs were witnessed by Elizabeth Bowen at the turn of the twentieth century:

> The large plum-red brick houses, with their porches and bow windows and gables, were mansions; they stood apart in lawns behind carriage gates, with evergreen bushes to screen them in. Here trams were quite out of hearing; the residential silence might be taken to be either null or rich. Between the mansions the roads ran almost empty, as though a premium were set upon walking here.[7]

These bourgeois houses are also representative of Dublin's shifting urban politics during the nineteenth century, which propelled a form of 'Unionist flight' to the suburbs. A series of independent townships hemmed in the impoverished and crowded inner city, stifling its efforts to expand and modernise. This situation continued for much longer than other cities in the United Kingdom: Glasgow's suburbs were absorbed into the city by 1912, but Dublin's townships were only fully annexed in 1929. Thus, while a predominantly Catholic working class populated the city centre, much of Dublin's wealth lay in the hands of a mainly Protestant autocracy, who paid their taxes to their own independent suburban townships. As a result, Dublin Corporation operated within much tighter constraints than other cities on these islands, as it was starved of the necessary tax revenue to provide services. How did the rising Catholic merchant class, the Meades, Carvills and Crosthwaites, who were building houses for a predominantly unionist population, fit in with these neighbours? Although these families gave generously to Catholic-funded institutions, they probably had more in common with their middle-class unionist neighbours, than they did with the working-class Catholic population in the tenements. As Ciarán Wallace has found, religion was becoming less of an identifier in local politics, while class was increasingly significant for the wealthy suburban dweller. Middle-class Catholics were frequent supporters of suburban unionist commissioners, showing the degree to which social class trumped traditional political loyalties.[8]

The lives of the Carvills, Crosthwaites and Meades were transformed by other changes during the Victorian age. Born into a new era of freedom for Irish

Catholics, they were one of the first generations to benefit from the lifting of the property restrictions, enabling them to lease plots in the growing suburbs. The housing market was central to their rise in status: John Crosthwaite made a 'large fortune' from speculation, while Michael Meade built houses in the Pembroke estate, which earned him a substantial income when he let them to his upper middle-class neighbours. These properties were absorbed into their children's marriage settlements, boosting their wealth and status. Joseph Meade benefitted from his father's success in business, and built up an even larger property portfolio; by the time of his death in 1900, he had acquired over 122 properties in Dublin city and county. These men were also part of the first generation to shape their environment through local politics, either in the city council or in the township. As chairman of the Kingstown Township for many years, John Crosthwaite played a leading role in local politics. Meade senior was vice-chairman of the Pembroke Township, but his son Joseph was elected to Dublin Corporation and rose to the highest rank in city politics, where he held the mayoralty for two years in a row. Joseph Meade's life, which spanned the Victorian age, is representative of the heights that were achievable for Irish Catholics, growing up in the post-emancipation period. The reformist drive of the nineteenth century opened doors and boosted Catholic business confidence, strengthening the case for returning the Home Rule parliament to Dublin. As nationalists argued, if Irish Catholics could succeed in commerce, then surely they could administer their own affairs in a devolved regional parliament within the empire.

William Carvill's story is a reflection of Ireland's international trade, and of the benefits that Catholics enjoyed as part of the British empire. He was a young man when full Catholic emancipation was granted in 1829 and set sail for Canada seven years later, leaving one British colony to forge new opportunities in the empire's largest. On both sides of the Atlantic, he and his brothers were involved in building ships that carried passengers from Ireland to Canada and returned laden with lumber for European ports. In Dublin, New Brunswick pine formed the skeletal frame behind the city's new red brick façades, built in large numbers during the nineteenth century. These roof timbers, cut from forests 4,000 miles away, reflect the wider supply routes that supported the building of the Victorian city. These houses are the products of exodus and enterprise – exodus to a New World to benefit an old one, all the while facilitating one family's rise to nouveau riche status. Within sixty years, Michael Meade, John Crosthwaite and William Carvill had all gone, into the earth surrounding the tomb of Daniel O'Connell, 'the great liberator' of Catholics in Britain and Ireland. Marked by the 171-foot-high round tower in Glasnevin Cemetery, their final resting place is among some of the city's most prominent citizens, a 'who's who' of Catholic middle-class Dublin. Challenging the accepted thesis of Irish Catholic poverty, oppression and exile, the achievements of the Meade, Carvill and Crosthwaite families still remain, in the high-quality houses that they built around their homes.

* * *

Using a range of sample houses built in the south Dublin suburbs, this book has established some general patterns in the evolution of the nineteenth-century house (Plates 5 and 18). Mutating from the Georgian precedent, the most common typology was the terrace, with new semi-detached forms becoming increasingly popular. This was a lower density of development, more suited to the desires of the 'middling sort', a reduction of the aristocratic townhouse in the city. Early examples were reminiscent of their Georgian predecessors and were sparsely ornamented, with parapet roofs, plain façades and blank gable ends (132–135 Rathgar Road). Over time, the formality of the terrace was interrupted by the introduction of vertical breaks in the façades, in the form of bay windows, projecting entrance doorcases and render bands (150–153 Rathgar Road). The end plots began to develop, exploiting the extra space to the side by inserting openings in the end walls and widening to form larger three-bay units. The design of Crosthwaite Park went one step further, by providing generous plots facing Tivoli Road, and reorientating the plan to form grand entrance fronts on the ends facing the sea. Classical sobriety gave way to Victorian eclecticism, as house designs became increasingly decorative, in the form of polychromatic brick and stone cornices that began to appear across façades. However, within the context of these general patterns of behaviour, these changes did not occur in a clearly ordered, linear progression throughout all of the south Dublin suburbs. Rather, the introduction of decorative entrances and polychromatic materials was as much a factor of budget and location, as it was of the particular architectural trends of the time. Houses in the Pembroke estate tended to be larger and more decorative than in Rathmines, drawing in the wealthiest of the city's suburban dwellers. Large semi-detached houses were built in Rathmines at Palmerston Park in the 1870s, but plainer brick terraces continued to emerge in Dartmouth Square (Rathmines) in the 1890s.

These buildings have been analysed mainly through the lens of the builder-speculator. However, the Victorian age also marks a growing professionalisation of architects, with the establishment of a professional institute and the emergence of university education. Compared to the eighteenth-century townhouse, which was erected mainly by speculative builders, architects' increasing involvement in domestic design is reflected in Dublin's Victorian streetscapes. The architect's hand is evident in the manipulation of the façade at 150–153 Rathgar Road (Plate 4) and the careful modelling of the plan and elevation at 46–52 Northumberland Road (Plate 8). His hand is also inferred in the articulation of the corner, a reflection of the architect's skill in dealing with the complexities of three-dimensional design. The rare archival drawings analysed in Chapter 2 show that architects were engaged in designing different classes of home, from the modest terraced house (132–135 Rathgar Road), to the large semi-detached villa (Northbrook and Shrewsbury Roads). Charles Ashworth was architect to the Artisans Dwellings Company, but he was also designing homes for the wealthy bourgeoisie in Shrewsbury Road, reflecting his ability to negotiate the complexities of social class.

Building control varied, depending on the landlord and the value of the ground in question. This played an important role in determining the overall form, materials and articulation of the suburban house in Dublin. Lord Pembroke's estate agent imposed strict control in the western sector, which is reflected in the high-quality housing erected there. The impact of the lease is clear in Ailesbury Road, creating a wide boulevard with large semi-detached structures clad in some of the most expensive materials. This marked a change in building control practice; in the eighteenth century, the same estate had been subjected to a looser form of building control, where individual builder-speculators made most of the decisions in anticipating the desires of its upper-class residents.[9] Loose building control was also characteristic of Rathgar, reflected in the architecture of the houses in Rostrevor Terrace, which are relatively sparse in their decorative detailing. Although Carvill built without lease restrictions in Rathgar, he could have maximised profits by laying out his field in terraces. Instead, he built large semi-detached villas, similar in scale to those emerging at the same time in Ailesbury Road. Therefore, while the semi-detached form was a requirement of many leases in the Pembroke estate, its emergence at the same time in other suburbs not subject to such stringent control shows that the typology had entered the mainstream of the domestic building aesthetic.

Aspects of this new building form are unique to the Dublin context. During the nineteenth century, the basement rose halfway out of the ground in English suburban houses, most likely a result of the Public Health Act of 1848. However, in the higher-quality houses in Dublin, the service floor continued to rise up, until it was fully above ground, accessed via a flight of steps leading to the entrance floor. Dublin's low-lying coastal location made it impractical to sink a basement storey in undrained green fields outside the municipal boundary, due to problems with flooding and the provision of sewers. It lagged behind other cities in Britain in providing long-term solutions to this problem:[10] a pumped system of drainage was complete in Rathmines and Pembroke only in 1879, and in Kingstown by the 1890s. In the meantime, drains were provided in an ad hoc manner, and houses were generally built without subterranean floors. This was a specific policy of the agent of the Pembroke estate, who prohibited the building of any floor below the road. Thus, in reconfiguring the Georgian house typology, which in itself was a unique Irish variant of the London template, the city gave birth to an equally unique Victorian architectural landscape.

These houses are three-dimensional manifestations of the industrial age, reflecting the reach of the empire during a time of rapid mechanisation. Prior to the Victorian era, domestic architecture was largely a product of its immediate environment. The standard eighteenth-century Dublin townhouse was faced with local hand-made brick, and stone cut from nearby quarries.[11] Thus, the particular geology of a city determined the character of its domestic architecture: Glasgow had been a sandstone city since medieval times, while Bath's houses were clad mostly with the local cream coloured limestone.[12] The industrial revolution was a key turning point in architectural design, as new forms of transport and technology produced an increasing variety of factory-made materials, which could be transported faster and cheaper than ever before. The standard house could be assembled with a range of materials from the far corners of the empire, which, by 1860, covered over 8,500,000 square miles. In Dublin, houses in Ailesbury Road were faced with red brick from Bridgewater or Belfast, and yellow bricks from Scotland were used to build chimneys and corbels. The advancing technological tide brought a profusion of coloured brick and stone to the market, and this, combined with increased mechanisation and the ideals of the Gothic Revival, encouraged increased decoration in house façades. Added to these findings is the relationship between construction technology and domestic design, where the depth of the front reception rooms are often sixteen feet. Relating to the limitations of a standard timber joist, this shows how the home is shaped as much by functional factors, as it is by stylistic trends and formal influences.

The articulation of the upper two floors in red brick over stone is another unique design feature of the suburban house in Dublin. In other British and Irish cities, houses commonly combined brick with stucco, but its juxtaposition with stone is unusual. On the west side of the Pembroke estate, these materials were imposed on speculators through the lease system; but it is also found in the better-quality housing schemes in other suburbs, such as Palmerston Park in Rathmines, or Grosvenor Terrace in Monkstown. Despite the possibilities afforded by an increasingly mechanised age, geology still played a role in influencing the character of Dublin's domestic architecture. To the south of the city was the largest granite district in Ireland; and this stone had been used to clad some of the city's most important eighteenth-century structures. This tradition continued in the Victorian period, where granite was used to clad the lower floor of Dublin's higher-quality suburban houses. Thus, Meade's houses in Ailesbury Road are a product of these combined forces: a local tradition of granite, combined with the opportunities afforded by the industrial age where polychromatic brick, stone and timber could be sourced from abroad.

Architecture often provides us with the only tangible link between the present and the past. Today, a child born in the twenty-first century goes to sleep under the same rafters as a Victorian middle-class lady, or her scullery maid. The original plans of these houses show the way in which domestic space was manipulated to articulate the relationships between different members of the household; between master and servant, male and female, adult and child. Of particular importance is the divide between the server and the served, expressed in the use of a separately defined entrance, service area and sanitary facilities. At Shrewsbury Road, valuable habitable space was sacrificed to serve this class divide, by inserting two parallel corridors, where servants could pass unseen on the other side. This is further emphasised by the spatial hierarchy; large, high-ceilinged spaces for the family, with more confined rooms for the servants, and segregated, narrow staircases designed solely for housemaids, cooks and nursemaids.

In the late nineteenth century, about 71% of middle-class families in Dublin kept servants, who were not only essential in supporting their employers' lifestyle but were also a statement of social status.[13] Nevertheless, the evidence suggests that the division between master and servant was more nuanced than might first appear. Although the service floor was designed as an entirely separate domain, there is evidence to suggest that it did not operate under such strict parameters. The fictional Charles Pooter, living in a lower middle-class suburban house in London in 1888, confirmed that his friends always knocked at the side entrance, so that he could 'save the servant the trouble of going up to the front door, thereby taking her from her work'.[14] Servants lived under the same roof as their employers, often for many years, and were witnesses to the families' private world. Such was the affection that the Carvill family had for their employee Margaret Woods, that she was buried in the prestigious family vault at Glasnevin, the inscription recognising her forty years as 'the faithful servant of this family'. Equally revealing is the letter written to *The Irish Times* in 1882, regarding a fire at Clarinda Park in Kingstown. The owner lavished praise on her housemaid Lucy Fannin, who in raising the alarm acted with 'presence of mind, and great calmness', and was lauded in the newspaper as the family's 'life preserver'.[15] Thus, it is clear that the plans of these houses tell one story of intentional class divisions, but further research from other written accounts would reveal to what degree these architectural constructs operated in practice.

The analysis of the plans also reflects the rapid transformations occurring within Victorian society at large, from the growing polarisation of the classes, to the rise of consumer culture and increased mechanisation. For example, the plans for Rathgar Road (1851) include an internal water-closet, but there are no bathrooms indicated. By the time the Northbrook Road houses were built thirty years later, a pumped system of main drainage and water had been installed in the two southern townships of Rathmines/Rathgar and Pembroke, reflected in the appearance of plumbed bathrooms. Furthermore, stables are a feature of the houses in Rathgar Road (1851), catering to residents arriving by horse and carriage, but they are absent in the Northbrook Road houses, which were served by tram. In 1905, the residents of the Shrewsbury Road houses were arriving home by motor car, which would utterly transform the planning of cities throughout the world.

* * *

In the Victorian age, the semi-detached house first made its appearance on a large scale. Suburbia promised a refuge from the disease and overcrowding that characterised urban living, while simultaneously providing links with the commercial and social opportunities afforded by the city. It was a space in between: neither urban nor rural, it promised the best of both worlds. The semi-detached form emerged out of this compromise, being neither fully attached (like a terrace) nor fully detached (like a villa). This metamorphosis created a distinct suburban aesthetic, breaking away from the tall red brick terraces of the urban core. The semi-detached form also influenced its terraced neighbours, where the end plots took the shape of wider semi-detached houses. Today, the 'three-bed semi-d' continues to be a popular choice for the average Irish urban family. Between 2001 and 2011, more semi-detached houses were built in the Irish Republic than any other house type, making it the largest category of urban accommodation, next to apartments.[16] These homes have inherited many qualities from the Victorian house typology. The paired house finished in a hipped roof and set back from the road to form a semi-public garden to the front, are all familiar to modern dwellers. A hierarchy of space is echoed in the standard plan; the front characterised by two back-to-back reception rooms and adjacent hall, with the kitchen to the rear. Standing in a semi-detached suburban house today, these factors can be traced back through time, to the Victorian house typology that emerged over 150 years ago.

Notes

1 A. Rossi, *The architecture of the city* (Massachusetts, 1966), p. 72.
2 J. Summerson, quoted in H. J. Dyos, *Victorian suburb, a study of the growth of Camberwell* (Leicester, 1977), p. 7.
3 M. Craig, *Dublin, 1660–1860: the shaping of the city* (Dublin, 1952), p. 305.
4 *The Irish Builder and Engineer Jubilee Number, 1859–1909* (Dublin, 1909), pp. 6–8.
5 A. Royle, 'Workshop of the empire, 1820–1914' in *Belfast 400: people, place and history* (Liverpool, 2012).
6 *The Irish Builder*, 15 December 1869.
7 E. Bowen, *Seven winters, memories of a Dublin childhood* (London, 1943), p. 20.
8 C. Wallace, 'Local politics and government in Dublin city and suburbs 1899–1914' (Ph.D. thesis, Trinity College, Dublin, 2009), p. 308.
9 D. Dickson, *Dublin, the making of a capital city* (Dublin, 2014), p. 167.
10 M. E. Daly, *Dublin, the deposed capital* (Cork, 1984), p. 255.
11 C. Casey, *Dublin, the city within the grand and royal canals and the circular road with the Phoenix Park* (New Haven and London, 2005), p. 4.
12 C. McWilliam and J. Newman (eds), *The buildings of Scotland: Glasgow* (London, 1990); J. Gifford, C. McWilliam and D. Walker (eds), *The buildings of Scotland: Edinburgh* (London, 1984); L. F. Cave, *The smaller English house* (London, 1985), p. 135.
13 M. Hearn, *Below stairs: domestic service remembered in Dublin and beyond 1880–1922* (Dublin, 1999), p. 7.
14 G. and W. Grossmith, *Diary of a nobody* (London, 1892), p. 31.
15 *The Irish Times*, 10 June 1882.
16 Irish Central Statistics Office 'The roof over our heads' (Dublin, 2012), p. 10 (Accessed 15 July 2016: www.cso.ie/en/media/csoie/census/documents/census2011profile4/Profile_4_The_Roof_over_our_Heads_Full_doc_sig_amended.pdf).

Index

Page references in italic type indicate relevant figures and plates.

Ailesbury Road, Pembroke 40–5, *41–4*, 48–9, 79–80, 117, *118*, 119, 156, *Plates 12–13*, *Plate 18*, *Plate 29*; brick, stone and timber work 134–7, 138, 143
architects: as speculators 108; *see also* design drawings
Ashlin, George 116
Ashworth, Charles, Shrewsbury Road 50, *50*, 66–73, 155, *Plate 18*, *Plates 25–28*

Baggot Street Upper, Pembroke 16
Ballyknockan granite 139–40, 142
basements 7, 16, 18, 49–53, *51*, 156; *see also* service quarters
bathrooms/toilets 60, 64, 68, 72, 73, 158
bay windows 17, 24, 49, 68
Beckett, J. and W. 61
bedrooms 64, 71, 72, 73
Belgrave Square, Kingstown 83, 84, *85*
Belvedere Terrace, Sandymount, Pembroke 81–2, *81*
Bentley, Mark 98–9
Bolton, Samuel H. 99, 140
Bowen, Elizabeth 153
Bray 108, 117, 123
brick/brickworks 133–8
bricknogging partitions 137
Brown, Robert 136–7
builders and speculators 107–9; *see also* Carvill, William; Crosthwaite, John; Meade, Joseph; Meade, Michael
building materials: brickwork 133–8; stone/granite quarries 138–42, 157; timber/saw mills 107–8, 110, 114–15, *115*, 116–17, 144–6, *145*
building trade, carpenters/labourers 108, 126–8, 143

Burlington Road, Pembroke 35, *35*
Byrne, Patrick 20

Caldbeck, William 116
calp limestone 140–2
cantilever roofs 35–6, *36*, 79, 81, *Plate 12*
carpenters/labourers 108, 126–8, 143
Carroll, James Rawson 114
Carson, E. H. 108, 136
Carvill, William 9, 98, *113*, 117; family connections 109, 110, 112, 114–15, 116, 122, 128, 146, 154, 158; Orwell Park 48, 99, *Plate 14*, *Plates 16–18*; Rostrevor Terrace 46–8, *47*, 48–9, 89, 99, 119, 138, 141, 156, *Plates 14–15*
Catholic nationalists 4
Catholic speculators 109–10, 153–4; *see also* Carvill, William; Crosthwaite, John; Meade, Joseph; Meade, Michael
cattle market 116
cellars *see* basements
chauffeurs 70–1
chimneys/chimneypieces 31, 59, 136–7
china storage 60, 65, 69
church buildings 20, *21*, 91, 114, 116
city politics 4
Clarinda Park, Kingstown 26, 85, *86*, 95–6, 97, 142
Clontarf 6
Clyde Road, Pembroke 37, *Plate 10*
coal stores 61, 70
Cockburn & Sons 107–8
commercialisation 4
corner terraces 29–30
County Grand Jury 93–4
Craig, Maurice 3, 151
Crosthwaite, John 9, 96, 109, 110, *112*, 117, 120–1, 128, 153–4; family connections 114, 122
Crosthwaite Park, Kingstown 23–7, *23–6*,

31–2, *31*, 85–7, *86*, 94–5, 97, 121–2, 155, *Plate 5*
Cunningham, John 142
Custom House 1

Dalkey granite 142
death rates 8, 119
deliveries/tradesmen 61, 64–5
Denny, Abraham 20, *22*, 22, 58–61, *Plate 3*, *Plates 19–21*
department stores 65
design drawings: Ailesbury Road *41*, *43*; Crosthwaite Park *25*; Northbrook Road 61–6, *Plates 23–24*; Northumberland Road *19*, *28*, *38–9*; Rathgar Road *22*, *51*, 58–61, *Plate 3*, *Plates 19–21*; Rostrevor Terrace *47*; Shrewsbury Road 66–73, *Plates 25–28*
De Vesci Terrace, Kingstown 83
dining rooms 59–60, 62–3, 67
doorways/entrances 17, 25, 29, 31, 33, 45
drainage: Kingstown 97–8; Pembroke 91–4; Rathmines and Rathgar 100
drawing rooms 26, 59, 63, 68
dressing rooms 71, 73
Drumcondra 6, 7
Dublin Artisans Dwellings Company 123
Dublin Corporation 93–4
Dyos, H. J. 5

Elgin Road, Pembroke 17, *Plate 1*
England *see* London, England
English garden wall bond brickwork 134
Ennis Lunatic Asylum 116
entrances/doorways 17, 25, 29, 31, 33, 45
estate landlords 77–8; Kingstown 82–7, *84–6*; Pembroke 78–82, *81*, *Plate 29*
Eyre estate, London, England 32

façades 14, 17, 157; brick and stone work 133–42; semi-detached houses 37, 40, 44–5, 46, 48, 48–9, 79–80; terraced houses 22, 23–4, 25, 27, 29–31, 49, 83, 155
Farrell, James 108
fireclay goods 136–7
Fitzwilliam Square *Plate 5*
Fitzwilliam Street Upper, Pembroke *30*
Flemish bond brickwork 134, *135*
flood risks 53, 156
floor construction 143
Fogerty, William 116
Four Courts 140

gable ends 29, 40, 45, 81, *Plate 3*
Galvin, John 27
gardens 70

Georgian townhouses 5, 14–17, *15*, 18–19, 26, 29–30, 57; basements 49–50; Henrietta Street 124–5, *125*; as tenements 7–8
Gibson, John 121
Glasnevin 6
Graham, Alexander 81–2
granite quarries 139–40, 142, 157
Great Famine (1845–50) 3

Haddington Road, Pembroke 16–17, *16*, 51–2, *Plate 2*
Harcourt Terrace 32
Hayfield Brickworks 136
Henrietta Street 124–5, *125*
Heytesbury Street, Portobello 7
Hibernian Brick and Tile Company 134

Inchicore 7
Industrial Revolution 133, 143–4, 156–7
infrastructure 89–90; Kingstown 94–8; Pembroke 90–4; Rathmines and Rathgar 98–100
inner city poverty/overcrowding 7–8
interior design 57–8, 73–4; Northbrook Road 61–6, *Plates 23–24*; Rathgar Road 58–61, *Plates 19–21*; Shrewsbury Road 66–73, *Plates 25–28*
Irishtown 8

Kelly, Joseph 108
Kelly, Patrick 122
kerbs: Kingstown 94–6; Pembroke 90–1; Rathmines and Rathgar 98–100
Kerr, Robert 62–5, 67, 68–72
Kilmainham 7
Kingstown estate 2, 8, 13, 33, 86, 142; Belgrave Square 83, 84, *85*; Clarinda Park 26, 85, *86*, 95–6, 97, 142; Crosthwaite Park 23–7, *23–6*, 31–2, *31*, 85–7, *86*, 94–5, 97, 121–2, 155, *Plate 5*; drainage and water supply 97–8; land tenure 82–7, *84–6*; roads, paths and kerbs 94–6; *see also* Crosthwaite, John
kitchens 60–1, 65, 69–70

labourers/carpenters 108, 126–8, 143
landlords: estate landlords 77–87, *81*, *84–6*, *Plate 29*; private landlords 87–9, *88*; rental income 77–8, 79, 80, 119, 121–2, 125
landscaping, Pembroke 90
land tenure 77–8; Kingstown 82–7, *84–6*; Pembroke 78–82, *81*, *Plate 29*; Rathgar 87–9, *88*
Lansdowne Road, Pembroke 35–6, *36–7*
leases *see* estate landlords; private landlords; rental income

libraries/studies 59, 64, 68
life expectancy 8, 119
limestone 140–2
linen rooms 72
London, England 14, 20, 32, 121; comparison with Dublin forms 49–53, *50–1*
Longford Terrace, Kingstown 83–4, *84*
Loudon, J. C. 32–3, 59–61
lumber *see* timber/saw mills
Lyons, John J. 114

McAulay, Eve 16, 17–18
McCarthy, James Joseph 114
McCurdy, John 108
maps: Dublin 2; Kingstown 86; Pembroke 6, *Plate 2, Plate 29*; Rathmines and Rathgar 6, *21, 88, Plate 14*
Martin & Son timber merchants 145–6, *145*
Meade, Joseph 42–5, 46, 66, 80, 94, 119, *120*, 122–6, *124–5*, 127, 128, 154
Meade, Michael 9, 42, 80, 91, 93, 109–10, *111*, 114, 128, 140, 153–4; Rathgar Road 20–2, *21–2*; saw mills 115, *115*, 144–5; *see also* Ailesbury Road, Pembroke
Merrion Square, Pembroke 1, 8, 14, *15*, 17, *30*
Mitchell, William Mansfield 61–6, 139–40, *Plates 22–24*
Moran, Peter Joseph 25–6, 87, 108
Morley, Frederick 80
Morris, Thomas 52, 67–8
mortgages 121
motor cars and chauffeurs 70–1
Murphy, Michael 98
Murray, Arthur 20, 22, *22*, 51, *51*, 58–61, *Plate 3, Plates 19–21*
music, drawing rooms 59
Muthesius, Hermann 14, 20

Nash, John 32
Northbrook Road, Rathmines and Rathgar 158; brick and stone work 137, 139–40, 141; interior design 61–6, *Plates 22–24*
Northumberland Road, Pembroke: semi-detached houses 36–7, *38–9*, 58, *Plate 11, Plate 18*; terraced houses 17–20, *18–19*, 27–9, *28*, 30, *Plate 2, Plates 5–8*

Ordnance Survey *see* maps
oriel windows 25, 27, 48, 49
Orwell Park, Rathmines and Rathgar 48, 99, *Plate 14, Plates 16–18*
O'Toole, Patrick 108
overcrowding 7–8
Owen, James Higgins 114

paired houses *see* semi-detached houses
pantries 60, 61, 69
parapet detail, eradication of 35–6
partitions 137
paths: Kingstown 94–6; Pembroke 90–1; Rathmines and Rathgar 98–100
pediments *24, 25*, 32
Pembroke estate 2, 5–6, *6*, 13, *30*, 100, 123, 152–3, 156, *Plates 1–2*; development of semi-detached houses 33–40, *34–9, Plates 9–13, Plate 18*; drainage and water supply 91–4; flood risk 53, 156; Haddington Road 16–17, *16*, 51–2, *Plate 2*; land tenure 78–82, *81, Plate 29*; Merrion Square 1, 8, 14, *15*, 17, *30*; Northumberland Road 17–20, *18–19*, 27–9, *28*, 30, 36–7, *38–9*, 58, *Plate 2, Plates 5–8, Plate 11, Plate 18*; Pembroke Road *15*, 33, *34*; roads, paths and kerbs 90–1; *see also* Ailesbury Road, Pembroke; Meade, Michael
Phibsborough 7
'piano nobiles' 19, 50
Pim Brothers & Co. 65
politics, city 4
Portobello 7
poverty/overcrowding 7–8
private landlords, Rathgar 87–9, *88*
Protestant elite 4, 20
public health 8, 52, 91–3, 97, 100, 119
Pugin, Edward Welby 116

Raglan Road, Pembroke 37, *Plate 9*
railway suburbs 4, 82–3
Rathmines and Rathgar 1, 2, 5–6, *6*, 13, *21, 88*, 156, *Plate 14*; drainage and water supply 100; land tenure 87–9, *88*; Northbrook Road 61–6, 137, 139–40, 141, 158, *Plates 22–24*; Orwell Park 48, 99, *Plate 14, Plates 16–18*; Rathgar Road 20–2, *21–2*, 27, 30, 51, *51*, 58–61, 155, 158, *Plates 3–5, Plates 19–21*; roads, paths and kerbs 98–100; Rostrevor Terrace 46–8, *47*, 48–9, 89, 99, 119, 138, 141, 156, *Plates 14–15*; *see also* Carvill, William
Regency style houses 32
rental income 77–8, 79, 80, 119, 121–2, 125
Ringsend 8
roads: Kingstown 94–6; Pembroke 90–1; Rathmines and Rathgar 98–100
Roche, Edward 121
roofs 29, 33, 35, 36, *37*, 40, *42, Plate 6, Plate 9*; cantilever 35–6, *36*, 79, *81, Plate 12*; chimneys 31, 136–7
Rostrevor Terrace, Rathmines and Rathgar 46–8, *47*, 48–9, 89, 99, 119, 138, 141, 156, *Plates 14–15*

Royal Terrace, Kingstown 85, *86*
rubble stone 140–2
Ruskin, John 17

St Michael's House, Ailesbury Road, Pembroke 117, *118*
Sandymount, Pembroke 81–2, *81*, 92, 93, 100
sanitation 8, 52, 91–3, 97, 100
saw mills/timber 107–8, 110, 114–15, *115*, 116–17, 144–6, *145*
sculleries 60–1, 69–70
semi-detached houses 13, 32–3, 48–9, 156, 158–9, Plate 18; comparison with English forms 49–53, *50–1*; development in Pembroke 33–40, *34–9*, Plates 9–13, Plate 18; interior design 57–74, Plates 19–21, Plates 23–28; Orwell Park 48, 99, Plate 14, Plates 16–18; Rostrevor Terrace 46–8, *47*, 48–9, 89, 99, 119, 138, 141, 156, Plates 14–15; service quarters 60–1, 64–6, 68–71, 72–3, 73–4, 157–8, Plate 21, Plate 23, Plates 25–28; see also Ailesbury Road, Pembroke
service quarters 60–1, 64–6, 68–71, 72–3, 73–4, 157–8, Plate 21, Plate 23, Plates 25–28; see also basements
sewers 91–3, 97, 100
Sexton, Walter 70–1
shipping 110, 112, 114–15
Shrewsbury Road, Pembroke 50, *50*, 66–73, 155, Plate 18, Plates 25–28
sideboards 59–60, 62–3
sleeping quarters, servants 72
Smith, Charles Manby 59, 64–5, 121, 143
Smith, George 142
speculators *see* builders and speculators
stable buildings 61
stairs 37, 42, 58, 62, 67, 72–3
Stokes, Frederick 7, 89
stone/granite quarries 138–42, 157
Studd partitions 137

studies/libraries 64, 68
suburbanisation 4, 5–7, *6*, 16
Summerson, John 5

technological age 4, 156–7
tenements 7–8, 123–5
terraced houses 7, 13, 14, 27–32, *28*, *30–1*, 155, Plate 5; Belvedere Terrace, Sandymount 81–2, *81*; comparison with English forms 49–53, *50–1*; early suburban terraces 14–17, *15–16*, 51–2; Henrietta Street 124–5, *125*; Kingstown 23–7, *23–6*, 31–2, *31*, 83–7, *84–6*, 121–2; Northumberland Road 17–20, *18–19*, 27–9, *28*, 30, Plate 2, Plates 5–8; Rathgar Road 20–2, *21–2*, 27, 30, 51, *51*, 155, Plates 3–5
timber/saw mills 107–8, 110, 114–15, *115*, 116–17, 144–6, *145*
Tivoli Road, Crosthwaite Park 31–2
toilets/bathrooms 60, 64, 68, 72, 73, 158
tradesmen/deliveries 61, 64–5

unionist townships 4
Upton, Dell 5

Vernon, John 34–5, 53, 78–9, 80, 90–1, 93
Victorian age 3–5; Dublin in 1865 1–2, *2*; and historiography of domestic architecture 5–8, *6*

Waldron, Patrick 87–9, *88*
Walker, Thomas 108
Ware, Isaac 50
water supply: Kingstown 97–8; Pembroke 91–4; Rathmines and Rathgar 100
Wicklow granite 139
windows: semi-detached houses 48, 49, 63, 68; terraced houses 17, 18, 19, 22, 24, 25, 27, 29
working-class housing 7–8, 123–5, 152
Wright, Gwendolyn 5